Coffee, Cigarettes, Death & Mania

REVIEWS*

"This amusement park ride, strapped in next to Richards, shows a deep, well-developed thought process, with rock-solid manic logic that always ends in disaster.

Based on this literary MRI of Richards' brain, his caregivers can challenge his attitude and sincerity. They have learned how he tricked them, and they can try to head him off at the pass. This is the valuable contribution that this book makes for all mental health practitioners."
— Robert Harris, Clinical Laboratory Software Executive, Administration, retired, and firsthand observer

"We have many accounts of mental illness by psychologists, psychiatrists, and other mental health professionals. We also need to hear directly from those who experience mental illness first-hand.

Rodney Richards' book is a passionate, personal account of one man's journey living with bipolar disorder. It is raw, honest, and powerful.

Mr. Richards' story of wrestling and coming to terms with bipolar disorder doesn't sugarcoat the difficulties, but it also proves that these individuals can live full and rewarding lives."
— Kathleen M. Pike, Ph.D., Clinical Professor of Psychology, Columbia University

"Rodney's book about his struggle with bipolar disorder is a revealing account which is blatantly and refreshingly honest. It describes the havoc and chaos caused by mental illness not just on its innocent and unsuspecting victims, but also on their families and the people who love them.

Above all, this is an inspirational tale of Rodney's drive and determination to overcome the ravages of the illness and is a testimony to the love and support of family and friends who were there with him along the journey."
— Dr. Susan Fuchs M.D., Hamilton NJ, psychiatrist

* Reviews of *Episodes A poetic memoir*

Coffee, Cigarettes, Death & Mania

Existence lives between extremes

Rodney Richards

An ABLiA Media Book

IMPORTANT NOTICES

Copyright 2021 Rodney Richards

Published with assistance from ABLiA Media LLC in the U.S.A.

ISBN-13   978-1-7341084-0-8

Library of Congress   LCCN 2020923219

Front cover art designed and created by Jesse Richards with iStockphoto

First edition

DISCLAIMERS

This book is a rewrite and reformation of *Episodes A poetic memoir* published in 2013 (out of print), and it contains revisited dialogue, thoughts, emotions, descriptions, and scenes to the best of the author's notes and   recollection. Some d etails may not be exact but are close approximations.

The author is not a spokesperson for anyone or any organization.

Statistics and medical information on bipolar   disorder, its treatment and effects, change. Always seek advice from current medical and psychiatric practitioners   and reliable sources.

Other publications by the author

Solving the World's Titanic Struggles, copyright 2018. One hundred opinion essays on personal and social topics citing spiritual principles and texts. Available on Amazon. Volume 2 due November 2021.

TO THOSE I'VE HURT

I am sorry if I hurt you, no matter the cause of my behavior. You deserved better treatment. I pray those hurts will lessen.

TO MY FAMILY

Janet, my first love and stalwart companion. Natural leader, educator, creative talent, nurturer, and succorer. My supporter, defender, protector, and greatest cheerleader. I would have failed in life or died long ago without your love, care, and constancy.

Jesse and Kate, independent, wise, and accomplished. Joys of my heart in ways seen and unseen. You endure my antics with divine acquiescence.

Mom, kind-hearted, patient, and giving. Your unshakable faith and love are eternal reassurances.

Dad, Rodney Senior, an important temporary caretaker. Dad too, Ralph Daloisio, provided for Mom, me and siblings for over fifty years. May you each abide in peace.

Stephen, because you were true to yourself. Ralph Jr., Carleen, and Charles, best friends and beloved brothers and sister. Congratulations on the success stories you are. You braved misfortunes and created loving, united families.

Beneath my reserved exterior, I love and cherish each of you.

Truthfulness is the foundation of all human virtues.
— 'Abdu'l-Bahá

Truly, there's absolutely nothing in this universe
including ourselves,
that isn't perfectly timed.
— Dr. Wayne W. Dyer

To find our voice and inspire others to find theirs
is an idea whose time has come.
— Stephen R. Covey

There are eight million stories in the Naked City.
This is one of them.
— ABC TV show

When the pendulum swings
when you're in the blackest pit,
one thought:
Escape!

CONTENTS

PREFACE   i
NOTES TO READERS   iii

1.0 EPISODE ONE
   1.1 SOMETHING'S NOT RIGHT   1
   1.2 GOTTA GO   5
   1.3 YES LORD   8
   1.4 THE FIRST DEPARTURE   11
   1.5 SECOND DEPARTURE   14
   1.6 THE APARTMENT TALKS   17
   1.7 SLEEPING WITH A GHOST   20
   1.8 UNEXPECTED ARRANGEMENTS   22
   1.9 GRANDMOM'S BROKEN   27
   1.10 DRESSED TO KILL   30
   1.11 JOINING THE HEROES   34
   1.12 WINDFALLS   37
   1.13 WHISKED TO ANOTHER REALM   39
   1.14 FROM BLACK TO BLACK AND WHITE 44
   1.15 INVENTION CORP   48
   1.16 SUICIDE WATCH   52
   1.17 GOLD'S CURE   55
   1.18 ITS MISTY OUT   60
   1.19 BACK TO BUSINESS   63
   1.20 POP THOSE PILLS   67

2.0 EPISODE TWO?
   2.1 HAIFA VISITS CHICAGO   69
   2.2 JOY AND FEAR EMBRACE   74
   2.3 ACTING LIKE AN ADULT   77
   2.4 RED SCARE   81
   2.5 SHAKEUP OR SHAKEDOWN?   84
   2.6 A MODICUM OF STABILITY   87
   2.7 THE VISION   90
   2.8 STICKING A NEW POSITION   92
   2.9 THE FIRST SPILL   95
   2.10 A FAMILY THAT PLAYS TOGETHER   97
   2.11 CRASH AND LEARN   100
   2.12 DEALMAKERS   102
   2.13 ADDITION(AL) STRESS   105
   2.14 IT SEEMS ABSURD   107
   2.15 ANOTHER DEPARTURE   110
   2.16 "DOCTOR, DOCTOR!"   114
   2.17 THE DREAMS, OH, THE DREAMS   116
   2.18 TROUBLES   118

3.0 EPISODE THREE
   3.1 POLITICAL CORRECTNESS ASIDE   123
   3.2 MILESTONE?   128
   3.3 SNOW COVERS DEEP   131
   3.4 ROCK-AND-ROLL WITH THE PUNCH   134
   3.5 PRELUDE   137
   3.6 NOT FOR THE WEAK   140
   3.7 LAYOFF GLOOM   144
   3.8 BATMAN RIDES   149
   3.9 A SPY IN BLACK   154
   3.10 SOUL STIRRING   158
   3.11 BATMAN ASCENDS   161
   3.12 IN A GOOD PLACE   163

4.0 EPISODE FOUR
   4.1 CAN'T THINK STRAIGHT   169
   4.2 MORE DAYS WITHOUT DATES   174
   4.3 FOSTURING DIVINE EDUCATION   180
   4.4. EUROPEAN INTERLUDE   182

5.0 LAST EPISODE?
   5.1 "FOOLED YOU!"   191
   5.2 FLEE   192
   5.3 SEARCH FOR PASSAGE   195
   5.4 THE BRITS OFFER AID   197
   5.5 RENAISSANCE MAN   199
   5.6 DELAYED BY BEAUTY   202
   5.7 A FRIEND'S ADVICE   204
   5.8 GRAVE OF TEARS   206
   5.9 THE SOULS OF ROMA   208
   5.10 THE PROMISED LAND   215
   5.11 JUMP   218
   5.12 NOCTURNAL JOURNEY   220
   5.13 GARDEN CITY   223
   5.14 A STEEP APPROACH   228
   5.15 A NEW COMMAND   230
   5.16 EXILED   232
   5.17 ISRAELIS RELENT   233
   5.18 LIMBO   236
   5.19 ESCAPE   240
   5.20 EXPOSED   243
   5.21 LIBERTY   247
   5.22 CARRIED AWAY, AGAIN   250
   5.23 SAFE FROM MYSELF   253

6.0 EPILOGUE   255

7.0 INSIGHTS AND TAKEAWAYS
     7.1 WE NEED MENTALCARE   257
     7.2 WE ARE NOT ALONE   259
     7.3 BIPOLAR NEVER LEAVES, BUT…   261

8.0 RESOURCES
     8.1 MENTAL HEALTH INFORMATION   263
     8.2 INFORMATON ON THE BAHÁ'Í FAITH   265
     8.3 ABOUT ME   266
     8.4 CONTACT ME   267

9.0 ENDNOTES
     9.1 EPIGRAPH SOURCES   268
     9.2 REFERENCES AND NOTES   268

10.0 ACKNOWLEDGMENTS   275

PREFACE

Have you heard of the term "psychotic" or "psychotic break?"

Psychosis is a symptom of a condition, like sneezing is a symptom of a cold. But psychosis is worse than sneezing or sniffles. Many people who have bipolar disorder like me experience psychosis during their high, or manic, episodes. In a psychotic state a person can experience delusions or hallucinations that risk death. I wish being manic was like a sneeze or cough.

In psychology, a delusion is a persistent false psychotic belief regarding the self or persons or objects outside the self. Delusions maintain themselves despite indisputable evidence to the contrary, for example the losing gambler convinced he will win "the big jackpot." Hallucinations are sensory perceptions (visual images, sounds, or sensations) that occur without actual external stimuli, such as hearing voices when no one has spoken, or seeing things not actually there.

Bipolar disease, with its chemical imbalances in the brain, can cause delusions and hallucinations and more. These thoughts, scenes, and ideas aren't real. But to a person with mania, or depression, they are as real as what you hold in your hand this moment.

My psychiatrist advised me, "Rodney, your grandiose thoughts, what we call delusions of grandeur, will never go away.

"However, something is in your makeup, your genes, or your determination, not to let this illness rule your life. Perhaps its your own effect on your epigenetics, I'm not sure. But in my experience, what you've achieved and the marriage you have is not common for those with bipolar.

"Just the opposite. Too many have a manic episode. We stabilize them on antipsychotics, and then they cycle down to severe depression. We treat them for that and hope they return to normal. Weeks or months later another manic episode follows, and it starts all over."

That was 2013 after five episodes. I've had two more. I am lucky.

Facts: You or someone you know may be bipolar.

The disorder is lifelong.

It is the sixth leading cause of disability worldwide,
  with over twelve million people affected in the United States,
  and it costs the U.S. economy $45 billion annually.[1]

Correct diagnosis is difficult, and not definitive through blood, x-ray, or laboratory tests. The average period from onset of symptoms around age twenty-five to clinical identification is ten years. Mine, undiagnosed, manifested itself at age fourteen with risky and delinquent behaviors.

There is no cure.

One in five patients with the condition commits suicide.[2]

It's not pretty. "Horrible," is another fact. That is the word my wife Janet used to describe it.

She felt the full brunt of my mood swings, cruel words, and crazy behaviors, and she dealt with them even as I was deaf and dumb to her concerns, worries, and hurts. Others around me suffered as well.

At times, although physically present in this world, mentally I was in a world without physical or social constraints.

What we now call bipolar disease was unknown until an article published by psychiatrist and Frenchman Jean-Pierre Falret in 1851. He described it as "circular insanity," from which a patient experienced cycles of manic excitement and cycles of depression. It became known as manic depression. Since its origins, the disease remains misunderstood, misdiagnosed, and mistreated, although more information is available now.

Despite its debilitating effects, the disease is manageable. Lithium, a natural salt not widely prescribed by the American medical establishment until the early 1970s, proved effective. Science has developed other medicines since. Helpful thought and behavioral control techniques exist in CBT. Before these, we were in mental institutions, prisons, homeless shelters, or out terrifying those who loved us. Many of us still are.

Our families and friends, police, and society, are not sure how to handle us when either manic or depressive episodes strike.

The upshot?

Life is meant to be happy and fulfilling. It should be, and I believe this memoir shows that. There are more successes than failures. I held onto a career with New Jersey state government for thirty-nine years, during which time I received state, regional and national awards. I earned the trust of superiors and the loyalty of staff despite disappointing or hurting people, as you'll see.

Bipolar disease, horrible as it is when it strikes, need not destroy individuals, families, relationships, careers, hopes, or dreams. When people are open about the illness, and society dispels its stigmas, significant steps can attack it. With understanding, patience, and care, normal living results.

The key?

We deserve and require a universal social and mental health program to close gaps, identify symptoms earlier, and inculcate best practices to treat it. In the United States, we have Medicare and Medigap programs for seniors, Medicaid, CHIP, and more.

We, and the world, require a Mentalcare program for all ages.

NOTES TO READERS

1. I wrote this memoir from the first-person point of view so that you'll experience what I experienced firsthand. Therefore, all occurrences of "I," "me," and "my," may not appear where expected and should be inferred. You'll find the royal "We" for example, as well.

The average human brain produces sixty- to seventy-thousand thoughts per day or fifty per minute. A thought results from a mental process in which a psychological association or a model of the world forms. A manic brain processes thoughts and associations more rapidly than normal, resulting in expansive streams of thoughts and emotions that explode without ceasing. They ramp up to extreme levels. Also, know that an average person speaks 125-150 words per minute. A manic brain is faster than this, and a telltale sign is rapid speech.

It's as if the brain is high on methamphetamine.

Information on bipolar in section 7.0.

2. As a longtime Bahá'í, there are many references to the Bahá'í Faith (pronounced Buh-high), founded by the nobleman Bahá'u'lláh (Ba-ha-ol-lah), in mid-nineteenth century Persia. Although its roots are Islamic, the Bahá'í Movement is a recognized independent worldwide religion, with an expanding 7.3 million adherents who live in 221 countries and principalities.

Its watchword is simple, but not simplistic: "The world is but one country, and mankind its citizens."[3]

Information on it in Section 8.2.

3. My thoughts in the text are often in *italics*.

4. Original haiku-like verses intersperse the narrative as succinct recaps, insights or emotions gleaned from hindsight and are my commentary where they appear.

1.0 EPISODE ONE

1.1 SOMETHING'S NOT RIGHT

A firecracker amusement park of spinning, rolling, speeding rides jammed with screaming children and teens, mixes with tired-looking carnies crying "Step up! Step up for the ride of your life!" Worn-looking teens at their wheels of chance booths divert my attention with yells of "Here ya go, only a quarttah, win the big prize!" Sounds of arm-swinging, rapid-talking, boisterous boardwalk walkers and bench sitters mingle in a loud cacophony. Look at my spot on Steel Pier and react to the pot-pourri of intrusive images just as... open eyes.

6:20 read the clock hands. Rise from bed, slip out, deliberate, cautious, silent as a mouthless ghost. *Let her sleep.*

Whistle... wheeze. Whistle... puff. Whistle... puff. Her breaths are gentle winds blowing sanctuary across her REM dreams. God bless her. Hope He fills her every wish. *Why in the universe does she love Me?*

Whisper the bathroom door shut and perform rituals, not flushing. Slip out and pad back. Slide open the closet door and lift sharkskin suit pants out, don them then weave a black belt through the loops. Pull a white long-sleeved shirt off the wire-thin dry cleaner's hanger, lift a tie off the rack and fingers knot by rote. Stretch into black cotton socks, carry black rubber-soled shoes to the dining room and push size eleven feet into them. At the kitchen door pull on jacket, grab wallet, keys, and fit glasses over nose and ears. *Did I have to go? Why Me? I know, it had to be You.*

Turn the ignition on in my faded yellow Chevette with its jury-rigged rusted circular saw blade locking its left shock absorber in place, buckle up lap seatbelt and put the gearshift in D. Drive six miles on narrow Trenton streets, five miles of skirting jaywalkers, ruts and potholes, and shout over the radio's insistent commercials. Sing out the memorized lyrics of classic pop and rock icons or one-hit wonders streaming from the new FM stations. *The music died when you died, Dad.*

"Hah. I know you're listening, don't give a shit." The Watchers record my spoken words on their hidden dashboard microphone, ready to intervene. Mimic lyrics until they echo in a House of Mirrors where reflections from lip-syncing singers fold and extend to infinity.

Park in State Lot 15A across from the New Jersey monumental War Memorial building. The slots are semi-empty as drivers queue up. Exit yellow money pit and light a Kool, five left. Climb Willow Street's hill and turn on West State to the Towne House Restaurant owned by personable Greeks, a dark one-room Jersey diner amid low and middle-

1

class storefronts, apartments on their upper floors. State and Broad, the hub of Trent's Town, lies a block and a half up.

"Mornin' ladies." Hank and Mary stop their caterwauling.

Take a last suck. Tamp the cigarette stub out in a thick glass ashtray on the mottled brown Formica counter in front of seven spinnable stools.

Mary nods, "Mornin' Rod." She pours sugar and cream into a thick paper cup with Greek designs, adds steaming coffee from a spigot on one of two steel urns, and presses the lid tight. She lays it on the corner with the chicken-scratch check. Leave a dime tip.

"Thanks, Mary, later." *What if you smiled?* They resume their barbs and jabs at each other's serving prowess. Hand Spiro two quarters at his well-guarded register from which he never leaves, shuffle out past the street-level boarded windows of bronze-colored thin steel plates, and head south on Willow. Enter Taxation building's glass doors, pass a uniformed state security guard, stride to an elevator, push UP, one opens, and turn and punch 2 from the choice of ten.

Doors glide open in a swoosh sound into the foyer. Enter BDP's windowless door, trudge down the hallway, turn left into familiar gray fabric-coated cubicle, walls five feet high, amid dozens of interlocked clones. Alone. Sit, grip face in chilled palms. "Up. Is it possible you went there? Ugh, Dad, should've known you better." *How soon before I follow you? Is my heart bad too?*

Tighten eyelids, smash head on arms, stare at royal purple shapes and yellow blobs as they float and swirl in rimmed black nothingness. Can't focus, can't stop on just one. They don't pause. *Is this...?*

Empty. Nothing but swirling contours. *What chance do I have?* "Rod. Souls are eternal. You can't die."

Pick up pen, print on blue-lined yellow work pad.

MEDITATION#1: NOONDAY PRAYER:
WHAT EXISTS?
NOTHING EXISTS
WHO EXISTS?
GOD EXISTS

Scrawl seven more pages of verses. *Stop your sobbing.* "Death, you found Me." *My turn.* Janet, Mom, Jess, everyone's disappeared, even the dead. Can't help it. Can't avoid it. Days ago, a dutiful son. This the remnant I'm left with.

"Why a void? Why can't I hope? Can I at least hope?" Soul's irrelevant.

"Life's a bitch made from addictive Oreo cookies with cream-filled centers, and we stuff our face then die from gluttony. Don't want to live." *Slow down... Easy... Concentrate.*

"Ahh, coffee."

"What were Bahá'u'lláh's words? 'He should forgive the sinful, and never despise his low estate, for none knoweth what his own end shall be.' Got that right!

'How often hath a sinner attained at the hour of death to the essence of faith, and, quaffing the immortal draught, hath taken his flight unto the Concourse on high!'"[4]

Dad had drunk his last draught with a vodka chaser. *On what day will I drink from the immortal cup? Will it taste sweet or bitter, cold or hot?*

But then the rest of His words strike like a thunderbolt.

"And how often
  hath a devout believer,
    at the hour of his soul's ascension,
      been so changed
as to fall into the nethermost fire!"[4]

"Brrr…." *Who wants that? Snap out of it.*

Shuffle a five-inch-tall stack of file folders, open one, examine IBM's equipment inventory row by row. "What the hell should I do with this piece of shit?" Close it. Flip through minor reports. Black letters and numbers blur. *Why afraid?* Daylight through the coated windows and artificial light from the fat overhead fluorescent tubes stream their muted radiance through frosted plastic covers. Hide from office colleagues as they enter, unless confronted.

Don't dare open mouth except to inhale hourly Kools outdoors.

Timex shows half-past four, time to go. *Made it.* Smoke mandatory cigarette as hurry past the Masonic Temple and the War Memorial to the parking lot.

Drive and brake, drive and wait with a thousand other state employee drivers backed up on Trenton streets as a flurry of contrived scenarios and what-ifs charge like bulls chasing cows through a rock-strewn field.

"Slam!" Almost ram the Buick ahead when he brakes. Accelerate at last, maneuver until on County Route 524, make turns by rote. Park in our driveway behind Jan's Corolla. *Five of five. Pretend to be normal.*

Something's off. Like the time damn near sliced my left fingertip off, clipping handfuls of dead lavender salvia stems in the garden. Didn't realize it was bleeding until red splotches fell on the surrounding brick path. Wrapped it in a dirty hand towel and drove to Emergency. Six stitches. Ever since, no feeling in that fingertip.

Why have feelings now?

As she serves Kraft Macaroni & Cheese for Jesse and stew for us from the crock pot, Janet recounts her day with our toddler in tow, their errands, and completed chores. "Rod, I swept the basement floor, don't forget you have to finish painting it."

I don't care.

3

Two hours later, floor paint drying, smile as she reads *Goodnight Moon* and tucks Jess to sleep. Collapse in our mahogany bed, pillows upright against the two-foot-high scrolled headboard. We turn on *M*A*S*H* with its catchy tune and oxymoronic Korean wartime humor, then *WKRP in Cincinnati* and chuckle again. Unready for normal sleep at ten, turn onto left side, away from her, shut eyes, and remain motionless. *What should I do? Who am I? Why wait? Should I share this with her, before the world cowers in fear from its self-inflicted follies? Should I leave?*

Janet turns off TV, walks her empty teacup into the kitchen, checks the backdoor lock, and turns off the kitchen light, her usual routine. She reads and clicks off her lamp at ten-thirty, curls under the covers, and turns to rest her busy body and mind for another day of ministering to Jesse, to Me.

Run the tip of a sword-like tongue between my teeth. Scrunch on left side, an extra pillow between legs. Conjure a world where comfortable sheets, blankets, and soft pillows cuddle everyone in peaceful dreams.

They deserve days of comfort too.

1.2 GOTTA GO

Raise head.

2:10. *Damned clock.*

Blinds and curtains conceal constellations as conjure their sparkles in a fast-spinning empyrean outside my bedroom. Only spacewalkers can appreciate what's out there all around us.

Rise, *careful don't wake her!* Ginger-like, grab jeans and Tee-shirt from the chair. Close door with a whisper. Tiptoe to the bathroom and place them on the hamper. Pull the hollow lauan door, press on it with left fist, pull and downturn doorknob with right hand, pull tight with the jamb, and upturn knob. Release. Flick the light switch.

Sit, pee into American Standard's cold-seated bowl, protected in a cocoon of 1950s pink-tiled safety. The urge itches. Unload.

"I'm your damn worst nightmare. Hell. That's for you, China, invading Vietnam. Can only guess what you would have done, like Tibet."

Again.

"Poof! Feel My Power." Heels raise above the pink-tiled floor. Muscle spasms shake left leg like an air jackhammer, up down, up down, up down....

Unload again. "Soviet Union, you too. Domination destroys. Must you both scare us with your atomic tests?"

Boom! Another. "What's it feel like? When will you stop shaking us?" Leg stops. "Smell my stink."

Right hand, hand of power, wipes. Flush, wash, pull up jeans, push arms through shirt, hit switch, inch doorknob open.

Push. Listen. *Don't step on cracks.* Pause by his room. *Gotta go, Jess. Sorry, gotta go.* Slip into loafers by the kitchen door. Grab wallet, keys, glasses.

Rev Janet's Corolla, roll down windows, shift into reverse, drive through empty Yardville outskirts under moonglow and headlights. Streetlamps and telephone poles are at attention like Roman Centurions lining the Appian Way. Drive past the semi-Victorian homes in Allentown. Turn onto two-lane County Route 539 toward the Jersey shore.

A man's hyper voice on the radio implores, "You'll love the Sparkomatic! Our new digital AM/FM Cassette car radio, with exceptional reception. We can convert your eight-track units as well. Order in the next hour before we sell out. Call one-eight-hundred..."

"Fuck you, sell out. You can't tell me what to buy. Why in the name of should I trust you? Excellent reception My ass." Push button.

"...and Pope John Paul II's visit to the United States is historic...."

"Let the priests marry for Chrissakes! The Apostles married, and they're saints. Are you even aware some priests are queers?[5] Dammit. Only thirteen, but that didn't stop Father B. Hell, I wasn't the only altar boy in his stable."

"I need music." Mimic syllables and sounds as they stream through cranked-up speakers. Join in unchained melodies and popular lyrics, upbeat, or downtown, sixties rock, or seventies pop. Chilled wind gusts blow and rush in.

"Puh-puh-puh, tap, tap, tapity-tap," on the steering wheel. Pull out a smoke. Cup hands to face, draw, toss match out the window. Drag.

"Ugh! Black tar. This shit is foul. Nuthin' but a damn chimney stack at a coal plant spewing cancer cells. Need to stop."

"Oomph!" Pitch pack and matches into crisp chilly October air.

"13...14...15...16..." as telephone poles wing past at 75 like the USS Enterprise jumping through space using warp drive on *Star Trek* reruns.

Whizz around the few moving vehicles. "Wonder where they're headed? He's got a tie on. Could be on his way to work. To *The Times* or *The Trentonian* 'cause it's so early?"

Shoot through the yellow blinking traffic light, needle at 80.

SPEED
LIMIT
50

"Yur kiddin' me."

Ahead, on the right, "A billboard? Here in Pine City? Your R.C. Maxwell logo should be RMIYC, 'Read Me If You Can.' Hawking real estate no less. Your reds stand out against short green pines, but... Bah, distractions. Ineffective. Who can remember a phone number speeding by? Whaddya want? Pull over on the shoulder and write it down?"

Other drivers glide in turtle cars as if it were a family Sunday outing.

"Let's pass you...and you...and you." Sail by like a speedboat, performing laps around rowboats. Register each finite movement, the short branches, outlines and shapes of dark frozen pines on the roadsides. Flashes of green plates with small white numbers connect.

"Milepost 24, so noted." Sandy, narrow, two-wheeled lanes shoot off through the endless pine forest on both sides.

"Where might you go? Passed you dozens of times. But can't scratch the car. An adventure for another time." Like a Ferrari at Le Mans, adhere like rubber cement to the county road driven so many times to the shore, as it dissects a million acres of the Pine Barrens as wind, weave, goose the accelerator on straightaways, round curves, and avoid crashes.

"They'll escape East Germany's barbed walls, mark me. The Prisoner of Venda is free. Uganda too, depose those dictators. See, solved it. I can solve them all." Odometer spins like a whirling dervish. "How many miles in the past five minutes? Gotta keep track."

Round a blind corner. "Perfect knew you'd be here." Zip up to the pump. Sunoco attendant is chatty; hit it off.

"Regular, my man, I've got a long trip ahead." Four minutes later, hands back change. Leap forward on spinning tires.

"Oh, poor world. Will you please stop bickering? Oh. To never see Janet or Jesse again! But Bob and Barb, they'll look after you. You'll be okay. The Bahá'ís will help." Legs, stomach, chest, arms, quake.

"What if they can't? Shit, what then? But they will."

Wipe raining tears. Hands wet, rub on jeans.

END IT

"Agree, this is pointless."

Lamp shines. Megan's Bar Party poster screams out… **LIVE MUSIC.**

Brown telephone pole beckons.

Dashboard needle climbs… 70… 71… 72…

Begin swerve…

   four-wheeled bullet leans right…

      finds target…

"Megan… Oh Megan… I'm going to crash your party!"

1.3 YES LORD

A whisper filters through the cabin…

NOT YET

Careen past. "Fuck you Megan's Bar!" Regain control. "Step on the gas Rod. Get away from this shithole."

Ride the crest of the road ribbon through waves of pine trees like a surfer glides through the Pipeline. Jet past silhouetted awry sentinels and short, scruffy scrubs, a hodgepodge that blankets tens of miles of flatness peppered by low sandy hills that undulate in misshapen treetops like an endless ocean of green, gray-black shadows.

A rambunctious Grey Squirrel in a valiant attempt to cross darts into Toyota's beams. "Watch it buddy," and it freezes, tail in the air like an ice pop then retreats into the Pitch Pines and Red Cedar faster than Flash can circle Central City.

A fork. Low green sign reads CRESTWOOD VILLAGE. Shoot left into still limitless Virginia pines, Atlantic White Cedars, and Sour Gums, short, tall, thick, thin, gnarled, black as the pervasive night. County Route 530 leads into a methodical development of cookie-cutter dimensions.

"Is this near Toms River?"

Spy a Cape Cod with lights glowing behind green shutter windows with thin white curtains. Skitter into its driveway. Jolt car to a stop on the concrete apron, stride to the Tic-Tac-Toe windowed white door.

"Bang, bang, bang."

A short man lifts aside the frilly yellow curtain. *He's looking at Me.* The wooden door opens wide. A welcoming couple stands expectant on a faded blue carpet. The short wiry man, dressed in tan slacks and white shirt, her in a pale robe matching her thinned white hair. Both their wrinkled faces, arms and necks show age spots scattered like shotgun pellets on dusky hides.

"Hi, I'm Rodney. Can you tell me the quickest way to the shore?" They smile. *They can see I'm not a serial killer.*

"It's chilly out. Come in for a cup of hot tea," she invites. Enter the sparse beige living room, kitchen straight ahead.

"Oh, no tea thanks, but it's a dear thought." Rub left-hand fingertips and nail ends from pinky to index back and forth across thumb.

"How do you like the neighborhood? Can I get to the shore from here?"

"Son, turn around, make a right, and then make a left at the stop sign back onto Route 530. You'll be there in no time," says Mister Cape Cod.

"Thank you both, in a hurry, bye."

Drive east. Smell the water. The radio blares, "Baby, heaven must have sent you…." It has.

Close eyes.

HAIFA

"Must…get…to…Haifa. Gotta get there, can't stop."

SAND CO. sign looms as clear as the exposed side of the gibbous moon overhead. "Where there's sand there's water."

"Screech…" Veer right onto a wide-rutted packed dirt drive. In twenty yards make out three large red dump trucks parked like gladiators, ready for the crowd's cheers or hisses and Nero's thumb up or thumb down. Reach an open space ringed by brown-green pines in deep shadows.

"Uurchh." Unbuckle, jump out, "WHO DO YOU THINK YOU ARE! YOU DON'T KNOW SHIT!"

Pace, "Damn these clothes." Kick-off shoes, pop shirt buttons, unzip pants, all of it. Bunch them up. "Unghh!" Throw them mightily into the woods.

"I'M COMING! NOTHING CAN STOP ME!"

Toss gold ring? Keep it? Toss it? But it's engraved, *Alláh-u-Abhá.*[6]

"Where's the beach?" Search in headlights' low glow. *Is that water? Don't need a boat. Ocean waves will float Me.* Stomp further east.

"YOU CAN'T STOP ME! YOU CRAZY FUCKED-UP PLACE!"

Yellow-white moon face listens, nods, acknowledges Who I Am. Right hand raises, then left, nod to Him in return. Spread arms. Reach. "Forgive them. Forgive Me. I should have come sooner."

The blowing breeze pushes backward.

"The next manifestation of God![7] Humankind needs to hear this. Able to generate peace and cooperation. Not just possible, but probable. THIS AIN'T NO PIOUS DREAM DAMMIT!"

Delicate repose drifts down like a silk kimono hugging bare flesh. Power rises, crests of submission wash through ears, mind, spirit…listen….

"Yes, Lord! 'O Lord! Increase my astonishment at Thee'"[8]

Breathe in the valley of wonderment and amazement.

"Like You Bahá'u'lláh,[7] I was '…asleep on My couch, when lo, the Breeze of God wafting over Me roused Me from My slumber. His quickening Spirit revived Me, and my tongue was unloosed to voice His Call.'"[9]

Stand in the silent coliseum except for the slight echoes of wind. Limbs vibrate with overwhelming power and supreme omniscience.

Peer outward above the ring of pines, the outline of a massive dark shape emerges.

9

A mighty Lion stands framed in tawny fierceness, long thick mane
  blowing, he's five times the size of the planet
He straddles Earth, silhouetted amid a black expanse
  containing countless blazing suns.
On powerful hind legs, front paws outthrust, massive head
  raised, the King of the Animal Kingdom, ferocious, fearsome,
  reveals his wide, sharp-toothed jaws agape.
The continents tremble and seas churn...

"ROOAARR"

Reverberations take root.
"I've risen as Your Lions have in the past 'to make the limbs of
mankind quake.'"[10]

    eyelids close, leap into black depths
  soft explosions surround and engulf
    once drowning in earth's miasma . . . now floating . . .
   imbued . . . permeated . . . exbued
  stillness and motion combine
    thoughts of peace . . . heartbeats . . . blood . . . quicken and ease
      inhale the fragrance of the Ancient Beauty[7]
   a clear Voice surges . . .

HAIFA AWAITS

"Yes Lord!"

    Peace settles like a cotton blanket on a newborn baby...

blackness   envelops

1.4 THE FIRST DEPARTURE

[Four weeks earlier, Monday, September 24, 1979]

"Who can this be?" Janet lifts the phone from its cradle by her side of our bed, lips frowning, her curly red hair in clumps, cute freckles as adorable as when we first met in Mister McMullen's eclectic art class.

Listen. She's intent for a full minute as she straightens and sits upright. Turns and watches me dress, her eyes concerned.

"Rod, it's your mom. You need to speak to her." Not like her to call this early.

"Rodney, I have sad news." *Heck.* Recognize the tone. Someone in the family has died. Know the drill; just not who. With my large family, it may be someone close, someone I met only once—or never heard of.

Plop on our bed with just a shirt and tie on.

"Donny just called."

"Dad?" He's the only one sorta care about in California.

"Um. Yes, I'm sorry. Donny told me your father died in his sleep. Donny checked on him and found him just past midnight."

"But he's so young!" Gaze up as Janet hovers. Dad, a faraway nebulous figure. Have only received a few note cards and Polaroids of him and his girlfriends. He's ex-Marine, divorced twice, lives in Irvine, California, and is, was, a school custodian. And a bachelor—and weekend alcoholic.

How will Stephen take the news?

"The EMT told Donny it was a massive heart attack, a silent myo, ah, my-o-card-i-al infarction." Hear every syllable as she continues with meager details. Janet's absorbed in what this means.

Rodney Carroll Richards Senior, namesake and progenitor; once brimming with confidence and love for women, gone. Whether a whimper, a gurgle, or a shout, no one heard.

Busy. Preoccupied. But I'll hafta go, put everything on hold. It'll mess up everything. Costly.

And time away. The new house and the scraping, spackling, painting and work it needs; our higher mortgage and nine percent interest rate; Jesse's care and toddler needs; car repairs, especially my Chevette; paying off credit cards for paint, supplies and living room furniture; my lowly computer operator salary the only income; what little savings, depleted; now, this.

But death doesn't give a damn about circumstances or the implications of losing someone. Or cares over what actions need to be taken when a loved one leaves family or friends hanging. Or whether there's a will. Or, or, or, and a million things.

No room to vacillate or consult my diminutive high school sweetheart.

"Mom, I'll leave today and take care of things. You call Stephen." *Someone must go.* I'm the only logical one who can; Mom has her own family with a husband and three kids.

Stephen can't afford it. Besides, he's never met Dad. He left us when Stephen was a toddler. I met him at fifteen, lived with him two years, and at least got to know who he was. Janet can't come because she left her Hamilton Township teaching post to care for Jesse. Besides, her severe air and motion sickness would make it too difficult. They don't need to go; they've never met Dad. Grandmom would find it difficult too. Who can say about Aunt Joan, his only sibling. *Bet the rest of the relatives won't fly three-thousand miles from Jersey to attend his service.*

Can't imagine Grandmom's pounds of sorrow. Mom is a thick-skinned Irish Catholic with a magnanimous heart. Both inured to hardship and trouble as mothers and wives. *No, this is our obligation. No way can I ask them to pay for the funeral. We'll hafta. Janet will understand.*

"Rodney dear, I trust you can do it."

"I'll do my best, Mom." Hang up.

My astute redhead of eight years of marriage says, "I'm so sorry, Rod. Do whatever you have to. Can I help?"

"Yeah, thanks, hon." Hug her petite frame for comfort because it's expected. "Best to leave today and make final arrangements, or at least be there. Can you get me a plane ticket? I have to call Chris too."

"Let me check on Jesse first."

Haven't been to Orange County since dropping out of college. Will be semi-alone there. Sift through past funerals. Never handled one, always an onlooker. The grown-ups took care of them. At least the State provides paid leave for up to three days for a death in the family, plus accrued paid sick and vacation days will help if needed.

Wait for Chris to arrive at eight-thirty. Dial her desk number and share the news.

"Do what you need to, Rod. Just go and the State will wait. I'll tell Virginia you'll be out and why." Kind; a change from her demanding, driven, intelligent, and efficient self. As Chief of Planning and Technical Services for the Bureau, Chris devours tasks like a contestant at a hot dog eating contest who piles on responsibilities as if they are tasty condiments. She doesn't believe in the common state employee maxim, "Close enough for government work." She expects it done right.

Phone adept and able assistant Alice with the news. "So sorry, Rod. What can I do to help?"

"Please follow up with Gene on the IBM equipment inventory. He promised a schedule today. Then go over that with Chris since she's waiting for an update. Oh, and call Jack Hoyer for status, Tony's waiting to hear about the ADR Librarian waiver of advertising, and the other system programmers are itching to get it too." We discuss other projects. Too much to check on, too much to do.

12

Hang up, walk to our living room bookcase, and pull out our two-inch thick medical dictionary. Thumb through its index for Myocardial Infarction. Page says part of Dad's heart had "seized within minutes." *And wouldn't ya know it, Donny found him, another bachelor breaking hearts.* Although Donny is twelve years younger, the two of them barhopped and caroused together, and were best buds.

So, it was quick. A blessing. *Hope my fate is similar. Only why so young?* The old joke surfaces: "Yup, my Daddy died peacefully in his sleep, and I hope to go that way too, at least, not kicking and screaming like his bus passengers."

Had he been with a woman? Too strenuous, maybe? Not funny.

Janet, past bookkeeper at Mercury Travel Agency in Trenton to pay her way through college, calls United and charges two-hundred-and-six dollars on our credit card. We agree paying for this will happen later, how much it will cost, no idea. Or where the money will come from but obligated to do what it takes. *Doubt Dad had assets, doubly doubt he had savings.*

It's raining. Enter the garage, lift the door, and light a Kool. "Ahh," the sucking drags tastes reassuring. Nicotine courses through addicted bloodstream. The throbbing buzz in my head and quickened pulse remind me I need it. Mind fuzzes.

Bitchin' California. Last there in '68. *Are you still carefree?*

Not for this, not by a furlong.

"A race to bury the dead."

Must host a good show
in his always sunny place
Doubt will take home a win

13

1.5 SECOND DEPARTURE

Janet pulls the car to the curb like others doing the same. Jump out and unload at United's glass doors at Newark Liberty Airport.

"Wish me luck." Hugs, first Jess in his car seat, then Jan. Jesse's innocent smile says he is too young to know what leaving or death means. Jan's smile is pragmatic.

"Be careful, Rod, call me when you get there."

"Okay, hon." *What will Southern California be like?*

Enter the terminal, buy coffee, walk to the gate, check-in, sit and wait to be called, and board. Scoot into ticketed window seat. Revel in the powerful thrust of takeoff as New Jersey spirals away. Settle in and speed to LAX in Los Angeles. The DC-10's seat is a comfortable fit for my hips as scan the blackened sky outside the jet's tiny window. Absorb emergency flight prep demonstrated by the mechanical stewardess.

Ahh, Dad. What does it mean? Don't love him, but don't hate the guy, despite leaving us. No reason to hate. Cutting off an Ewing police car when fifteen while driving without a license, with open package goods in the front seat, wasn't too bright. *You took me in then, or, sure as my name is the same as yours, would have landed in jail for something else.*

How laid back the west coast lifestyle. And the sex! How readily available. You even introduced me to Betty, a five-minute partner three times my age, and we had the strangest sex as she talked nonstop. The pot, drugs and alcohol too, all casual accouterments. Part and parcel of the culture, even though you didn't smoke pot or throw parties in our apartment, you gave me almost unlimited freedom because you treated me like an adult. Equal but not.

Regardless of feelings, I'll do my best for you.

> *Bitchin' teenage thoughts*
> *during three-hour flight*
> *pass as swift as clouds, like Dad*

Watch reads quarter after eight. Donny's at the gate. My older second cousin by nine years has kept his clean-shaven, dark Italian good looks. Shorter than Dad in stature but not in glibness for the ladies, his thick black hair recedes too. His look of recognition is like the stare from a glassy eyeball of a dead trout on a fancy dinner plate at the historic Coconut Grove, where Dad took me once.

Over ten years since last here and seen palm trees.

Donny and Dad shared the bachelor's creed: take advantage of every opportunity to take advantage. Uncle John, Dad's uncle by blood, a DOM, is the third in their triumvirate. He's been married to Aunt Charlotte forever.

Inhale a Kool on the way to the car, slide in, and Donny jumps on the twelve-lane Santa Ana Freeway to Irvine. First drove this freeway at age sixteen. Past midnight it was walls of white fog so solid had to roll down the window and poke my head out to see. The region we head to in Orange County is three-dozen miles south, near where I had lived in fall of '65 to spring of '67, and again when attempted Fullerton Junior College in '68.

"Married yet, Donny?"

"Heh, not yet, Junior, having too much fun. Since you left, I still work in janitorial services, but I'm a regional manager." *Does he want me to say something?*

"That's great, Donny, congratulations." Although family, we had been arm-length friends because throughout sojourns here he had hired me. Cleaned Motor Trend Magazine offices in Anaheim on second shift. Large color photos of silver Ferraris and red Lamborghinis hung in matching-sized glass and silver frames along private hallways and in offices. Wiped and dusted them without an ounce of envy, then did desktops and windowsills. Emptied the small blue trashcans then vacuumed the dark carpets, walled office by walled office. Spent paychecks on pot, Kools, and cafeteria lunches, first at the brand new and progressive Estancia High School without doors or windows in classrooms, then at older Tustin High, then at college.

"So, what've you been up to all these years, Junior? Where do you live? Rodney told me you had a son."

Relatives persisted in calling me Junior out here, even Dad, as if I were ten years old. The only ones who addressed me that way, but never minded. *Hah! Nobody in Jersey even knows I'm a Junior.*

Describe Jesse's cheerful personality. Describe Hamilton's safe mediocrity and explain how our newly mortgaged rancher and half-acre property needs tons of work. Gloss over new duties in computer-purchasing and equipment maintenance with the Bureau of Data Processing in the Treasury Department. Mention pretty and insightful assistant Alice.

He turns his head, his ears perk, and his eyebrows rise. *He thinks I'm popping her on the side, I'll bet.* Same hot-blooded Donny.

Don't tell him why Jan and I moved to the rural outskirts of Hamilton Township outside Trenton. How one afternoon driving down busy Nottingham Way we came upon flashing lights and found two police cars and an ambulance at our house. A driver had crashed his early model Ford into our mighty oak tree and died on our front lawn. A local Carothers tow truck was hooking up the smashed vehicle.

"Jan, we should move, for Jesse's sake."

Sad to discover later the older gentleman who died was Dave Carothers's dad.

15

Donny doesn't ask further questions. Mention the Bahá'í Faith and how involved we are and sense he's not interested. Typical Donny, Catholic only when asked.

"Any arrangements for Dad's funeral?"

"We had to contact somebody, Junior, so your Uncle John called Donegan-Beckenbauer Mortuary in Orange to handle the arrangements. I'll leave you their number when we get to your dad's place."

We speed forward with a music station on but silence in the car. Stare out the windows studying the souped-up 50s, 60s, and 70s muscle cars, and the speeders, weavers, and no slowpokes. Garish billboards flash and the bland highway landscape is monotonous green except for occasional towering palm trees and the mountains ahead which look like low hills. Meander through hedonistic months spent here as a youth. As we enter Irvine, major differences appear as the southbound lanes narrow from six to three.

"Donny, what happened to the orange groves?"

"Yeah, construction's boomed since you left, Junior. Wait till you see."

When we had lived in the area, Irvine comprised two words: EL TORO. The Marine Air Station, a sprawling, 4,600-acre military aviation base built in the 1940s, managed the largest aircraft known. Dad had hung out at its Non-Commissioned Officer's Club. Orange and grapefruit groves had surrounded the base for dozens of miles, the wide swaths of fruit trees originated the county named after them.

Now, groves gone too. *Heck, it used to be lush and beautiful.*

All unfamiliar territory. High stucco walls surround developments of single-family monstrosities and apartment complexes, with a strip mall on every other corner.

Recall drinking buddies Mike Gorman with his green GTO and Ray Hamburgey with his open-top raw-gray Jeep in need of paint and our trips to Disneyland, the boyish unchained weekends on the sands of the Pacific, dancing in the nightclubs of Newport Beach and L.A., and the suntanned sculpted girls eager to share intimate acquaintance.

And you too Dad.

Arrive in L.A.
to shocking ten-year changes
Where are past delights?

1.6 THE APARTMENT TALKS

Donny's not kidding.

Irvine. You used to be sleepy and deserted; now your a sprawling megalopolis. Only wealth and crowding bring that.

No near slums like downtown pockets of Trenton, no roaming beggars, no buildings over three stories except scattered offices, and no orchards. The adobe-walled complexes filling every block look like Army camps. We exit the freeway ten minutes later onto Culver Avenue. Donny pulls into a one-row lot on Pinestone.

"Check out that Chevy parked there, Junior. That's your dad's, and you should use it while you're here. I guess you'll have to sell it." The 1975 midnight blue Impala, twice the size of my Chevette, appears unscratched. *Maybe I can drive it home. I'll take Route 66 like Martin Milner. Could use a three-day vacation.*

The stucco building that looks like a motel has sixteen units. We trudge up wide, freestanding concrete steps to the second-floor walkway.

"Number twenty-three." *He lived alone, but not on weekends—not if he could help it I'll bet.* Donny unlocks the creaky door and hands over a Budweiser key ring.

"The car keys on it too."

"Flip." The ceiling light exposes a doppelganger of our 1966 pad in Tustin. A block from the high school, we had resided in a garden apartment complex after he and Marilyn separated. This living room is also shadowy tan with only two paintings, the 18 x 24-inch rising white stallion with front legs pawing the air on black velvet bordered by its chrome frame the most prominent. Dad bought it in Tijuana, Mexico, for four bucks. Eye-catching, although dusty now, its presence is a stark reminder of his Italian Stallion persona. His RCA stereo turntable sits on a short metal folding table under the picture, with stacks of LPs leaning upright against its spindly legs.

Song after song echo from the velvet voices of Bennett, Dino, Williams, and Mathis, and of course, Ol' Blue Eyes, The Chairman of the Board, Sinatra. A small black TV set with rabbit ears sits near it on another thin metal folding table next to the wall. A rectangular wooden coffee table sits empty-topped in the middle. Mismatched end tables with matching green lamps and faded lampshades mark bookends for a cheap spartan brown foam-cushioned sofa, no pillows.

A surge of déjà vu carries thoughts back to a particular night. He's dressed to go out.

"So, Dad, you listen to this classic music all the time. What's your favorite song?"

17

"Ah, "Spanish Eyes" by Al Martino. He's the greatest."

Recall the refrain serenaded so often, "You and your Spanish eyes will wait for me." The perfect description for Dad's love 'em, leave 'em, keep 'em hangin' style of romance.

Spy the light blue Princess Phone on the end-table. In that same spot a bulky black rotary had sat ready. That rotary, and that spot on the couch next to it, a bottle of Smirnoff's and his little black book, fixtures of Dad's Friday Night Procedure.

Weekend nights by five-thirty he takes a shower and gears up in clean navy slacks, wingtips under black stretchy socks, colored pressed shirt open at the collar, often a tie, and navy blazer. Ready to go gallivanting or to welcome a lady friend. He sits on the corner of the couch by the black rotary and smokes a Marlboro as he thumbs through his black book. Pours a shot of Smirnoff's from the bottle next to him, raises the glass to his lips, jerks back, and downs it in a gulp.

Phone call...shot. A rare Marlboro. Until successful.

"Hello? Jennifer?... It's Rodney...Yes, how are you?... Would you like to meet me at the NCO Club say in an hour?... Good, that's my girl... Looking forward to it too, see you there."

Then, I might drive him to the El Toro base in his '57 Chevy, even forage in the immense NCO kitchen refrigerators and make a sandwich until hoisting him drunk onto the backseat of the Bel Air two hours later. Or on other nights, drop him off at a bar. Then go milk a black cow at A&W and waste time until closing, observing with envy the hot rodders as they cruise through, pop wheelies, and lay rubber, or lust after the shapely servers in short-shorts and roller skates.

When a lady came to the apartment, would scoot to Ray's or Mike's, or take a drive to Newport Beach, walk the ocean sands under thousands of stars or poke into bars, or drive fifteen miles on the dark rocky coastline to Laguna Beach tethered like a migratory bird until time to return.

Breakaway.

Enter the kitchenette with its speckled-yellow dinette set, then pass the bathroom, as an 8 x 9-foot bedroom, also spartan, completes the scene. Toss my travel bag on the stripped-down bed, a stain on its left side.

"Thanks for the ride, Donny, and thanks for your help. You were a close friend to Dad and me years ago, especially those two months at your place when Dad was tapped out."

"Yeah Junior, we had good runs when you were here except when you hijacked my phone." *He used to get so angry he won't let me forget.*

AT&T long-distance charges to Janet were four dollars plus then, for ten minutes. Called her twice a week—in secrecy—on Donny's phone. Dad wouldn't permit using his. Didn't believe in handouts. Said, "Work for it." Had returned from Jersey to live with Dad and registered part-time at Fullerton Junior College for the cost of a few textbooks. Janet lived home in Ewing, as an education major at Trenton State College, our romance separated by ten states.

Break out of reverie.

"Donny, about Donegan, I'm sure they'll be fine. Thanks for contacting someone. Are Uncle John and Aunt Charlotte still in Garden Grove?"

"Yep, same place. Here's their number." He writes it on a yellow legal pad on the kitchen table, with Donegan's number.

"Junior, I have to go. I'll be out until after midnight, but you can reach me at noon, okay?" He hands over his business card.

"Yeah, thanks for your help. I'll call them early tomorrow."

"All right, bye kid." Place the chain across the door and lounge on the nondescript sofa, strike a match, and light up. *Tomorrow. What's it going to be like? Decisions and dollars, that's what. Funerals don't come cheap.*

Return to the bedroom and pull out a worn wooden dresser drawer that reveals folded black socks, folded white Tee-shirts, and folded white skivvies. In the closet hang pressed white and solid-colored long-sleeved shirts, a few casual print shirts, two blazers, and two dusky suits side by side. Few clothes for a bachelor's wardrobe.

Two pairs of polished, unmarred black wingtips line up on the floor facing in. A Kiwi shoeshine box lies nearby.

Princeton High School friends of his had nicknamed him "Sharpie"—always dapper—everything cleaned and pressed, like his public grooming. The Marine in him meant he always dressed and shaved except for gray sweatpants, a Marine Leatherneck blue sweatshirt, and white flip-flops whenever alone or with me in the apartment. A neatnik otherwise, nothing out of place.

Think of Donny, still a confirmed bachelor, Dad's only close friend beside Uncle John.

Yet here I am, a confirmed husband for four years longer than Dad's two failed marriages. Mine on solid steel-forged rails set on solid 4 x 6 pressure-treated ties by Janet's practical organization skills. *If I could just, please her, by responding to her and Jesse's needs. I'd be solid too.*

Thoughts of trials to come tomorrow race like A. J. Foyt competing on the kidney bean-shaped Trenton Speedway in its heyday. Visualize A.J. manhandling his stock Ford as another driver rides his bumper down the straightaway at over 150 mph to maximize draft. Two-dozen NASCAR drivers follow or attempt to pass him low then high until he zooms under the checkered flag when remember to phone Janet.

A bachelor's life
can be austere or decked out
for late-night trysts

1.7 SLEEPING WITH A GHOST

Janet's been waiting.

"Sorry, hon, should've called earlier. I made it. The flight was fine, great in fact. Cousin Donny picked me up and I'm at Dad's apartment now." Share sad impressions of California's bourgeoisie demise.

"I'll call your mom in the morning. She's worried about you. Any plans for the funeral?"

"Some. The family already contacted an undertaker, named Donegan-something. I'll visit them tomorrow. I'll reach out to Uncle John first and find out what else they've arranged."

"Good and try to sleep. Call me tomorrow when you know what's going on. Please don't go wild on the costs, Rod."

Yeah, sure, don't go wild. Is it even up to me? Funerals can be outrageous.

"You got it. I'll be back as soon as possible. Give my hugs to Jess. Luv you, bye."

Find her list and move to the yellow padded metal chair at the kitchen table with its matching yellow Formica top.

> *Make arrangements*
>
> *Order flowers from us and Grandmom*
>
> *Check Dad's papers for bills, checkbook, and a will*
>
> *Call Uncle John and Aunt Charlotte*
>
> *Check at school for pension or life insurance*

Grab pen, add **FLOWERS? SELL CAR OR DRIVE BACK?**

Step to the bedroom dresser and pull open drawers. Nothing resembles a will and testament. Find his checkbook.

"Some funds left at least." Few souvenirs or mementos. No knickknacks anyplace, either. He wasn't sentimental except for his crooners. Not cold, not talkative, but always direct. Crisp. "Unless it came to charming your women."

Open a letter we had sent. Inside, a Polaroid of Jesse sitting on his bed, legs out, arms wide, tussled black hair, wearing print pajamas and a blue-striped robe. Huge grin. Dad's only grandchild, whom he never met. "How will I lose you, Jesse? Will I die first as I'm supposed to?"

These tiny paper heaps seem meager for a man's legacy. *Too young. Fifty!* "Dad, were you in that terrible shape?"

Turn a page in his dog-eared brown address book, four times the size of the one I once knew. "Hey, Donna and Leslie." Dad, fifteen years older than Donna, wooed his buxom blonde bombshell with large gray-blue eyes like the pro he was after he separated from his second wife, Marilyn. I dated Leslie, Donna's quiet best friend.

"There's no point contacting these people, I have no idea who they are. None would have a clue who I am. Besides—too many. And where does Marilyn live?" They had separated nine months after I arrived from Jersey. He must have felt free again, his innate and natural mode unleashed, unable to change his prowling, female-chasing ways. We moved into the garden apartment next to Tustin High, and I transferred in from Estancia.

He teaches what I had already assimilated about driving and in May 1966 with the male Examiner in the passenger seat, take the test and hop two curbs in Dad's two-tone salmon Chevy Bel Air with its steering wheel as wide as a car tire. Earn a California license anyway, fourteen days past my sixteenth birthday. Jubilant, full of anticipation. Know Dad doesn't use the Bel Air much, since he walks across the street to school for work.

He lets me run with the pristine Chevy as I'd hoped.

But it's with the proviso "Junior, be there when I need a ride."

For the first time wonder, why didn't you enjoy driving? *I loved it, even in that big 'ole '57 boat.*

So, carted him places or pick him up. Every Monday morning though, he's poker-faced sober. No matter his weekend exploits, there are no signs of drunkenness from the night before, and he's ready for work on time. The V8 juice he gulped from miniature cans helped. He doesn't hit the vodka once during the week. "Dad, you deserve credit. You were reliable, neat, and organized."

Light up. Contemplate his sudden, inglorious end. Turn on his TV to ease growing low-key jitters. *What's going to happen tomorrow? Can I put it all on a credit card? Will they bill me?*

Fuzz out during a Dragnet rerun with Jack Webb and Harry Morgan in their monotone deadpans. At its conclusion, carry smokes and ashtray into the bathroom. Take a piss but too tired to brush teeth. Enter bedroom, turn the mattress over so the stain will be underneath, and put on clean sheets, no top cover, undress, climb on.

Sadness, an emotional construct. But duty, son to father, is a societal norm. Duty over feelings. The natural cycle. Death isn't supernatural, it's natural. Nothing here to be sorry about or spooked over.

"Tomorrow will be a pain at Donegan's. Hafta be on my game." Toss the challenge into a growing bin of death-related questions. "Where did your soul start on the continuum, Dad?"

"Ahh." Take a last hit of nicotine and stub the Kool out. Switch off the lamp and coil into position, left arm under the pillow. *Can I handle this?*

He died in this bed
24-hours ago
Death unlikely twice

21

1.8 UNEXPECTED ARRANGEMENTS

[Tuesday, September 25, 1979]

Head and body hum with renewed vigor under cascading water streaming from the showerhead. "Ahh, needed this."

Dry off, shimmy into Levi bell-bottoms, pull on a burgundy polo shirt, and slip into brown loafers. Press palms together and straighten fingers to find that quiet sacred spot of inner humility. Think of Dad.

"O God! Refresh and gladden his spirit, purify his heart, illumine his powers. I lay all his affairs in Thy hand. Now Thou art his Guide and Refuge...."[11] Finish the prayer I'd said so often to bolster my spirit.

Open eyes. "Dad, it's not morbid making your funeral arrangements, just necessary. I'll handle this like all fastballs thrown my way—hold the stance, wind up, and swing." If one strikes my body hard, or in this case wallet, won't ask 'Why me?'

Dial the number Donny left.

"Hello?"

"Hi Aunt Charlotte, it's Rodney." Aunt Charlotte, one of only five relatives out west.

"I'm so sorry, Junior, your dad was special to us." She should realize he wasn't that close to me.

"I know, thanks. So, you called a funeral home?"

"Yes, Donegan's. We've used them before. We set the viewing for tomorrow afternoon, not sure what else to do. Besides that, I don't know what to say, except that we're broken up about your father." *Please don't share the gloomy details.*

"Ah, is it okay that we set the viewing?" *It's done. Whaddya want me to say?*

"Sure, no problem. I'm calling them next. I'll share more details about the service as soon as I find out."

"Ask for Richard, the owner. We thought you would like to make the final arrangements. Is that all right?"

"That's fine. I owe him that." She's rushed. A nurse longer than I can remember, she worked long hours.

"Oh, and Aunt Charlotte, thanks for watching out for Dad."

"He was like a son. We'll miss him."

"I know you have to get to work."

"Yes, thanks, Junior."

"Okay, bye." Don't hanker for small talk. This will be a memory in a couple of days and won't see or hear from them again. Now that Rodney Senior is gone, Junior will disappear too in a few days. No reason to communicate exists.

Dial Donegan's. "Richard? This is Rodney Richards, ah, Junior. You have my father there."

"My condolences, Mister Richards. Can you please stop by here, say in an hour? I can answer all your questions."

"That'll be fine." He offers directions, on Chapman Avenue, the main drag in Orange, next to Santa Ana. Remember high school jaunts there to parties. At nine-thirty start the Impala, which thrums with horsepower.

"Hmmm, nice. Should drive this back home." To hell with gas and motel costs. Heck, I'll sleep in the backseat like I used to in high school when out late nights. Could be a helluva trip. Three days across the continent? Heck, only this time with no agenda and not cooped up on a graveyard Greyhound bus back to Jersey like '67, or driving here non-stop with Dave in his VW Beetle in August '68. How enjoyed singing to Grace Slick and Jefferson Airplane's *Surrealistic Pillow* on 8-track tape, excited about college.

In Jersey, juvenile delinquent episodes had landed me with Dad, since they were too intense for Mom and Ralph, especially after our fistfight. By summer's end in 1965 that and other outlandish behaviors paused with a United plane to live with Dad and Marilyn, her son Freddy, also fifteen, and his younger brother Warren in their Costa Mesa townhouse.

"I can sell the car after returning home. That money can help with expenses." Costly and problematic funeral scenarios creep in. *Too many decisions. How much do funerals cost?*

Jan had said, "Use your common sense and try to keep costs down." *Sure. How?*

Deathly arrangements
hard on those few left behind
to decide what's fine

In twenty minutes, see the low sign on the right and park in front. At the red doorway of a large converted, white-painted brick house appears a middle-aged man with a full head of blonde hair. We shake hands once; he introduces himself. *Hmmm, Richard's helping the Richards'.*

He holds the door, we enter, and he leads toward a doorway with the **OFFICE** sign above it.

"Mind if I look around?"

"Of course not." Glance through Donegan's large entrance lounge with its drab salon couches and high-backed wing chairs, four muted grays, two burgundies, a cookie-cutter home for the dead. Enter the main viewing room, supposed to look like a low-ceilinged chapel without stained glass. Walls, covered in matte gold lame paper in red rose and green leaf print, are shrouded in heavy red velvet curtains framing windows that only allow pittances of natural light. Two long blond credenzas line up under the windows, with square tissue boxes centered on top.

23

Four dull forward-facing club chairs crouch in front, displaying forlorn moods. Thirty white wooden folding chairs with padded gray seat cushions line behind them like ghosts from viewings past, in strict formation like white crosses at a military cemetery, awaiting orders from their captain.

Only I'm the Captain on this revolving ship of death, Dad an errant sailor relegated to the soil, not the sea. Even Janet hasn't arranged a funeral, so no tips there, unlike her usual advice-laden personality. We are both moderate, no-frills wanted or required, basics good enough. *But heck, we can't pay for this, whether glitzy or bare bones.*

Insha'allah. Be content with the Will of God. Trust things will pan out, no matter our plans. God is the best of planners.

We step into his white-washed office with its ebony desk, bookcase, and chairs. He offers a seat in a plush, high-backed, swivel office armchair covered in shiny and smooth faux leather. Comfortable and comforting. Built to ease the tension. *Ha, I'm not relaxed.*

Richard reviews the papers in front of him. "Do you like the facilities?"

The interior's fine except for the blood-like velvet curtains matching those from the mansion on the old Dark Shadows TV soap opera.

"Yeah, copasetic. Nice."

"Very well. I'm, I'm, sorry for your loss. I understand how unexpected it was." *How many times has he said that?*

"Yeah, I still can't believe he was only fifty." In shock for the third time. *I'm only twenty-nine. Does that mean I have twenty-one years left?*

"Charlotte told me you'd be handling this. Would you like us to call you Rodney or Mister Richards?"

"Rodney will do; Dad was Mister Richards." Always Dad to me.

"You're a Junior, right?" *Oh no, he just said Junior.*

"Right. Guess Dad became a Senior when I was born in 1950." *Just add "Sr period" to your last name and by magic it makes it legit?*

"Should we start with the information I have for Rodney Senior?" *Heh, you may have more than I do.*

"Yep, go ahead." Richard recites his full legal name and address. He confirms Dad's employment as a head custodian at Rancho San Joaquin Middle School in Irvine.

"I knew he was a custodian but not the school." *I need a smoke. Coffee would be nice too.*

"Had he been in the military?" *Was he. Can never forget.*

"He was a Marine. Last night I discovered he was a master gunnery sergeant. He had an honorable discharge in 1953." All a vacuum to me. *Need a smoke.*

"Because he's a veteran, one option we offer is a burial plot in a military cemetery, including a standard service and grave marker."

"How much does that cost?"

"Nothing. He's entitled to it by the government. We transport the body to the site, and they take care of the service and burial. By any chance, do you have his discharge papers?" *Costs nothing?*

"I do, that's how I knew he was a sergeant. But I don't have them with me." *Thank goodness I found them.*

"Can you call me with his service number and we'll confirm the arrangements?"

"Definitely. That's great. Costs nothing? Let's do it. And which cemetery is it?"

"Riverside National Cemetery, in the San Bernardino Mountains about forty miles northeast. A beautiful location. It just opened within the past three years and is part of March Air Force Base.

"Sounds good."

"We'll proceed then. We've worked with them multiple times."

"Great." *Whew. This could be a big problem solved.* The cost should be much less. Janet will be pleased, and Grandmom will appreciate the military send-off. *Maybe this won't be so bad.*

Richard leads downstairs where caskets lay on pedestals with open lids that boast fancy white frilly faux-silk interiors. It's Dracula's basement lair, only brighter.

"Richard, I want genuine wood." Pick cherry for its distinctive tint and grain, but expensive. Return to his office. Order flowers from Janet, Jesse, and me. Richard unshelves a blue binder with sample programs and prayer cards with to choose from. *More damned choices. More costs.*

Flip through the plastic-sleeved pages and select the cover and content for twenty-five prayer cards and an equal number of bifold **IN MEMORY** programs. *Do words hold meaning when you're dead? Guess the difference is if you hear them or not.*

Richard offers a limo to drive the immediate family to Riverside and back.

"Yes, that's appropriate. Me, Donny, Uncle John, and Aunt Charlotte, and their daughter Janie. Doubt their son Muffie will join us." *More expense. Need that smoke!*

He rattles off details: obtaining death certificate copies, something about the County, and issuing an obituary. Realize—there's nothing to add—don't know his accomplishments. *Sorry, Dad.* Richard shares the estimated cost, twenty-six hundred dollars. *Wow. Janet won't like that. That hurts.*

"And that includes your services?"

"Yes, everything."

"Okay." *I tried. It would've cost more for sure.* Realize it's no one else's duty to pay but mine—even though neither Janet nor I have the money. We set the final service at Riverside for Thursday at eleven, in two days. Richard confirms tomorrow's viewing at three o'clock for the family and the public. *Boy, they don't waste any time here.*

He pushes across the contract for signature. Register the line items, some costs penciled in to be inked in later. We agree they will bill me. Sign. *Need that Kool.* We shake hands. *Well, that much accomplished.* Must prepare for the public viewing and service. *Can I handle them?*

Light up the second I reach outside. *Am I grateful for this smoke or his help?* Take the freeway through Santa Ana and Costa Mesa to Newport Beach. Park two blocks from the pier where hung out in the bars, clubs, and surf shops. Homes are bigger, fancier, all custom with huge ground-level decks and half-glassed-in upper decks. It's quiet except for the white and gray gulls that squawk and scramble for scraps on the shore and in the sea, and clusters of surfers, swimmers, and sunbathers. Occasional walkers and bicyclists meander by. The biggest ocean in the world hasn't changed its immensity.

Amble up and out onto the almost deserted pier except for the line of casters interspersed along the railings, trying to hook their catch of the day. The wide pier overhangs the blue-green Pacific's frothing waves. Midnight trysts on hastily laid-out beach blankets below stir boyish libido. Memories reappear of lighthearted, sun-filled days engaged in affable banter with tanned girls in thin spaghetti-strapped bikinis accentuating their curves. Had encountered a statuesque hourglass-shaped brunette from Las Vegas sunning topless on her smooth belly on these hot, sifted white sands. Struck up a conversation praising the perfect weather. She was visiting for one day, after which her mom was driving her back.

Gave her my number, and she called later.

"Hello, Rod? It's Michelle. Since you offered, I was hoping we could go to the clubs tonight. Can you pick me up?"

"Compared to Vegas it may be tame, but sure can."

After we hung up, asked, "Dad, I have an unbelievably hot date. Can I borrow the car?"

"Junior, Donny needs you on the job tonight."

"But Dad, she's special, and a Las Vegas showgirl. I won't get another chance to be with her."

"An obligation is an obligation. No." Felt like a punk calling her back and reneging. Anger welled up. Thought he, to whom women were so important, would understand.

"What if we had hooked up that night? Would we have bonded? Would we have married and live in a cute bungalow in Nevada now?"

She was an exquisite woman with her congeniality, long siren hair, fine legs, and tanned sweet chocolate skin.

Janet doesn't mind if I look, just so I don't touch.

Women worth pursuit
can't skewer a heart's true bond
when under love's spell

1.9 GRANDMOM'S BROKEN

At the apartment, ecstatic to phone Richard and convey Dad's service number. Call Janet who's eager for updates. Share the bottom line and why funeral costs are lower.

"That's great about Riverside, but did you need prayer cards AND programs? And twenty-six hundred, that's a lot."

"I wanted to remember him."

"Well, when you get here, we'll set up an account. I'll help you with it. We'll figure it out." *Love her positive attitude.* Not as optimistic, but her background as an accountant will ease the chore of reconciliation.

Phone Mom.

She hasn't seen Dad except for a few brief times since 1954 when they divorced. She hadn't had a simple time raising me and Stephen, but not once did she bad-mouth Dad, although he'd broken her heart with his cheating. Strong and kind-hearted, she held secretarial jobs to provide everything we needed, even summers at day camps, while she worked.

"Things are proceeding well, Mom." Fill her in.

"Rodney, how are you taking it, emotionally?"

"Fine. Not bad. It's been many years."

"I'm sorry you have to go through this."

"It's okay Mom. He did the best he could, and he was straight with me. We'll have a nice service at Riverside National Cemetery. He would appreciate that. I'll be home in a few days." Say goodbye.

Stephen. Should've asked about Stephen. Dad hadn't met his youngest son, not since he was two, or over a brief visit. Dad didn't know Mom's new family either, Ralph—Dad, Ralph Junior, Carleen, and Charles. All as close as my life vein.

Time to call Grandmom. *How do I talk about her son's funeral?*

Picture seventy-five-year-old Grandmom Richards astride her black Princeton rocking chair in her thin gray frock and short brownish stockings covering her ankles. Her saggy face with gloomy circles under soulful eyes belies a senior life of both widowed and retired loneliness. Dial.

"Hi, Grandmom. It's Rodney. I'm in California." *Do I sound positive?*

"How are you taking it?"

"Me? Okay, I guess. But I'm concerned about you, how're you?" *I'm sorry, Grandmom.*

"I'm ah, all right, Rodney. It happens to all of us…. I will miss his weekly phone calls though…." *What can I say?* Instead, describe Donegan's and how their place is fitting. Share the bounty of his veteran's burial, and she's pleased.

"Rodney, can you order a spray of red roses from me for the casket?"

"Of course, Grandmom, honored to." Hear her invisible tears. *Or are they real?* But she's tough. Never seen her rattled. Another strong woman. Like too many others, deserted and alone to deal with harsh realities. And they all deal with them. *Oh, what prices they pay!*

"And Rodney, your Aunt Joan would like one red rose to be from her, placed in his coffin. Can you do that?"

"Of course."

"I trust you to handle everything."

"I will, for you."

"Give my love to Janet and Jesse when you talk to them, please."

"Yes Grandmom, love you Grandmom, bye." When Dad was a teen, he lost his father, and she lost her young husband. His car plowed into a stone bridge abutment on Route 206 heading to Princeton. *Husbands, fathers, and sons shouldn't die so young.*

This load, not one carried before, but... *have to do this.* No different from meeting deadline pressures for Chris. But that's not life or death. This, something else. Step outside on the second-floor walkway. Light up. Chinese proverb pops up.

"Grandfather dies, father dies, son dies."

There's an order to death. Children aren't supposed to die before their parents regardless of age or cause, yet starvation, neglect, disease, and war decimate their innocent numbers. *God will care for them.*

"Well, down to business." Call Richard, order the roses.

Phone Donny, share the arrangements, ask if he wants anything of Dad's hoping he will.

"I can use most of the furniture, Junior, for a friend. She's looking for furnishings."

"Great." *Better than being stuck with it. If your girlfriend can use it, so be it.*

Call Uncle John. "I'd like his LPs Junior if that's okay with you."

"Fine, I may keep a few though."

"Also, Janie's boyfriend has offered to buy the Impala if five-hundred sounds all right with you?" *Hell. No adventurous trip.* Someday, Janet and I will go on a third honeymoon. *What a bust our second one was.*

"That sounds fine, Uncle John. Cash only though." *What can I do? Dicker?*

Phone the electric and gas companies and Ma Bell and close the accounts for September thirty. Trot downstairs, meet with the super, and arrange for the apartment inspection and return of the security deposit. Ask and he tells me Dad isn't liable for rent payments since he died midterm. Ask if he has any cardboard boxes, and he has two.

"Thanks." He adds nothing about Dad.

Begin sorting Dad's belongings. Conflicted about disposing of them. "Are they mine to keep as the eldest? Should I share them with Stephen? Picky as he is, would he want anything?"

28

Fold Dad's long-sleeved midnight blue Marine jacket into one box. It has red trim, a standing collar, white web belt, lighter slacks, and place two medals on top. "Bet you were proud. I wonder what duties you had, where you served, what you saw. Did it make you tougher or smarter?"

Scan through then pack his sparse photo album, two framed pictures, personal effects like jewelry and his address book, five LPs, and handwritten letters still in their envelopes. Mementos for Grandmom, me. Bag the sheets and towels, wrap breakable dishes in loose newspaper and add pots, pans, silverware and utensils except for what I need. Add foodstuffs and other clothes for the Salvation Army. Save two beloved Pepsi's from the six-pack I bought. Comb through the phone book and the Trailways Bus Station in center-city Santa Ana jumps out.

"Oh, and better file a change of address."

Load the trunk and start the Impala. Find the post office first, file the address change, then drive until locate Trailways and arrange for delivery of Dad's boxes to the Trenton Bus Station for pick up later. Drop off bags at Salvation Army and receive a contributed receipt for ten bucks.

Spot the Tustin Car Wash on the way back, bigger and fancier. Pull in line, get out, walk along the short cinder block wall inside, glass-enclosed, and watch the Impala pass through. Spent sweaty days at age sixteen washing and drying cars, or damp-wiping smoke-filmed interior windows.

Never minded. "A paycheck's a paycheck." Learned that selling magazines door-to-door, my first summer job. *One of my first break-ins.*

Cruise past Tustin High School and the adjacent garden apartments where we had lived. "Oh Marlene, so sorry." My stocky jock girlfriend, with her bubbly, take-no-prisoners personality, must've been dismayed and angry. One night when she was out of town, stole her faded green apple 1955 Chevy and smashed its grill and rear bumper squeezing past a dumpster. Without a license, scared to admit it. Parked it back in her numbered spot, flipped up the car mat, replaced the key, and scuttled into our apartment, not a word said.

"And look at Tustin now. Built-up, congested, no open areas, despite wide streets and avenues. You paved over my youth."

Pull into 7/Eleven for coffee.

At the apartment, strike a match and light up.

"That's it. Hope it's enough. Must trust Richard." Only one problem.

"How do we pay for the coffin and everything else?"

Take a deep drag.

Children dying is rough
on parents. Tough also
on parent's children

29

1.10 DRESSED TO KILL

[Wednesday, September 26, 1979]

Awake before first light, sweep front curtains aside, fire up a Kool.

"Plenty of time. Don't have to be at Donegan's until two-thirty." Scroll through hapless TV local programming.

"That's enough." Leave, start on the sidewalk with the sun shining. The block, lifeless, except for a few brisk dog handlers who nod but don't want to chat, and cars moving on the streets.

Return, half pay attention to TV, smoke a few, as annoying commercials aggravate eyes and ears except for mean Joe Green accepting a Coke from a well-intentioned fanboy. Watch reads ten-forty. In the middle of Bob Barker's Price is Right, a male contestant with wide sideburns below his earlobes spins the massive wheel hoping for the green magic dollar slot.

Oh no! The courthouse. The second most important thing to do!

"What did Richard say about probate?"

"As next of kin, you'll have to file paperwork at the Santa Anna Courthouse tomorrow morning. Just fill out their form and provide a certified copy of your Dad's death certificate. Stop by here first and I'll have copies for you."

Rush to Donegan's, pickup certificates, then dash to the county building and zip into the first open slot. Inside, wait in a short line for forms, fill out blank spaces with what I've learned. Five minutes later, hand them back with ID and a death certificate. *Hope this goes through.*

Wait.

"Richards?" Hop to the counter window.

"Sign here and here." Sign. *Am I in the clear?* "That'll be ten dollars, payable to the Clerk." Hand over cash. Take ID, receipt, and proffered certificate. *Great! Easy.* With so few assets, perfunctory. But callous. The state offers nothing to dead citizens that I know of. The living poor may qualify for welfare or the generosity of churches.

Outside, lean on the Impala, enjoy fifth smoke. Maybe this will all work out.

Head to a Bank of America branch. Enter and find an associate. "My father passed, I'm next of kin, and want to close his account please."

"Yes sir, I need his account number, death certificate and your Driver's License, please." Hand them over. He Xerox's a copy of each along with the county certificate. Thought to bring Dad's checkbook and bank statement. Sign a dense form. Associate goes to an idle teller, returns, and forks over two-hundred and twelve dollars. A poor showing for a fifty-year-old man.

Thank him and hit the parking lot. Sit in Impala. Light up. Inhale and pause, exhale and pause some more. Even if I perform the right motions, what about the right emotions? *So much crap to get through!* Dad, once you were animated, hardworking, interested in life, women uppermost. That's how I knew you. That's how I forgot about you. Now just another "Dear departed." Another name or picture on an obituary page, the last time it will appear. *Your heart attack, your fate. My fate to be here. I could've at least written or phoned you once from Jersey.*

Drive back to the apartment, the unfamiliar surroundings becoming commonplace. Inside, shower. Splash on Ralph Lauren Polo. Change into the white shirt, yellow tie lined with red polka dots, and black suit Janet had folded, careful to avoid creases. Meet Uncle John and Donny at the funeral home at two-forty-five.

Uncle John says, "Aunt Charlotte had to be at her nursing job, Junior. She sends her regrets. Janie's working too." *Cudda guessed that.*

"We'll just stay out here for a bit, Junior," says Donny.

Inside at the front of the room, a macabre view of closed eyelids stares at the white popcorn ceiling. His body lies in the open cherry casket with Grandmom's spray of ruby roses on top, hanging like a drape covering the lid. Their attar, the aromatic smell of permanent slumber, permeates the empty room. Pull loose a long-stemmed one and place it on his right shoulder and arm for Aunt Joan, a talisman from their childhood together. *Wonder if she considered flying here?*

A floral arrangement of gladiolas atop thin green legs is on the right, "From Rodney, Janet and Jesse with Sympathy." John and Charlotte's, Janie and Muffie's are on the left. One too from "Joan, husband Pete and daughter Suzanne with Sympathy."

No others.

Pace the length of his 5'9" body, one inch taller than mine. He's well-heeled in his now cheerless blue suit, starched long-sleeved cobalt shirt with gold cufflinks showing engraved letters "RR," red paisley tie with gold tie clasp, and polished black featherweights over black socks. He lies in state waiting for the masses to file by. Dressed to kill for a date, and this, his last date with the living.

Squeeze his ice-cold right hand, a hand that hadn't touched me in a sign of warmth or affection. *Or struck me in anger.*

Ashen, his mouth is tight-lipped. A whisper of rouge blushes from his high cheekbones. Stoic for one who had a loose, easy-going lifestyle. His head and body are stiff and straight as a plank as is his aquiline nose. Even at fifty, jet black hair, although receding on both sides, in a rare suit, his corpse provides charm and self-esteem for a confident man.

Release his hand. Plop on the club chair and glaze over the months we had together, not even two full years.

Outside, John and Donny shoot the bull.

31

Ten minutes later, a thin brunette woman saunters in from a side door. Not bad looking. Like so many Barbies in southern California, she's wearing a sexy, short, burnt-red cocktail dress accenting her well-defined, unblemished, tanned face, shoulders, arms, and legs.

"Hi, I'm Rod Junior. Are you here for my Dad?"

"Yes. I saw the notice in the paper. I'm sorry." Hand her an **In Memory** program with funeral details and Mary Lee Hall's words on the reverse side, "If I should die and leave you here awhile, Be not like others, sore undone...." Add a prayer card, a picture of the white marble Pieta on a jade background on the front, a Saint Francis prayer "Lord, make me an instrument of thy peace..." on the reverse.

The mystery woman takes them, strides up, hovers over Dad, gazes down, nods, then departs the way she came.

Check—didn't sign the guest book. Check—no Sympathy card. Can't, or can only, imagine their relationship.

Although Dad, Catholic in name and not religious, still, no one called a priest. Had combed through his wallet, found membership cards for VFW, B.P.O.E. Elks, and a few more, but thought nothing of it. Guess it wouldn't have mattered if they'd shown up for their five-minute programs. No one else here to hear them, anyway.

Shrug, move to the gray brocade love seat facing the lonesome bier. Stare at his prone body, flinch at the thought of thirty empty padded folding chairs behind me. Ghosts of mourners and well-wishers who passed through. Open my Bahá'í Prayer Book to the Prayer for the Dead and say the lines without repeating the refrains nineteen times. *It's the most I can muster, Dad. Sorry.*

Don't touch his cold flesh again. *Is something wrong with me? Did you love me? You never said so.* Never told you either, never thanked you for taking me under your wing. Owe you that. Fond isn't quite right.

Heh heh, you called me "Shithead" often. After one squabble, was livid and stormed out. Hitched a ride to friend and co-worker Willie's and his "aunt." Hibernated in their one-room/kitchenette rental for a week. Refused to phone. You just let my anger simmer and cool, like turning off the gas burner under a small pot of Campbell's chicken soup.

Admire you? Although you excelled as a reliable worker, your woman-chasing and alcoholism weren't for me in the long run. *Respect?* You treated me that way. *Understand you?* How can anyone grasp someone they've only been with a few impressionable months.

"And poor Mom.

Seventeen and a half, beautiful, kind, and naïve when you both met at Princeton High School. Dad, always handsome, you swept her to Washington, D.C. and there I was born. But you couldn't settle down. Mom had to negotiate alone, hold jobs, and take care of Stephen and me for eight years before marrying Ralph to start a second family. *Dad, did you consider our well-being?*

32

Understand. You can't answer that. When we meet in the world of spirits I'll hug you, our first father-son hug. You should know I tried not to judge. You were being you. *Anyway, who am I to forgive? Am I a priest or a son?*

Near four o'clock and still alone.

Donny and Uncle John enter. "Junior, did a chickee in a red dress come in here?"

"Yes. She paid her respects."

"Did she leave a name?"

"No. She was Miss Anonymous."

Missus?

Should've looked for a ring.

Dad often said,
"Junior, treat all women well."
He loved them all—
briefly

1.11 JOINING THE HEROES

[Thursday, September 27, 1979]

Bloodless dummies. The four of us are bloodless dummies with plastic vacant eyeballs during the forty-mile ride. No one fidgets or utters a syllable.

The air conditioning is as comfortable as it is uncomfortable contemplating Dad's heart-crushing demise. We dip and rise through the monotonous Santa Ana Mountains and canyons, our short black limo trailing one silver hearse, and pass desolate and scorched earth, forested in spots, as dirty clumps of chaparral dot the steeper San Bernardino Mountains. Sporadic dwellings poke out among undulating outcrops of hardscrabble stone. Impolite to smoke, no one else smokes.

No flower car. The attar from the shock of roses doesn't accompany us either. "Can't be used," Richard had said, "No flowers can be." Janie's home babysitting Muffie, her fifteen-year-old retarded brother, my powerful cousin who wears a man-sized diaper and bellows or grunts as if rocks fill his mouth.[12]

No cars with headlights on radiate behind us.

Arrive and pass the rough-hewn fieldstone National Cemetery signs on both sides of the drive as the limo follows the main circular road and stops at the crest. A man in khakis and matching shirt open at the collar greets us with a nod. Aunt Charlotte stares at us, as, with help from Donegan's pallbearers and Uncle John and Donny, we lift the coffin from the hearse onto a thigh-high metal cart.

But it's not just a coffin. It contains the dead body of a man, the man who gave me birth, genes, and blood.

The silent man in khakis rolls it to its designated spot under a tall, wide, white concrete canopy supported by two white posts. The shadowing canopy of Death. He gestures for us to move to the single wooden bench that resembles a church pew, then drapes Dad's coffin with a wrinkled flag as we take seats eight feet in front of it.

He moves behind us, standing, waiting.

Surmise it's a cue, so rise, step behind the casket, turn, face the frozen bodies sitting or standing before me and the acres of soldiers' bones lying beyond, listening with their spirits for comforting words addressed to them too. Words that will bring their crumbling bones to life.

Intone from memory the consoling words in as clear a voice as can marshal, "O my God! O Thou forgiver of sins, ah, bestower of gifts, dispeller of afflictions! Verily, I beseech Thee to forgive the sins of such as have abandoned the physical garment and have ascended to the spiritual world…" Tears well up "…and, and, grant them… to… to behold Thy splendors, on the loftiest mount."[13]

You left us, Dad. Decades ago. Wisps of memories all that remain. I could only observe your outward behavior. Your true character stayed hidden.

"Uh." Want to drop to the flagstone beneath my feet, on this dreary shadowy spot, hallowed by the blood sacrifices of thousands under a luminous durable sky, twenty-seven-hundred miles from actual family and friends. Stare at the flag-draped coffin.

Like mimes frozen onto a plate-glass window, no one utters a word or flinches in the stillness. *Dad, what I didn't know about you!*

Crane forward, scan the grassy fields of low white crosses in a futile search for… something. What I don't know about myself. *Can I say I love you and mean it? Or am I drowning in dreams for what could have been a closeness never broached?*

Eyes water, breathing pauses, cheeks streak. No one rises. Return to pew, sit.

Silent Khaki Man steps back behind the low wall and switches on the loudspeaker. He moves to stand behind us and the two Donegan staff. Taps start from a recording. It sounds rushed. The three of us on the bench stare ahead with folded hands, indifferent to its soulful notes. The trumpet moans its oft-repeated tune, then sputters off.

Khaki Man pushes the casket behind the low wall. He returns, steps up, bends, hands over a pre-folded flag, this one not wrinkled. "On behalf of the President of the United States, the United States Marine Corps, and a grateful nation, please accept this flag as a symbol of our appreciation for your loved one's honorable and faithful service."

No further words are forthcoming or sounds play for this onetime warrior and lover. The buried uniforms covering bleached bones beneath the surrounding white crosses clothed their hosts for a brief time and now they reside in an eternity of Mistress Fate's making, listening in silence.

Silent man. Silent white bones, even in the living. A few scripted words with silent meanings. A silent flag. Taps amid silence.

Traditions scatter through time like the dust of Dad's physical remains laying on rotted satin will be in a hundred years. Four stinking relatives, a functionary, and hired hands. Not even flowers. And another funeral cortege has pulled up, waiting. Silent Man motions us to leave.

No time for a eulogy, even if could muster one. *And who would speak for He Who Cannot Speak?*

Finished. Whether or not commensurate with your life. *Someday, Dad, I hope to return, find your plot, and say the Congregational Prayer for the Dead.*

Rigid reserve lingers in the limo like smoke-stink on the return trip to Donegan's. *I need a smoke.*

Cookie-cutter services
convenient for the living,
paltry for the dead

After goodbyes at Donegan's, buy coffee on the way to the apartment. Sip and smoke in the car using its dashboard ashtray. Wonder. *Is death cruel, just, or indifferent? Or all three together?*

Once back, change into jeans and a Tee-shirt, light up another. "Wish Barb, Bob, and Janet had been here. Hope Dad's spirit is adjusting."

Inside, phone home. "It's done. I'll call Mom and Grandmom later." Jan wants details but too drained to recount them.

"Hon, I'll be on a plane tomorrow if you can book a flight." End our crisp conversation with, "Luv you."

Sink into remorse on the sofa as mind whirrs into what I should have done differently. Gulp last lukewarm drops of coffee.

We'd hoped for enough money to pay for this and expenses like plane tickets and meals, especially because Janet hasn't held a salaried job since Jesse's birth. She sacrificed and left her teaching career for us. *What have I sacrificed in return?*

There'll be little income from Dad's estate to offset costs, not even a fourth. *How will we pay this off?*

Lay head back for a rare nap.

Memories of the living
linger until
what ifs no longer haunt

36

1.12 WINDFALLS

[Friday, September 28, 1979]

Try to nap, can't. As elusive as finding a hardened criminal who just made his escape crawling through a hard-dug hidden tunnel from a federal maximum-security penitentiary in Texas.

"Bringg... bringg... bringg..." Pick up the receiver next to Dad's bed. "Rodney? It's Richard."

"Yeah Richard, everything okay?"

"Well, I'm not sure. Your dad worked for the Irvine Unified School District, right?"

"Yeah, but not sure how long. He worked in Tustin Schools too."

"That means he should've had a pension. Have you inquired into that?"

"Wow, no, I forgot." *Holy shit, he probably did.*

Janet must remember commitments, what needs doing, and appointments, even those I'd set up. How often heard, "Rod, shouldn't you be at the doctor's soon?" She doesn't and wouldn't show up late for a meeting or scheduled activity. Neither did Dad.

"Here's what we need to do...."

Richard honks at nine-thirty, run out, and he drives to the district administration building in central Orange County southeast of Santa Ana and Tustin. Richard says it's a huge district. Once there, it's obvious the staff are efficient as behind the counter they set good examples. Accept their condolences.

"A good employee, and you're his son?"

"Yes, thank you."

The clerk, Celia, confirms the name listed as beneficiary on Dad's pension. *He named me? Are you serious?* Had thought his companionship with Uncle John or Donny came uppermost. *Why only me? What about Stephen?*

Celia asks for a driver's license, a death certificate, and a copy of the county document. Place them on the counter. She scans and Xerox's them. She types a form and when finished slides it over. It has Dad's full name and information, and mine, and a line with the number $14,000 on it.

Fourteen thousand?! It's almost my annual salary. Besides paying for the funeral, this money will help with our home improvements, pay off credit cards, and fix our cars. *Heck, Janet will throw a party.*

Hand falters as scrawl incomprehensible signature.

Celia adds, "Also, Mister Richards Senior had a fifteen-thousand-dollar life insurance policy, and you are the sole beneficiary." *O my God. Thank you, Dad. Did you ever imagine how this could change our lives?*

37

We could almost pay off our thirty-five-thousand-dollar mortgage. *I can deep-six the beat-up Chevette. We could go to Disney World!*

With Celia guiding things, complete a new form and scribble signature. Thank her twice, in shock and gratitude at Dad's largesse and our good fortune.

Richard pulls in at the apartment. Shake his hand with both of mine. "Thanks for all you've done, and for Dad. Janet and I and the Richards family appreciate it." *We will have to send a bonus.*

Inside, phone Janet, who's flabbergasted and relieved. "See, Rod, I told you it would work out." She further advises, "Perfectly normal that Donegan's would help with that, Rod. They want to get paid sooner." Of course, that would occur to her practical mind.

We're both surprised and happy about the boons, especially being able to pay Donegan. She recounts her chores, updates on Jesse, family news, and Bahá'í activities. Grateful for her constancy. She confirms the United plane ticket and departure time.

Phone Donny and confirm the late afternoon ride to the airport.

Dial Uncle John.

"You can pick up the Impala at two. I found the paperwork." Between a rock and a hard flight home, will grab the five hundred now. Tell no one about the inheritance.

Snap open the last Pepsi and strike a match for a Kool. A long, satisfying draw. Take a lightheaded swig. Relax heart, brain, and muscles for the first time since Mom's call. *Quite the gift. Was this your payback?*

Whimsical thoughts dash by, like buying a pool table. Extreme wishes flit in as if hold the winning ticket to the New Jersey debut Pick-4 lottery.

Venture out and splurge at a Chinese restaurant. Love the Hunan fried pork dumplings as appetizers and shredded pork with vegetables, mixed rice, and peppers as an entrée. The egg roll is hot and spicy.

"Yum." Ice water cools tongue and lips before peeling orange slices to taste their chilled pulp and tangy juice. Crack open the brittle fortune cookie and read its slip of wisdom:

When winter chills, spring's warmth follows.

Uncle John and Janie's boyfriend drop by with the cash. *They know what a deal this is.* Hand them the keys and sad to see my alternate 1963 Corvette Sting Ray go. Still hope to drive across America someday.

"I'll mail the title in a week." They leave.

Wait for Donny.

Poor days have ended
Jubilees, excitement, and thrills
will soon explode

1.13 WHISKED TO ANOTHER REALM

Hungry greetings at Newark Airport terminal surround me as exit United's gate. Hug Mom, Janet smiles wide, and we share a puckered kiss. Shake Ralph's hand. "So sorry, Rodney."

Together they ask, "How was the flight? How are you feeling?"

"Flight went well, and I'm fine. Dad had an honorable service at Riverside. The funeral home was a terrific help, as were Donny, Uncle John, and Aunt Charlotte."

Jan says, "My Mom's watching Jesse for us," which drowns her in grandparent magic. We share goodbyes with Mom and Dad, place my bag with the folded flag in it in our car, and drive the Jersey Turnpike heading to Exit 7A. Chipper, run at the mouth with impressions of Southern California. Share memories at the beach, funeral details, and plane trips. Philosophize on death, add, "I can't wait to get back to work."

Janet asks, "Are you going to ask about Jesse?"

"How is he?"

"He missed you, but he's fine. Are you okay?"

"Ah, yeah, fine." Standard response. Recount more, jumping from scene to scene. On top of the world with the income from Dad's bequests. She listens, interjects little. *Be cool. Be methodical.*

An unrequited want surfaces. "Jan, I think we should take a vacation to Disney World."

"Rod, Jesse won't remember, so what's the point?"

"Oh." *Makes sense. She keeps me grounded, without sinking my spirits into the ground. We'll go when Jess is older.* Ramble on about Orange County's devastated orange groves and wide freeways. Thoughts spew like geysers and spin like wind-blown tumbleweeds across non-stop lips.

Janet stares, says, "When we get home you can sleep." She maneuvers local roads to her parents Cape Cod in Ewing. At the Hutchinson's, overjoyed to greet Jesse and cuddle his small energetic frame.

"Hi, little man!" Big grasping smile and arms. Hug Doris with thanks who let her British guard down with me a long time ago, but not her accent. As a war bride, she's lived in America since before I was born.

Once in our door, Janet commands, "Lie down," as she beds Jesse who's fallen asleep in his car seat.

Can't sleep.

The next three days spend hours deciphering bills I'd packed. First, send off a death certificate and copy of my driver's license to the car company for the Impala. Shocked when found out Dad had only owned it a year yet owed four thousand dollars. But co-insurance paperwork in its glove compartment paid it off upon his death, giving title to his heir. Call them and confirm my status.

With the seven-hundred-twelve in cash, we open a checking account for the estate. The school district won't send checks without Dad's divorce decree from Marilyn, so we enlist our seasoned lawyer, Mister Robinson, to investigate. He had drawn up our wills. Kind, wise, and considerate, he speaks from aged experience to our best interests.

One good thing, the title soon arrives for the Impala. Sign it and forward it to Uncle John.

Forwarded bills arrive. Can't pay Donegan until Irvine approves the funds, so write small checks to a dentist for thirty dollars, annual *Time* Magazine for fourteen ninety-seven, and a chiropractor for forty-three. Each one dredges up resignation and anger. Determined to knot loose ends, one credit card states outright, "Charges are forgiven in the event of death," but ignore it.

"Jan, I hafta pay this. I don't care what it says, it's the noble thing to do." She objects. But I write out the check and mail it.

Go to Trenton Bus Station to pick up Dad's two boxes, but they can't find them. Pissed as hell, file a claim. All I have from Dad had fit in my suitcase.

The next morning deep-six a half-pack of Kools. "I'm done with these killers." Janet doesn't comment.

Saturday morning, she says, "Rod, don't forget we have an Assembly meeting here tomorrow night."

A few hours later we visit Grandmom. She's subdued. Recount events. Present her with the folded flag. "We'll miss him, Grandmom, me too. So very sorry."

Just before our seven o'clock meeting, Janet says, "Why don't you stay in the bedroom? You can watch TV and relax."

"Okay, could use a break." Not important.

Our Assembly manages Bahá'í affairs in Hamilton Township and because of our central Jersey location, also serve south Jersey. Our elected nine-member council administers community affairs like the Sunday school and nineteen-day feasts, meets with individuals or couples who have personal issues, career questions, or financial problems, and we officiate marriages and grant Bahá'í divorces if the parties can't reconcile.

Hold meetings every other Sunday night in our living room, so it's easier to care for Jesse. The Faith is obscure but as Treasurer had fought the Division of Taxation to obtain our legit 501c Sales Tax Exemption as a subsidiary of our National Spiritual Assembly.

Shut our bedroom door and lie on our bed, back against upright pillows. Flip to HBO at the end of *The Gauntlet* with Clint Eastwood and a skinny Sondra Locke, his girlfriend I'd read. Scoop Breyer's fudge swirl ice cream out of the bowl as watch. Thoughts swirl too, like the ripples in the vanilla and the cascades of bullets zinging across the screen and blasting their protective bus. Ideas drip hot like boiled water in a Mr. Coffee machine and fire up aromatic ideas as they pile high, crisscross, and skitter away like jackrabbits.

Two tense days pass. Janet maintains vigilant silence. Edgy and irritable plot scenarios of universal global change.

What about a Bahá'í-based corporation? It'll be a major player, there's nuthin' like it, and it can't fail, no way. It'll be a powerhouse of international commerce. We'll mass-produce greeting cards, Bahá'í authored books, knickknacks, memorabilia, and tons more. With popular themes they'll sell like warm pancakes with maple syrup and smoked bacon at a church basement fundraiser. Can use quotations from prominent figures and religious teachers, past and present.

Jot notes in Sharpie pen in my usual block printing in the space of twenty minutes.

STEPS: 1. ESTABLISH CORP
   A) BAHA'IS/MANKIND CAN BUY, OWN STOCK IN IT
   B) PROFIT SHARING AND DIVIDENDS
   C) PROMOTE ENGLISH AS SECOND LANGUAGE
   D) RAISE $500,000–1 MIL FOR ESTABLISHMENT
      1) BUILDINGS 2) EQUIPMENT 3) SALARIES
      4) CONSOLIDATE INT'L AV CENTER AND ALL BAHAI PUBLISHING TRUSTS

Outline precepts and structure. Add departments using Bahá'í friends like Linda for art, Spud for media, and Bob for marketing and photography. Barb, his attractive young blonde wife, will be the spokesperson since she approaches people with a serene smile, measured tones, and is well-adapted as the Assembly Chair. She would make the consummate hostess.

Print **INSHALLAH** nine times for future growth and success. *The Corporation will be an instant worldwide success.*

"Jan, I have a great idea for a corporation. It'll involve all our friends and be so useful it can't miss." Show her the thirteen pages of notes.

"Rod, why don't we share this with the Assembly? You can meet with them and get advice. It can't hurt, and it might help. It would make me feel better if you did."

"Humph."

"They'll help. Please? I'm worried about you. You're erratic. You're not acting like yourself."

Can it hurt? They might say "No." Then what?

Hear

PROCEED

"Okay." *Not acting Myself? It's a fantastic idea. We'll donate some profits to the Bahá'í Fund.*

Jan calls Barb.

Enter our living room two nights later for the hastily called meeting as the other eight members rise, ring around me, and smile. I shake their hands. Barb beckons, "Welcome Rod, please sit." She's our best friend, but as Chair she's something else—impartial. *Nothing to fear. This assembly loves me.*

After a brief prayer, Barb recites the confidential nature of the proceedings we're all familiar with. Then, sweet as pumpkin pie, "Rodney, tell us why you're here."

Rattle off a rambling description of the Corporation and its departments for twenty minutes. Just beginning.

Barb interjects, "Rod, we realize this is important to you, but how would you like us to help?"

"I need to meet with the Universal House of Justice in Haifa. And not just a representative. Can you call and tell them I'll be coming?" No one flinches or raises an eyebrow.

Barb says, "Rod, you're familiar with how the Assembly operates. We'll study your papers and consult on your request. We'll respond in a few days. Would that be all right?"

"Of course, and..." then gabble on. Patient, they listen without expression for five minutes until Janet looks over at Barb. She puts up her palm.

"Rodney, thank you so much for sharing. Does anyone have a question?" Friends have none. Barb intones, "Rod, there's a power in turning to an assembly, and we promise to review what you've provided and to respond to what you've asked. The secretary will contact you in writing, okay?"

"I hope so, I hafta move fast."

"We understand. We'll close with a prayer." Cathy Weber recites the Short Healing Prayer. Jan stands to help me leave.

That's enough. They'll take care of it.

Jump up, turn, and head to our bedroom before the other members even rise. Know how it works.

The institution's first letter, dated October 9, arrives a week and a half after returning. The second arrives October 18. Neither suggests a visit to the Universal House of Justice and both state, "You should wait, settle down, and pray on it." *Ha! Give me a break.*

The latter one adds, "Although your desire to quit smoking now is commendable, it would not be a good idea at this time." A temporary pass. One thing's sure, as an ex-Catholic school kid, at mass every weekday morning at seven-thirty, my flesh can be obedient.

42

Buy a pack of Kool's the next morning, light the match, suck on it, sigh. Thoughts fly like lost loons in the middle of the Atlantic Ocean, searching for a rocky outcrop to rest upon. *But they won't tell me the truth! They hide it. They've construed elaborate schemes to convince me I'm like everyone else. But I'm special. That's why I'm allowed to smoke. Must be.*

"Sumpin's goin' down; not aware of it, doesn't matter, but guar-un-teed. They'll tell Me."

Next day, shocked, receive a bill for past-due taxes on Dad's 1977 California Income Tax return. Pay the thirty-seven dollars that day. Receive suspicious bankruptcy papers filed against Dad the day after he died. *A scam?* Another job for Mister Robinson. Each triggers helplessness and anxiety.

Days and nights flash by in grandiose schemes and intricate plans for breathtaking endeavors. Re-cement international relationships and recreate civilization. Crazy, racing, futuristic thoughts and pregnant ideas require immediate action. Expel boundless mental energy. Excise inner promptings in secret as words stream forth. Speak like a drunken politician extemporizing from a soapbox in front of a panting crowd of sycophants clamoring to taste "New and Improved" panaceas.

Symptoms of uncontrollable thoughts and feelings grow, and grow....

Just days later, on that fateful early morning before October's end, in the throes of racing thoughts and uncontrollable emotions, snuck out of the house and drove Janet's Corolla, talking, singing, exhorting, crying, and speeding through the endless Jersey pines. Swung it off the road into the clearing of silent metal gladiators and watchful pines surrounding the **Sand Co,** under the glow of the gibbous moon. Bare of any semblance to reality, shouted epithets at humanity's misdeeds.

Heard the one-word command and goal... **HAIFA**.

Stripped. Ready to swim the Atlantic Ocean with vigor to get there.

But whisked instead into that twilight realm that only poets and saints can describe. Conscious awareness disappeared like wisps of the setting sun, casting shadows overtaken by night as enveloped in paroxysms of serenity and reassurance that His Will, and only His Will, decide the fate of every creature.

Deserted this world. Entered a never before conceived realm and drowned in assurances that all would be set in order.

One Voice, One Mission
As the Messenger,
must fulfill pledge
to perform

43

1.14 FROM BLACK TO BLACK AND WHITE

"Where am I?" Head and blood pounds in syncopated drumbeats from a hidden village deep within the Brazilian jungle. At rapt attention, attune hearing to the supernatural thrumming of spirit shapes and peaceful voices reverberating throughout the tall rubber trees.

But I'm not in the midmost forest of the Amazon.

Encased in the blackest black cloud of mystery-laden mental fog, roused out of forgetfulness and otherworldly timeless dreams.

Stiffen.

The Toyota's headlight beams pierce the darkest-shadows of million-year-old Jersey pines three times as tall as Me. They ring the small circle of light around My body. The silent ancient orb shining above is as bright as a streetlight on a midnight-shrouded farm road. The enveloping hush is omnipresent, as the yawning Sea of Tranquility captures stardust with a faint blue tint. There's no breeze to cool burning pinprick sensations atop sensitive exposed skin.

Relax throat and jaw, shoulders, arms, and leg muscles as recognition dawns. *What's that?*

Engine sounds and heavy tires crawl nearer on the packed dirt and sand. The black and white Crown Vic, with no flashing lights, approaches and crunches to a stop five yards away. Two officers slip out and draw close. A short husky male, trim black hair, asks, "Um, why don't you sit in the car?" His silver badge reads DiPietro in blue letters.

"We will." Amble forward. Duck onto the rear seat. Sticky flesh molds to the plastic bench. Place palms flat. Sweat warm, cool, alive. The other policeman retrieves a blanket and lays it over glistening thighs.

They search. Find no clothes, shoes, or wallet.

"It's four o'clock, we'll get you home. Have to make a stop first."

"All right."

They drive in the dark, no siren, no strobe lights, to a brick one-story building. Brake, park, door opens, step out, blanket slides off. Enter and march down the short gray hallway, deep inside, to an unlocked barred gate the width of two persons. Officer swings its thick hinges, proffers a drab one-piece olive-green jumpsuit.

"Please put this on." Climb in, zip. The chill of the concrete floor on feet belies the starkness of the bare cell room. Sense light green cinder blocks behind, stare at smudged thumb-thick bars from floor to ceiling on three sides.

"You're in the Holding Tank." A heavy iron clang reverberates in the space, the key turns, footfalls from thick leather-soled shiny black shoes fade.

Silence. Deep breath in, exhale, placid. Turn about-face, grasp cold oil-painted flaked gray-green bars, clench firmer, bars turn tepid. *Cells at Juvie and County jail smaller than this.* At Juvie, ostracized for driving, without a license, with a local homosexual. At County hefted a mop in self-defense against an inmate agitator hurling curses at me as we swabbed the grated metallic deck. Sit on the wooden bench thick with layers of worn lime green paint. It's bolted to the cinder blocks. *What time is it?*

Observe as if looking down from the soulful moon onto Earth's crusty brown or blue or white outlines, questioning and alert, with no plan at hand for the invisible billions of scurrying figures below, yet aware of every creak and sound in the confined space. Fold hands and lay arms on thighs and in a flash, stare forward into scenes of a gleaming, silver-towered, faraway bustling city. Blink, and it becomes dull, brown-coated, no movements, no flying conveyances swinging through its crumbling towers. They fade and dissolve to dust.

Steps. Hear steps. officers return. One rests his body on a swivel chair. DiPietro stands two feet away and writes on a clip-boarded sheet. Reads rights aloud. "Do you understand these rights as I've conveyed them to you?"

Nod.

"I need your verbal assent."

"Yes."

"I need your attention." *Questions, of course.* "Name?"

"Rodney, Richards."

"Address?" Comply.

"Phone?" Tell him.

"Someone we can call?

"Janet."

"Your girlfriend, wife, mother?"

"Wife. Where am I."

"Berkeley Township Police Headquarters, Pinewald. Are you familiar with the area?"

"How far from the ocean."

"Two or three miles." He steps away, walks down the long hall. Disappears. *Losing time.*

DiPietro returns. "I spoke to your wife, and she was upset."

"Upset?"

"She'll be here soon." *Oh.* "I need your fingerprints." Unlocks holding tank door. "Can you come over here?" Shuffle to the gray-green counter. He lifts right hand over an ink pad. My friend rolls the tips of fingers onto it, then presses each onto a card.

"So how long ya been on the force?"

"Ten years. I've been lucky."

"Yeah, I've been lucky to be with the State for almost the same time."

Truth. Listen for cues from the officer to explore a new topic. Probe him, as an officer with a duty to perform. *Rational he should do this.*

Return to barred room eight feet away. Both leave. *Should I escape?* Spy meticulous clock hands on wall overhead as they strike five-three-five in silence except for faint tick-tocks that follow. Sit. Wait. Meditate. *The Buddha sat.*

Familiar voices enter the hallway.

"Hey! My jeans." Janet also carries a blue pullover, Bob next to her. DiPietro unlocks the clanky gate. Clothes pass through. Unzip, undress. Dress. Slip into sneakers.

"We're releasing you to your wife." Follow down the passage. Stride through double glass doors, held open by My angels. Sprint to Bob's car parked twenty feet from the station doors across yellow no parking lines. Spud taps rear seat—sit next to me, please. Slip in. Barb, pregnant, sits in the front passenger seat. Sense, hear, shushes, then soothing language, "We'll help you feel better." *Let them say what they want.*

Body, lips, hands, fingers, feet move at random. Pitch black outside. Yet spotlights illuminate the once silvery gleaming towers still filling eyes. Janet climbs in, anxious, shuts the door, "Okay Bob." Pull away, leave this temporary stop. "A neighbor heard you shouting and called the police. Do you remember that?" *Pragmatic.*

Bob states, "I'm driving to Mercer Hospital." *So what.*

They remain silent. Words tumble, rushed, some clear. Steady, low, high-pitched voice. Headlights pierce the misty low white fog as if they are hot lucid stakes piercing icy solitude. Curious pupils peer forward onto the two-lane county road ahead. Barb twists in a questioning glance. Stare through the gloom and fog.

"Why don't you sit back, Rod?" Ignore tender request and their mute expressions. Notice route, car speed, bumps, curves, oncoming headlights. Ignore, notice, ignore, notice.

"Where the fuck are we going?"

"You don't have to curse, Rod." Again, "Why don't you sit back?"

"Need to watch. Don't you know that?" Speedometer climbs to 55 like expectant soldiers on a battlefield eager for the command, "Charge!" and the legions of dark menacing pines arrayed to block them. Whizz by them, moving west like a locomotive, no past. Time has taken a hiatus.

In a flash the sun's spreading glow is dawn, not dusk.

Recognize Trenton outskirts, then streetlights and structures. The eight-story white and brick building on Bellevue Ave commands the city block.

Bellevue. I get it.

> **EMERGENCY ENTRANCE**

Enter. Night duty Doctor Jack Ward greets us. Alone with him, he peppers questions in mild singsong tones. *This is a test. He must be a psychiatrist.* Reply in clear, sane words matching his cadence.

Says "Here's something to calm you." Pop his pills, drink his offered water. *Look rational.* Study the green sink across from my high bed-like table that seems to oscillate, as ponder which scientific discovery will cure cancer.

He speaks with Janet, sends us home. *Does she have Power of Attorney?*

As we walk into the kitchen, Jan says, "Rest Rod, you need sleep." *Don't need sleep. Pay attention to Voices and listen.*

Eyes dart, move, peer at conjured words and seminal phrases drawn on cuneiform tablets, pictures of Tomorrowland, and scenes from dreamlands past and future.

"He should've put you to sleep."

No need to respond. No troublesome questions. No evasive answers. The air between us floats on cracked eggshells. Undress. Lie in bed. Lids close under the beige blanket pulled up to my chin that shields legs, lap, and chest as they warm.

Next morning she's miffed at Doctor Ward.

"He should have sedated you so you could get a decent rest instead of just prescribing stupid vitamins."

That afternoon, Janet and Jess go to visit her mum. Alone, squint out the rear bedroom window.

"Who's that?"

Home to rest
but rollercoaster continues
to disturb and stir mind

1.15 INVENTION CORP

FBI. Bet on it. Better not tell Janet.

Two stocky men in midnight blue suits wearing black wraparound sunglasses, white shirts, and black skinny ties lurk behind our nine-foot-tall lilac bushes at the bushy cusp of the backyard. *They must protect their investment.* Turn aside from the window and click through TV stations, catching bits of asinine commercials touting their miracle solutions in twenty-second spots.

Janet returns. *Try to act sane, Rod.*

She carries a tray of soup, crackers, salad, and Pepsi for lunch, as if this is a case of flu. She projects the best and is prepared for the worst. Controlled, refraining from interrogation, she also administers pills and water at appointed times with the precision of Nurse Ratched, and dare not balk. She departs, as neither food nor TV holds attention. Seen most movies. Swivel, lift the curtain, peek out the window again.

Are they still there?

Now agents are shadowed behind our tall, wide, Eastern White Pine.

Aimless thoughts percolate over two days, then shoot like Green Arrow's specialty arrows toward gyrating targets of silver-rimmed circles within brass ones. Emotions weave like soaring hawks searching for prey, even as extra sleeping pills attempt to offset hyper-drive.

Jan and Jess leave to run errands.

"How would you like to earn millions from your invention?" the TV hawker asks. "Call us, and we'll turn your dream into reality!"

Dial the 1-800 number, speak to a male voice, jot directions to Cherry Hill Mall area, about thirty miles away. It's sunny, sixty-five degrees. Pull up garage door, wheel out blue and chrome Honda 360cc motorcycle bought used at Sherm Cooper's reputable Cycle Ranch after Dad died.

Speed south on Route 295 then west on Route 72 to a dilapidated office building in Pennsauken and park sideways in a slot. The entrance lobby has a dirty, joyless Deli the size of a walk-in closet. Fork over a buck for a cup of dubious joe. Two sips, "Ugh." Too stale even for me.

Toss it. Ride the rickety elevator to the third floor, burning and in a rush. Enter a carpeted hallway of unmarked doors but find it.

Invention
Submission
Corporation

The square waiting room of brown paneling has four worn corduroy-covered office chairs, a corner table with lamplight on, and a few ragtag magazines. No windows. No receptionist. Just a lauan door. A cheap bronze-plated nameplate on it says PRIVATE. After five minutes a shaved man with brown hair, in his forties, opens PRIVATE.

Medium height and build, no jacket, no tie, plaid shirt. *Looks safe.*

"Hi, how do you do. I'm Mister Johnston. Do you have an invention idea?"

"Yes." Goes to his desk. Returns with clipboard, papers, and pen; hands them over. "Oh, brought My pen."

"Please take a few minutes and fill out the forms the best you can. When completed, we'll see how we can turn your idea into a commercial success." Reenters his office, closes PRIVATE.

This idea is excellent. Start on the forms, enter personal data on one, draw a bathroom sink on graph paper on the second, complete the top half of the confidentiality agreement on the third, and finish in less than ten minutes. The sink is mid-chest high when lifted by pulling a side handle. The added height ensures ease of use for the elderly to brush their teeth and wash up while standing upright without bending at the waist.[14]

Knock on PRIVATE. "Come in."

Sit on the only plastic chair in front of his 2 x 5-foot desk. Thirty-six inches separates us, the wood-paneling behind skimming my rear end. He reaches for the clipboard; hand it over.

"You're Rodney?"

"Affirmative."

"And where is your town?"

"Near Trenton. Grew up in Mercer County."

Asks for signature on Statement of Confidentiality and Non-Use. "It's necessary so we can consult frankly." *Makes sense. This will be a wild commercial success.* Sign, eager to start. *Our Corporation....*

"Like everything, Mister Richards, this is a process. First, we perform a patent search to confirm your idea isn't registered. If not, we draw your rough design according to established standards. Then, we canvas possible manufacturers to find out if they like your concept. If one agrees, we strike a deal and patent your idea in your name." This will cost big bucks.

"This sounds reasonable, right?"

"Ah, of course." *Thought this would lead somewhere big, not money in your pocket.*

"Based on those critical steps, and the incredible benefits that will accrue, a thousand is a fair price to begin what we need to do, don't you think?"

"Ah, We'll have to think about it."

"Do you use VISA?" *I'm not stupid enough to give you a credit card!*

Stand. Remember, wallet lost. "As I said, We'll have to think about it, ah, Mister Johnston. I'll call." Grab a copy of the confidentiality statement. Don't bother closing PRIVATE.

Light up outside. *Hope I'm back before Janet and Jesse. If not, I'll say I went out for cigarettes.* Hurtle north on Route 295 on My two-wheeled jet. "Good, nobody here." Climb under bedcovers after turning on the TV. It's a brilliant idea! "Will implement the Corporation at a future date. It'll still work."

Products spell sales
like saltwater taffy boxes
at the Jersey shore

Before dawn, sit at our downstairs desk, pull out blank paper and write, "President Jimmy Carter, Commander-in-Chief."

"Subject: Fixing America's social and political ills." Rail against the rigged two-party system and self-serving foreign policies promoting only U.S. commercialism, threaten retributions if don't change consumption attitudes and planned obsolescence, and urge more attention to protestors, decry environmental raping, all in harsh, commanding tones. Scold as an angry parent does a wayward child. Address five back-to-back pages to White House, 1600 Pennsylvania Avenue, D.C., a future state.

Sneak out and mail it before Janet wakes up.

Antidotes gush hot
for America's poisons
President must scurry

Later, over a dinner of lentil soup and PB&J sandwiches, Jan says, "Are you trying to hurt me?"

"No."

"Well, you've done a good job. You haven't had a kind word or spoken to me in days." She's angry. Uncommon numbness seeps in.

"Ah, I'm sorry. Didn't mean to hurt you. Just don't have much to say." Afraid. Afraid thoughts will spill out hot words of grandiose plans meant to change the world's current laissez-faire attitudes into action.

"Princeton House Behavioral Health Center can help you feel better. You need to go there, Rod." *Go or upset her. Which?*

"If you say so." She drives. Drop Jesse at Grandmum's first. On the way she says, "A PSE&G linesman found your wallet a few days later. I have it. Can I trust you not to lose it?"

"Yes."

She turns into the brick facility on Mt. Lucas Road and parks. At the front desk, she leans up and speaks to the intake person. Stand away, calm.

View a large open room with couches, chairs, and console TV. See a green-felted regulation pool table. Itching to play.

Approach counter, "Hi, My name's Rodney and I need to stay a few days. Can you help Me?"

Princeton House clerk turns to Jan, "We can admit him."

Do what she wants
Hurts, even unintended,
cause worries and concerns

1.16 SUICIDE WATCH

"I Am the next manifestation of God."

Channel the divine Missions of Krishna Lord, Zoroaster, Moses the Lawgiver, Buddha, Awakened One, Christ, Son of Man, and the Apostle, Muhammad, The Warner, Peace be upon each of Them. Bubbling omniscient spirit brims and seethes with power and authority. Strong kinship courses through blood and feverish brain, interlocked like unbreakable spider webs constructed from the infallible Word of God.

"Rodney, my name's Peter. I'm the head psychiatrist. Please have a seat." He smiles. In khaki shorts, open gray Hawaiian shirt with mottled-green palm trees, short tan socks, and penny loafers, he beckons to the open wicker chair and shuts the glass-topped door.

Welcoming, harmless.

Offer hand, he takes it. "Great to meet you, how's it going/ beautiful out today, isn't it?" Sit. Comfortable on a thin flower print pillow atop the squeaky high-backed, wide-armed, interwoven wicker chair. A King's throne.

Next steps clear. Tiny events have purpose. Convince him.

He pulls his sleek black desk chair on rollers to within three feet away, sits down, crosses his right leg, smiles wider. *Sincere.*

"Yes, gorgeous out. Rodney, I accept who you are and would like you to tell me how you feel. Can you do that? I guarantee no interruptions. Here's water in case you're thirsty."

Kind.

Take the glass.

He accepts Who I Am. Ah, at last!

"WecanachieveWorldPeaceeasilyAllwehavetodoisloveoneanotheras brothersandsistersinonehumanfamily One familyallcreedscolorsskintones culturesmergedintoonehumanrace…"

"Rodney, can you slow down, please?"

"Universal Love is innate. Once we love one another, unity is assured. All religions teach that. His Messengers are the same spirit and only differ based on the age in which They appeared and the capacity of people to understand Them. The Golden Rule is the foundation of all human interaction… *Must be precise. Help him recognize this…*

"Barriers to peace will evaporate. Full equality of women and men, universal education, and justice will buttress social amity and concord. Every person will work, have wealth, and uniform health care. English will be the auxiliary tongue. Communications will explode and be instantaneous. The world's federal system will function without flaws. Every organization and company will promote fairness in their best interest. Religions and ideologies will unify instead of fighting with words, fists, swords, and guns. Science will promote truth instead of arms…"

Peter's face is rapt, nods head, writes notes, utters "I see." "Sure." "Yes, that makes sense."

Continue to pontificate….

Don't remember sedation. Five hours later, wake up groggy. Wander out to the carpeted hall. Sidle up to counter.

"Where am I?"

Male attendant replies, "Princeton House, alcohol, mental health, and drug treatment facility." Turn back to bed, lay down, veg out.

Two days and nights pass. Deep blue skies rain the sun's rays through floor to ceiling windows and hooded eyes eschew the next morning's light. Breakfast of scrambled eggs and bacon is the only boon. Start a game of eight-ball on one of two pool tables with an inmate in a midnight blue robe. Break, orange five-ball in. Solids. Run the three, then seven, two, six, one, then four.

The all-black money ball hugs the long green rail. "Eight-ball, corner pocket." Exact thrust, follow through with a smooth stroke. "Clunk."

"Good game." Ready to play another…

LEAVE

Shuffle through the unguarded lounge to My shared quarters. Roommate lies on his bed, reading a magazine. Stand and stare until he looks up. "I'm bustin' outta here."

"Now." He jumps up, dashes out. *To tell someone. No matter.*

March up to the 4 x 5-foot window, interlock fingers into a balled fist, raise it high. With full might, tense back and shoulders, arms arc straight out, visualize pushing through glass, swing in single, taut, outward, forward motion… "BANG!"

"CRACK, clink, crack, clink, clink…" The rectangle of plate glass explodes outwards and inward. Hop on the two-foot-high windowsill, step into fresh air, cross the dull brown concrete sidewalk, sit on soft grass, cross legs. Look up. Clear skies. *Peaceful.*

Gaze down at hands—no blood; not a scratch. *A sign.*

Placed on suicide watch. Drugs administered, "For you, Thorazine and Haldol," he says.

Body, mind s l o w s d o w n. Sleep overcomes….

Mid-morning is a limbo of lost time. Look down on blue rubber-soled slippers as stumbling feet pad the hard linoleum floors. Drugs add increasing depression, restlessness, and agitation with no distinctions.

Two long-haired blonde girls, eighteen or nineteen, appear as escorts and accompany my every move from a distance.

Tell Janet, Mom, and Dad on their visit, "I have two guardian angels."

Next morning, reach pool table and opponent. Eyesight sharp. Body strong, maintain a steady stroke. Unbeatable. Unstoppable.

A bank shot will end the game. "Eight-ball side pocket." Smack cue ball hard into the eight, it careens off the green cushion. "Clunk."

"So easy!" Control hidden glee at such a large confirmation.

After lunch, lounge on the cushioned cloth couch in the Great Room, legs and feet up, slippers off. One of My escorts sits on the arm of a nearby chair. A polite brown-haired nurse pulls up a rolling tray and holds out pills in a white Dixie cup.

"No! I'm not taking that crap!" Knock cup from her hand with one swipe and pills fly across the room. "Your wrong! What are you lookin' at, jackass! I don't belong here! I should never have come. You can't keep me here!"

On fire. Rational Soul on fire.[15]

In minutes two orderlies pin upper body down, a doctor lifts sleeve looking for meaty flesh. The pinch stings. Clear liquid injected. The heavy fog of hostility dissipates like lapping waves rolling onto the long smooth beach of Wildwood by the Sea, where a short walk into the ocean leads to raised sandbars and chest-high, calm, refreshing cool ocean water.

> *Stretched out, dazed, crazy dreams*
> *as ambulance rolls*
> *Tug at manacles*

1.17 GOLD'S CURE

Will not let trouble harass Me.[11]

Fuzzy.

"Where... We... goin'."

"North. Summit Hospital," says the EMT. As the driver maneuvers over flat or bumpy roads, wriggle wrists then hands free of wide leather buckled restraints half-inch by half-inch, fold arms across chest, pull up gray wool itchy blanket to my neck, and lie stock-still. *Ah, so much better.*

EMT in white winks but doesn't move.

After some time, stop. He pushes open doors. It's overcast and dry. He hops down, pulls my gurney out. A bald fellow in white comes around, grabs the head end, both pull and lift. It unfolds, stretches, and hits asphalt.

Far from familiar rural Mercer County environs, we're on a sheltered estate, but family dwellings loom thick on all sides in a neighborhood of split-levels. Spy late fall's brown, veined, and pointy oak leaves as they litter the ground like candy wrapper trash after a rock concert. The EMT pulls off the coarse brown blanket and unbuckles leg and waist shackles.

"Can you get up?" Sit, rise, stand in a shaky haze. A young white smock wearing a stethoscope approaches. *Doctor?*

"We'll help get you better." Reminds me of classic words, "I'm from the Government and I'm here to help."

Burly bald attendant with embroidered letters *Fair Oaks Hospital* on his jacket holds my arm as trudge up concrete steps to its central doors. The multi-level orangery building looms like a grasping King Kong, with two-story brick wings protruding from its core looking like his outstretched arms.

Janet pulls up in our green Toyota. Inside, we enter ADMISSIONS in a blur, answer questions and sign documents. Interview follows, "Did you have a recent meal? How do you feel? What are you thinking? Do you have thoughts of suicide? What is your wife thinking?"

They ask her, "What has his behavior been like?" She recounts the last three weeks with hand movements.

Say goodbye to her in the lobby. Escorted to the male dorm room.

The black hands on the wall clock point at two and two. *Gotta get outta here.* Rise, fumble in dark for jeans, shirt, and socks, but can't find shoes. Four dorm mates, sprawled and asleep, are only visible from the white glow of their Tee-shirts. Pad to one of two thin windows, just wide enough to squeeze through. Reach high, brace palms and fingers on its edges.

"Ungh," hoist body onto six-inch wooden ledge.

"Bang, Bang, Bang." Inhale, tighten finger grips. "Bang. Bang. Bang."

No cracks. Right foot feels numb even through the sock. *Shit.* Climb down, lie on the single bed, frustrated. Sleep elusive.

Soon meet Joey, a strapping handsome Italian kid with thick black hair who's in for drug use. His second time. "Yeah, I'm hooked, but so what?"

Shoot the bull. He's an active listener, full of punch, and lighthearted. We snicker at the creeping slugs. Attend our second psychotherapy session together. Five of us, most in robes, sit on wicker chairs or white rockers on a semi-circular wooden stage. Our six-foot tall hourglass blonde therapist in her long white smock enters and takes a seat.

"Rodney, why don't you lay on the floor?" *Swedish model or therapist? Okay, weird, but up for the challenge.*

Curl into a fetal position on the linoleum in front of the stage. Think back to high school. Like sleeping on the backseats of unlocked parked cars instead of going home at three in the morning.

"Dig deep into your memories. Express how you feel." She moves her right hand to her chin, crosses her long legs, and rests her elbow on her right knee, showing skin above a tantalizing white stockinged thigh. *Hmm, what would satisfy her?*

Close eyes. "Mommy, don't leave." Moan, "Where are you going? Don't leave me here. Please, don't leave!" Relive the mist-filled morning clinging to Mom's arms inside her 1948 Studebaker.

"No Mom, please!" Two nuns grab waist and shoulders, drag me down the path into St. Michael's Orphanage.

Four years old, locked in, don't remember other children's faces. Contract chickenpox and quarantine in an institutional green room for a week, itchy, no TV, a solid door, and a barred window. Silent nuns bring meals, no books, no conversation. The thick white socks rubber-banded around my wrists don't prevent fingers from scratching.

Scads of white pockmarks on my torso confirm the nightmare.

"I'm so alone." *Is this what she wants?* "Oh... so lonely... abandoned." *I can tell, can she?* Fake cries, smirking moans, all bullshit.

"How are you abandoned?" goading us. *No!* Rise, sit in a rocker, cover face. Feel flushed, want to cry, embarrassed. *Hell, never let embarrassment show, never.*

Joey increases his moaning. The Indian girl cries out and shivers as well. *A good faker like Me and Joey?*

"Thank you, that's all for today." We're dismissed like a line of postal customers at closing time. *Do we have to do this again? Have to so we can earn privileges, I guess.*

Recall that much from Admissions.

Disposable days and nights pass following arbitrary, white-smocked directions. Then, the greatest prize.

I can smoke! Janet delivers Kools. Love her loyalty.

Fair Oaks has rigid class and break periods, and lots of solitary time, although opportunities for superficial friendships exist. Time to stew on unpleasant things. Time to realize how poorly life treats too many. It does and doesn't. Life doesn't treat us, we treat it. It just is, we react to it. *No use groaning that God chose me to be... sick... nor rich, nor the brightest.*

Doesn't help to blame parents, relatives, boss, anyone. Unproductive to cry. As a kid, pleasant, carefree, shallow. No concerns for consequences. Played out each day as whims and events dictated. Our near-poverty growing up on Trenton's back streets—not a factor.

A week of floating between boredom and group obligations passes.

Sit on a green padded table in an exam room. Doctor Gold, always in a white lab coat open to his knees with a dangling stethoscope around his neck, enters with a chart and manilla folder and closes the blue metal door. Young, short, even handsome, with thick brown hair, a child-like face, he's kind, with a ready smile. Looks at me. Opens his file. Fingers his stethoscope.

"You may get a kick out of what I'm about to tell you."

"Good news or bad?"

"Both."

"Okay, hit me."

"Rodney, you have Bipolar Affective Disorder."

"Yeah, I'm BAD all right. Badder than you, Doc." Neither happy nor sad. Just information, data. *Can't hurt Me.* BAD, a fair moniker years ago as a troubled youth. *But now? Hell, I'm respectable.*

"What's the good news?"

"We're starting you on Lithium, which should help prevent another episode. Are you all right with that?"

"Whatever you say, Doc. That would make it good, huh? Only wish I had an acronym for G.O.O.D." Had no fears as a youthful hippie. Sniffed glue, amyl nitrate, smoked pot, drank Lord Calvert, Ripple, and wine, popped uppers, dropped acid, smoked hash, and cooked opium. Didn't care about the consequences then. Drugs and alcohol not a concern. *How about God Only Orders Drugs?*

That night at her visit Janet says, "The first week you were here Doctor Gold wanted your system clear of drugs, so they didn't give you any. That enabled him to determine your natural level of lithium for a baseline. He also told me, it's a common salt and all plants and creatures contain trace amounts. It'll help stabilize you, Rod. During an episode your chemicals get out of sync."

In sync is best; *don't always feel the hottest.* Or too hot and full of myself.

Janet also says, "Finding the proper dose is very important. Too little, you'll flip out again. Too much, you'll stumble around dazed."

Toxic levels cause dehydration, kidney problems, or seizures.

Or death. *Great, simply great.*

"Meds time," calls out a nurse. Mealtimes and bedtimes handed pills. Down them with water from the bottomless supply of Dixie cups and water. The simple mood stabilizer calms streams of erratic thoughts. Each time nurses reiterate, "It's critical to maintain the proper dosage." *But the blood draws, whew.*

The crooks of arms are pink pin cushions. "I'm dying in here."

Still incarcerated, but who gives a shit about hours passing in boredom when enclosed by solid brick and concrete walls with locked windows and doors that don't budge. Looking out Fair Oaks windows it seems as phony as a Hollywood movie set constructed to fool the big screen viewer. Trees seem like 2D painted cutouts, as do the glossy cars in the parking lot from sunlight I can't feel. *I only need one car key.*

Days without dates pass in bouts of lethargy and fuzziness Clear thinking is a chimera. Shuffle like everyone else in a copycat George Romero movie in a stumbling, rambling, lost routine surrounded by jean-clad clones as shift body to meals, groups, dispensary, smoke breaks, lounge, and bed. Each night winds down like a battery-operated clock losing power with a desperate desire to recharge.

Ask a newbie for the date, says it's December something. Dad died near the end of September. Janet doesn't want to upset recovery, so haven't heard news of events at home, work, or in the world. These past two months, ride a rollercoaster cart teetering on the edge in a hemmed-in tomb-like Space Mountain, a rookie space cadet lost in the twisting, speeding catacombs of the pitch-black orb, its white attractive sphere hiding the chaos inside. *But this sure ain't Disneyland.*

Spend afternoons in the Arts & Crafts room on simple tasks. Sleepwalk through repetitive motions, depressed and dull-witted.

"Tap, tap, tap," hammer five-pointed stars and crescent-moon punches into a two-inch-wide leather belt, then make fat prong holes with an awl, while sitting at a wooden worktable. "Tap, tap, tap," mindless, soothing, concentrate on pounding.

Our workroom is quiet, only a few of us, not all busy. When finished, pick another project, and with careful placement, top off a light-maple jewelry box with fake multi-colored gemstones embedded in plaster-of-Paris. When that dries, overlay and glue a bas-relief-colored print of an 1850s high seas schooner onto a 9 x 11-inch wooden frame, score the edges with hammer and bevel-edge chisel, sand, then apply thick shellac that reflects the overhead light with a glossy shine.

"Ahh, nicely done," the monitor says. *Yeah, I'm an artist.*

We smokers watch the hands of the clock for lifesaving, life-giving breaks after breakfast, lunch, and dinner.

"Smoke time everybody!" someone calls out. In a clutch of panting wild slathering wolves, ready to attack warm flesh, we diehards gather in a clump at the courtyard door. Only an orderly can unlock it to let our ravenous wolf pack out. Whoever the orderly happens to be, some friendly, some stand-offish, he or she waits for the twelve of us to file in, then shuts the door and stands guard near it. Once in the penned area, we're hyper nervous until our guard uses their lighter to light each of us in turn, whoever wheedles through the mob first.

"Tastes like heaven," to a gaunt stringy brown-haired hippie who loiters nearby. Take a deep inhale, lower exhale, until hotbox it down to its nub and the dump the butt in a Smokers Outpost.

"Can you light me?" to the orderly for the second. On edge without them. Feel like a convicted criminal on a life sentence in Folsom Prison let out in the common yard for fifteen minutes of fresh air and exercise.

Janet brings packs, but no matches, no lighter. Smoking is the only pleasure to expect. Predictable days pass in predictable motions without emotional outbursts except for either super-agitated or loudmouth newcomers. Depressed admittees slink to corners to be alone.

Dr. Gold asks if Janet can address two combined family sessions. "She's her own person Doc."

She tells me on her visit afterward, "I said how disappointed I was it took so long to diagnose you. Family members there relayed how embarrassed they were at their loved one's behavior, and how hurt they were by them. They worried their families might be sick too. They were most concerned about what others might think." *Feel like shit.*

Like an emerging butterfly, surface from the smothering chrysalis of head-filled silky liquid called mania and depression. Can't worry about drugs I've never heard of and what they're doing to My personality.

It's a blustery sapphire-sky day with wisps of clouds that point the way out. We inmates walk through the main doors to a school bus resembling the Beatle's yellow submarine but painted blue. *A field trip!*

Step up and enter, take a padded brown seat, and sit high on the thirty-five-foot-long tour bus as we cruise downtown Summit. Off the reservation, unblocked air, with 3D glasses on, admire grass and wind-blown tree branches, independent shops, custom abodes, and average people treading sidewalks and streets. *How bright the colors!* No solid beige walls. No cramped and circumscribed courtyard.

"This is great. This is what privilege levels earn." Love window view especially on this bouncy ride, a voyeur, seeing citizens perform their single-minded day-in-the-life tasks. The only thing missing is the Beatles' lyrics in the background and their crazy costumes.

A few citizens note our electric Kool-Aid acid bus as it rumbles by.

Like Richard Farina wrote, "Been down so long it looks like up to me."

Gold's mild salt tablets
make manic impulses fade
Are they exorcised?

1.18 ITS MISTY OUT

Doctor Gold says to Janet, "He's stable."

Free! Soon anyway. Itch like a dog with fleas to push out from behind Fair Oaks doors into the bustling world I've missed for over a month. Fair Oaks—better than the cramped jail cell at County with its bars and screaming inmates, yet a prisoner just the same. Soft carpets and tiles just hide concrete floors.

On the auspicious day bag up things and don a dark windbreaker to match the sky. At the exit interview, Janet jots notes as the clerk intones directions, and we sign forms. The stoic female also hands over a script for Lithium.

Walk to the waiting attendant, who opens the main door. Expectant, push doors further out and step into December drizzle. *Oh, so excellent! Gawd, what happened?*

Stop on the middle front step and inhale the life-giving mist. Raise arms in the cool breeze. Turn head skyward and open mouth to gulp the tiny droplets and let them soak face and body. The mist dispels the stale air, beige carpets, and boredom that still emanates from behind.

Escaped. A captive wolf freed from a steel-toothed trap into a confusing forest of endless news cycles and their upsetting events, deeper and thicker than the Pine Barrens itself.

Returned to a world calling itself civilized. *Ha!*

With a light step, walk to our emerald Toyota. The invisible car. We joked about that car. Other drivers didn't see it—too many of them cut us off. Too many to be coincidental. Janet places my bag of clothes and craft items on the back seat. She comes round, opens my door.

"Thanks." Sit, Jan closes it. She strides to the driver's side, climbs in, buckles up. She doesn't start the engine, turns, and stares at me. *What's wrong?*

"Don't you need to do something?" *What the hell are you talking about?*

"Ah, I don't think so. We've got my things, right? Um, Doctor Gold told us I'd be all right."

"Don't you need to buckle up?" *Oh.* Typical Janet; alert, practical, observant. Ever mindful of what needs doing. Do it as soon as possible, or toss it and forget it, like junk mail. This reminder, like hundreds of times before, something mundane.

"Yeah, sorry." Mumble it often on the drive, more for being a pain in the ass these past months. Can almost hear her say, "Doctor Gold made it clear you couldn't help yourself. You didn't know what you were doing."

Tough to believe.

It's a great warmth to get back and hug Jesse. "Daddy!" We cuddle for some moments, big smiles and jabbering. The next few days Jan, leery and alert, juggles what's left of paid sick time with Chris over the phone. Thoughts of Fair Oaks jumble and become indistinct. Want to forget the whole bleeping episode. Hope Janet can as well. Nothing is that simple.

Adopt attitude moving forward from the Bahá'í prayer, "I will not dwell on the unpleasant things of life."[11] Thinks aren't that bad, feel, better. At least not a mental case anymore. But internal invisible microbes, in brain, guts, and blood, can still release self-destructive poisons.

Keep the garage door closed to smoke my nicotine poison of choice in at regular intervals and freeze my ass off. "Gotta stop these." It's my private sheltered treeless courtyard, free of larger burdens. Relish the time alone without crowding in with other smokers. Free to think nothing at all.

Hamilton Bahá'ís stop by the house, drop off food dishes, and lighten Janet's secretarial duties for the Spiritual Assembly. Hear her tell a few that pry, "Rod had a breakdown and is recovering."

Kitty, Bob's mom and our dear friend, mentions to Jan, "I don't understand it. Just tell him to get over it." Most don't ask outright. The episode has become a pariah, untouchable, unmentionable. Janet is the gatekeeper if anyone has questions since so little literature exists on bipolar. Can't imagine her worries. She knew before marrying me I wasn't one-hundred percent squeaky clean. *Who is? But what about now?*

Doctors said, "With bipolar, he could do something abnormal with no warning. Could harm himself or loved ones. If it happens again...."

Janet doesn't show fear though, nor doubt or indecision. She exudes confidence. Even with the label BAD, she treats me as an equal, fair in her appraisals. She never shows distrust, only love and concern. When she says, "I'm going to Triangle Repro to make copies, including our driver's licenses, insurance, and credit cards in case we lose them," think nothing of it.

Her loyalty—a rock—unshakeable. As long as tell her where I'll be.

Love, like Gibraltar,
deep, solid, strong. Hold on tight,
despite unseen cracks

When leaving, the stoic Fair Oaks clerk said, "Call the state's health insurance office to see about a psychiatrist." Janet finds Greenspring is the State provider, makes an appointment, and I'm assigned to a Doctor Argueta at their facility on Parkside Avenue in Ewing Township. Meet with him and we're impressed by his forthright and considered views.

Janet starts, "It wasn't until the police called and woke me up that I even knew he had left. It was a shock. The officer said a neighbor heard him screaming and called the station. Police found him nude.

"Then I had to call a friend to watch Jesse. Called other friends and picked him up at a strange police station, not knowing what was wrong. We drove him to Mercer Hospital, and he cursed and ranted the whole time. There, Doctor Ward only gave him vitamins, stupid man. He needed a sedative."

Listen as an observer, as if stranded on an atoll in the mid-Pacific. Conscious memory of the episode is like a chalkboard wiped with a wet cloth, just like I did at Sacred Heart Grammar School because Sister Agnes took offense to my clownish antics.

Doctor Argueta, short, brown-skinned, slick black hair, casual clothes, relaxed, says, "That is how it can happen with bipolar sufferers, without warning. But if he fights any abnormal impulses, calls at once if he feels he's slipping, and follows his medication regimen, future occurrences shouldn't return. We hope. But there are no guarantees."

Janet swivels and looks at me.

"Can you promise to do that, Rod?"

How can I say yes? How can I stay sane? Can't even stop lighting up for more than an hour. Both diseases will kill me as surely as swallowing cyanide-laced coffee if not careful.

"I'll try."

Admit it. You're bipolar.
Can't snuff it out
like a cigarette butt

1.19 BACK TO BUSINESS

"Hi Chris, I'm here. Clean bill of health, sorry I missed so much work." When she sits down, add, "I want to thank you. Janet thanks you too."

"Glad to have you back, Rod, we can use you. I'm sorry for your loss and what you went through. Janet is remarkable though, you're fortunate to have her. We have a lot to do, especially with Telex. We're expanding rollouts to ten more agencies, and we must get them right."

Exhausted sick leave and vacation days have almost cost me a career. But through many phone consultations with Janet, and using half-days without pay, Chris held on to my position. Grateful for that, and for her bringing me on at all. After being fired.

That was my first hard lesson at BDP. Our second-shift supervisor Bob Groom was out on a Thursday night. There was a lull operating my IBM 360/50 Mainframe Computer since the next job's thousands of eighty-column punched cards were still being sorted on the IBM 083s, a job I once did. Eugene and John were mounting 9-track tapes in rapid-fire succession for the string of Lottery programs on the IBM 145 Mainframe. Knowing everyone upstairs had left for the day, snuck into the Assistant Director's office. Rifled through his desktop folders searching for upcoming pay raises but discovered nada.

The next day, Computer Operations Manager Joe Marino called our house, and asked, "Do you know anything about it, Rodney?" Heart and mind whirred, pulse raced, "Nothing, Joe."

But once onsite at four o'clock, he summoned me into his half-glassed Computer Room office. Confronted, confessed. Blubbered like an alcoholic on a binge after a three-year dry spell, recounting apologies and "I'm sorry," crying with tears of remorse into a half-empty glass of cheap whiskey.

Cried as Joe, stone-faced, intoned, "Rodney, you're fired."

Desperate, Saturday morning knocked on Tom Moorcroft's house door, Joe's assistant. He let me in. "Tom, it was a monumental error in judgment. Won't ever do something like that again. I'm a good computer operator, Tom, you've said so yourself, and I've proved I can do the job. I'm loyal, despite this mistake. Tom, please, I've been with BDP for nine years. Will you consider taking me back?"

Joe did not, but in a stroke of luck, Chris Reid was looking for staff and accepted my transfer to her professional unit, Planning and Technical Services, formed just months earlier. "Chris, I'll be loyal and honest, I swear." She's demanding like Joe, and her data processing acumen soon penetrates my surface knowledge of DP terminologies and functions.

Chris, always in a mad rush, doesn't raise her voice, except to cry out from her office at the end of the hall, "Rod? Can you come here?"

My beautiful, intelligent, and young brunette assistant Alice, whom Chris extricated from Tape Storage Room duties in Computer Operations months before Dad died, has kept things afloat. She's organized and sharp. Pending action memos are in one pile, what she's handled in another. We consult on pressing needs like the BDP annual maintenance waiver and divvy up tasks. Optimize hundreds of Telex IBM-compatible 3270 controller and display rollouts. Ensure purchase orders for the equipment are in place, and divvy up phone calls to agency heads and contacts.

Alice says, "Gene from IBM, Greg from Telex, and a few others asked where you were, so I told them you were on sick leave and nothing more."

Janet had confided in her as well, but can't afford embarrassment, too busy. "Deal with what's in front of me, then move on," is all, like walking under pouring rain, shoveling a foot of snow, or sweating out a 100-degree Jersey heatwave of stifling humidity. It's the nature of existence. Fix it or forget it. Just like ignoring drivers who cut off our invisible Toyota when Janet says, "I guess Harry's arm or his blinker's broken."

At home, obligations fester. Janet nails down Blue Cross/Blue Shield reps over Fair Oaks' out-of-pocket charges. Still react to Dad's bills but funds finally received from both his bequests cover them.

Worry over my arrest charges on the night of insanity. Discuss it with our close Bahá'í friend and Assembly member Olive McDonald, Mister Robinson's secretary at Teich, Groh, and Robinson in Trenton. She recommends we see him. We trust his legal expertise, invaluable in resolving Dad's major estate issues like acquiring Dad and Marilyn's divorce papers for Irvine. He also had the California Bankruptcy Proceeding against Dad vacated.

In our meeting, ask him, "What about the lewdness and disorderly person charges that night in the pines?"

"As you requested, we contacted Berkeley Township. The Court dismissed the Complaint on December twentieth."

"That's a relief. Thanks. Can we wipe the charges off my record?"

"Rod, why don't you let it go."

"I agree with Janet, it's best to let it go. It would take time and expense, and we can't erase the arrest."

"Okay, Mister Robinson, if you say so," but disappointed. These things can come back and bite like malaria-carrying mosquitos.

Jan mails a thank you note and check for five-hundred-forty dollars for services rendered.

After sending a check to Donegan's with a note of gratitude and praise, we deposit Dad's pension and life insurance funds into savings and use a small bit to upgrade the electric service from 100 to 150 amps. Start a college fund too. Janet doesn't buy a thing for her frugal self.

At Jan's suggestion, splurge and take the train from Trenton into Penn Station in Midtown Manhattan. Cab it to 47th and the acclaimed Five Star Waldorf-Astoria Hotel and landmark on Park Avenue. The classy bellhop shows the two of us into a minuscule room on the fourteenth floor without a decent view of the iconic city, but the high bed and chocolate flower-print wallpaper reek of swankiness. We unpack, go downstairs, enjoy the elegant restaurant atmosphere, eat a light dinner, and wink at the high-priced tab. Upon returning, read, watch TV, and chat. After showers don the complementary and luxuriant white terrycloth robes.

"These are a pleasant touch."

"What's underneath is even more pleasant." It's stimulating and novel to be away and we enjoy each other's company.

The next afternoon, shuffle with the crowd to the ticket taker at the Shubert Theatre on Broadway, find our seats, and watch Cassie sling her tale as she fences verbally with her director Zach in *Chorus Line*. After the ensemble's passionate rendition of "One," head to Carmines up the block for an Italian dinner. Can't finish their lettuce salad wedges or family portions of cheese-filled ravioli on huge white oval platters.

Lying in bed later, ponder the song's lyrics, think of Janet, and realize she chose me as her one. I have to show her she's the one.

Stephen hires a lawyer, implying a lawsuit for his share. Turn to Mister Robinson who suggests he call Stephen's counselor. They speak at length. In his office, we listen to our lawyer's advice. Agree to send Stephen fifty-four hundred dollars, not begrudging the amount. *Stephen, you deserve it and much more.*

We receive his light blue notecard, dated March 1980, "Thank You" on the outside. Inside, its hand printed.

> Dear Rod & Janet,
> Sort of an apology for being disagreeable for so long—I guess it was all just too much. Get little Jesse a tricycle and let me know how much.
>   Love, Steve.

So, it's not just me. Understand what "too much" means. Hadn't ever called him "Steve" though. This moniker is new. Difficult to conceive how Dad's death affects him. *What could he feel? Loss? Indifference? Love would come hard.*

Dad left Mom when I was four and Stephen two. Stephen grew up in his Catholic school circles; me free-range on Trenton city streets and alleyways. Cordial, yet we never embraced. Tormented him as a kid, once barricading him in the bathroom for an hour, heartless to his cries of "Let me out! I'll tell Mom!" After leaving home at fifteen, heard little about him or his activities, and still don't pry. *Stephen is an enigma.*

We do not buy a trike.

The episode and incarceration at Fair Oaks fade as constant chores and tasks at home and on the job wrap me like the Waldorf's terrycloth robe in a comfortable mode of "Get down to business" that disperses grandiose thoughts. Feel protected from the flames of self-combustion caused by bipolar's spontaneous grips.

But one primary problem remains—too self-absorbed in black and white convictions. *You've got to stop rushing to judgment, Rodney, you do it all the time.*

As a young computer operator, mentor John Guido had often said, "Rooter, slow down! Think it over and think it out." My interruptions irked Janet. Can hear her voice, "Rod, will you let me finish?"

Friends and family act as if nothing happened. Knowing them, they aren't discussing it among themselves. By luck or intention, not treated like a lost golden retriever puppy found by a lonely child, fawned over and made special.

Reenter daily regimen.

Perhaps, shouldn't get too settled in the warm comfy robe of familiar and expected obligations.

> *Duties resume—*
> *employee, husband, parent,*
> *believer—safe and sane*

1.20 POP THOSE PILLS

"Rod, did you take your pills?"

"Yes dear."

Unghh! Can't stand the question. Must swallow the fat tablets and capsules like a religious fanatic four times every single day. That goes too for Janet's reminders. Both go down like chewing dry notepaper that sticks in my craw and want to spit them out before they choke me.

Still moody, finding the right concoction had been like balancing an egg on a teaspoon in a twenty-yard dash to the finish line at the Mercer County 4H picnic. Yet with Dr. Argueta's expertise, Janet's sharp eyes and ears, and shared feelings, the three of us settle on a cocktail.

The meds don't hamper my energy more than they should. Only a low hum of dullness marks my usual pensive demeanor.

"I'm good," is my canned response when Janet probes. From crown to toe, the prescribed chemicals drown emotions like a black suit worn for a funeral, including a starched white shirt, thin black tie, black socks, and black shoes. Dare not slip out of them into comfortable bell-bottoms, sandals, and a purple and yellow tie-dye Tee-shirt or cries of, "You look weird," will erupt.

A cocktail it is. First, Lithium, a mood stabilizer. Purple Wellbutrin too, an anti-depressant and smoking cessation aid that doesn't curtail urges in the least. Chlorpromazine three times daily is an antipsychotic. Geodon for schizophrenia helps level moods. It's like testing a new act at the circus, walking on a frayed wire stretched across a tenuous net stretched fifty feet below with holes the size of Ford F-150s and no balance beam to hold on to.

Janet's constant, "Rod, did you take your pills?" is the only confirmation I'm taking the eleven damn pills when I should. *How those words grate!* Feel akin to Yossarian in a Catch-22 afraid of his commander more than the enemy. *But who's the commander? Pills? Her? Doctor A?*

Encased in a hapless condition, hope these colored pills and capsules hit their synaptic markers. Thirst for opportunities to express emotions without fear of being labeled psychotic or having motives questioned.

Tread like a cat who's seen a mouse ten feet away and slinks toward it.

How to remain stable?
Impede eruptions with
morn, noon, and night nudges

Of late, Janet's concerned over laissez-faire attitudes. Pay no attention. Cry when watch poignant scenes in Disney movies or commercials for maltreated doe-eyed kittens or dogs but feel no emotional responses for the human condition. Apathy is my traveling companion.

"Rod, did you hear what I said?"

"I'm sorry Jan, what?"

Despite insouciance in response to her concerns, she doesn't load on guilt, doesn't poke, doesn't jab or dredge up past insane acts. She avoids references to October and November altogether.

"It's like this year only has ten months, not twelve." She's focused like a flashlight beam on nursing me back to health and raising our son in a loving household. A return to the status quo before the episode is what she desires most.

Is it possible? Had shocked and disappointed her, yet while manic had no control, and doctors' pronouncements reinforced that. Mania isn't an excuse but is unpredictable. It's concealed, a byproduct of the disease.

"It's more like a volcano," one Fair Oaks doctor had shared to scare us. "It lies dormant, ready to erupt scorching viscous lava and spew ash for miles that can maim and kill normal relationships. Mania releases layers of risky and dangerous behaviors accompanied by senseless words and deeds. Mania hurts loved ones down to the bone marrow."

Clueless how to reassure her it won't overtake brain and body again, or hurt her to the quick, again. *She deserves better.*

Doctor Argueta adds Desyrel as an antidepressant and sleeping aid. Waking up mornings at three o'clock wasn't healthy.

Somehow, hear that Joey, best friend while at Fair Oaks, had relapsed and returned there after surviving near death from an overdose of heroin.

It doesn't bode well. Count blessings.

Volcanoes prove that
Mania, like lava, leaves
loved ones burned to crisps

2.0 EPISODE TWO?

2.1 HAIFA VISITS CHICAGO

"Care for a drink?" The light-blue uniformed flight attendant is solicitous, and the urge to smoke itches a dry throat and tongue.

"Yes please, Pepsi, if you have it." *Good, she has it.*

Janet can't have anything fizzy, nor food, only water. Feel Barb's arm next to mine in the middle. On the other side of her, glued in the corner, stiff, paler than her see-through freckled skin, window shade drawn, Janet cringes, hands clenched and arms hugging her body. Eyes scrunched and tight-lipped, her head leans on a minuscule gray pillow against the bulkhead.

Oh, hon, I hope your head and stomach make it through this.

Severe airsickness wracks her. She isn't afraid of flying; it's her inner ear that's the culprit. It cannot tolerate unpredictable movements, like these buffeting winds. All remedies, like Dramamine, failed. *She may cope with her eyes clamped shut. Knowing her susceptibility to migraines, she may have one now.*

Her hyper-sensitivity to motion is why she always drives the car when we travel together, so she can see the road ahead and the horizon.

But excited! She is too, she's said so.

We're on United's flight to Chicago's O'Hare to attend the 72nd Bahá'í National Convention at headquarters in Wilmette, Illinois. The May 1980 election will commence in Foundation Hall under the impressive Mother Temple of the West, a stunning paean and tribute that inspires awe in tens of thousands of visitors every year. Delegates from the contiguous United States will elect nine new members to the National Spiritual Assembly, the NSA, our governing council since the 1920s.

"C'mon, we'll have a fun trip. They have a terrific guest program too. And the most fun, we'll be together," Bob and Barb had said.

I add, "It'll get your mind off the normal routine, Jan. You need a break. People we know from around the country will be there. Plus, I'd love to see the House of Worship again. It'll be memorable. I've been in decent shape for a while now."

Stable on my meds, Janet agreed. Grandmum and Grandad mind Jesse.

Bob, squeezed into a seat across the aisle, tries to find room for his oversized body and long legs. When first met him eleven years earlier, he dressed like an ice cream truck man, attired head to ankle in white pants and shirt. He towered at six-foot-six, had a two-hundred-fifty-pound frame, sported a bushy brown beard attached to wild curly shocks of brown hair, and thick glasses with black frames. Currently, clean-shaven and hair tamed, his still ferocious hugs greet strangers and friends alike.

Bob and Barb, our closest friends, married a year after us. Their precious daughter Abbey has reddish hair.

Janet has filled two bags with sickness, and Barb is an attentive solace.

We glide low over the warehouse district and airport hangars. Turn sideways and lean over Barb. "Hon, almost there. The shaking will stop in a minute, I promise."

It doesn't. Fierce winds blow across the mammoth Great Lake. Offer soothing words as the plane lands and taxis. We disembark and Barb escorts a weak-kneed Janet as Bob leads toward Baggage Claim. We hire a shuttle van whose sixteen-mile drive to Evanston exacerbates Janet's off-kilter brain and stomach.

The Orrington Hotel is close to Lake Michigan, and a four-minute walk to Northwestern University. We check-in to the once luxury accommodation and the welcoming clerk dispenses room keys and convention packets complete with itineraries.

"Are you all right Jan?"

"I have to lie down." Once in our room, she lies on our bed to recover. Go outside to smoke. *We're here!*

Back upstairs, tap on our friends' door. The three of us stretch out, watch TV, and converse, albeit less so until Janet recovers. She joins in for dinner after which we renew acquaintances with those we haven't seen in years as early attendees mingle in the lounge.

It takes twenty-four hours for her to reconstitute and assuage her upset metabolism. This was a good flight.

The next morning, while one-hundred-seventy-one diverse male and female delegates from around the nation meet in Foundation Hall under the Temple above, we four join delegate spouses and guests on a tour of the only Bahá'í House of Worship constructed in North America. In 1974, on our second honeymoon, we'd staggered into it when arriving here after a harrowing car trip from Jersey.

We had made it midway on the Ohio Turnpike heading to Indiana following the flow of traffic at 70 mph, chatting about the trip.

"Whoosh!" Billows of thick white smoke emanated from the hood, clouding the windshield and blinding me. Swing fast to the shoulder, get out, clouds still foaming forth, and pop the hood. A steam ball pushes me back and know what has happened. Heart sinks.

Our '63 Chevy Nova had overheated and died, a bitter stab to my ego. Mike Reilly and I had labored three days replacing its engine just two months before. Get a tow to the Clyde Rest Stop below Lake Erie. Despite my mechanical precautions and trip checks, a water hose had burst and without coolant, the cylinder head cracked. Sad to see it go, conveyed the title to the tow truck driver instead of his twenty-five-dollar fee.

Now we were stuck five-hundred miles from home with no transportation. But typical for my friendly talkative wife, who could engage a rock in conversation, she befriends a family in their broken-down RV. They chat.

"Rod and I were on our way to see the Bahá'í Temple in Wilmette, and now we don't have a car."

"Well honey, Jim and I and the kids live right up the road. You come with us. Let us take you there."

"Are you sure? We couldn't impose like that."

"No problem 'tall. We'd be happy to if you'd let us help."

Kind-hearted, they give us a ride to their home in Evanston, a five-hour trip, me in the back of their open pickup truck with their eight- and twelve-year old's, an adventure for the three of us. Jan rides in the RV tow truck cab. They even put us up for the night.

The next morning headed to the Orrington with our friendly policeman host driving, the one-hundred-thirty-eight feet high dome of the Temple startles our eyes as we round the bend hugging Sheridan Road along the lake shore.

"I thought I'd surprise you," Jim says.

After sincere "Thank you's" to our charitable hosts, we check-in at the Orrington, rest, then visit the sacred House of Worship for the first time.

Inside, the high dome interlaced with woven thin ribs looking like spider threads, culminates in a bronze Arabic symbol, the Greatest Name, in a nine-pointed circular star at its apex. We say prayers then circumambulate and marvel at the distinctive nine-sided Dawning Place of the Mention of God, clad in white quartz and intricate designs for such a vast edifice.

After a brief stay in the area, we ride a Greyhound Bus to Janet's Godparents in Kalamazoo, and they fete us for two days. Finish our trip back to Jersey in another stifling bus with my red toolbox and our luggage.

But the Temple! Magnificent. And a boost to our spirits.

And here it is, again. The details add splendor. Rich are the multilingual prayer chants as they echo through the hollow holy space, and we keep our heads bowed in reverence.

When the voices cease, our visitors group climbs a narrow circular stairwell leading to the clerestory and we look down upon the rows of chairs and across the circular expanse to the interior inscriptions above the nine arched doors. Then, Glenford Mitchell, Secretary of the U.S. NSA, escorts us out onto the roof.

Downtown Chicago with its spiraling office buildings stands far off in stark relief. Vistas of flat, close-knit suburban dwellings are laid bare to our curious view. The gargantuan Great Lake skims past a thousand feet away to the east.

Oh, if I could fly! Oh, to be an eagle and soar in limitless space!

That evening the four of us join the Evanston community's Nineteen-day Feast at an elementary school where standing room greets us. People hobnob, speaking and smiling nonstop with quick-fire hugs and cries of "Alláh-u-Abhá!" peppering the hubbub. From the front, prayers and quotations from the Writings are read aloud, competing with low chatters, followed by announcements which we can't discern. Afterward, the refreshments table, blocked by bodies, confirms our decision to head out. Bob and Barb still socialize inside since they have more contacts.

We reach the vestibule and halt before stepping into the pouring rain.

"Should we find an umbrella or a newspaper? Or call a cab?"

Janet commiserates with a nice older woman under the school door overhang. She and her husband are also staying at the Orrington and their black car, parked at the curb, idles. The friendly woman offers a ride.

"Oh, thank you, that'd be marvelous." The four of us converse in their spacious automobile along the quick route. We thank them again as we all exit at the Orrington's entrance.

After we enter our room, change, and relax, Barb knocks on our adjoining door. Unlock it with, "Hey, great Feast, huh?"

"Yeah, let's talk about who we saw." This meant for Janet's ears, of course. In a huddle, the girls sit on our bed in their pajamas. Bob lays at the foot of mine and covers a wide expanse as he interjects and adds tidbits of what he's heard. I watch TV local news.

Janet recounts to Barb how nice the older couple were.

Bob jumps up, "O my God! Do you know who that was?"

"Nooo, who?" *Huh?*

"It was Mister Charles Wolcott and his wife. Did they have a driver for their car?"

"Yes, they did. Who's Mister Wolcott?"

"He's a member of the Universal House of Justice." Appreciate now what a special lift it had been. Meeting members of the world governing body is uncommon. Janet adds, "We were like old friends discussing the weather and the topics of the day. No airs at all."

After elections and as we pack, we agree the trip is eventful on multiple fronts, and tons more relaxed than in '74. Our faith in the electoral process renewed, our friendship with Bob and Barb deepened, we can even say we've met and spoken with a House of Justice member and his wife.

Janet fares a bit better on the return flight, and we land in Jersey on time. Its firm ground, unlike the airy delusions I had once conjured. However, that Soulful Voice heard clear as a ringing bell, on that night encircled by the endless pine forest under the half-white moon, springs to mind…

Haifa

Home of the Universal House of Justice.

In our bed, six months after our return from National Convention, and twelve months beyond the October episode, Janet gets up and switches off the TV. She returns and sits closer.

"Rod, I have something important to tell you… I'm pregnant."

"Oh, hon! Fantastic! A baby! A companion for Jesse and a new life. Wait till we tell everyone. How are you feeling?"

"I'm feeling fine now, but we'll see."

"Just tell me what you need done and I'll do it."

We'd tried conceiving since the timing was right and had discussed how the optimum interval was four years for better child-raising and personality development.

We hug and kiss with expectation and happiness.

"Hon, I'll be here for whatever you need." Inner and outer spirit feels like dancing a jig to the tunes of Fairport Convention or the Small Faces.

As we share the news over the next few weeks, friends are happy for us too, as are our parents and the larger family.

Enthusiastic for Jan and our baby, no matter the sex, at least feel something akin to joy.

Baby announced
What about their future?
Health and happiness sought

73

2.2 JOY AND FEAR EMBRACE

"Whoosh, whoosh, whoosh, whoosh…."

"That's it, hon, blow. Blow it away. Just like in Lamaze class. Like you've practiced."

Prior techniques prepping for Jesse's birth are de rigueur for Janet as she pants. She had pushed twenty-four hours before he arrived, and because of her small pelvis had endured a Cesarean.

She's adamant. "I have to push. It's better for developing lung capacity." She's as determined as I am sleep-deprived, unable to keep eyes open, or attention focused. I slouch half-awake in the room chair.

Tolerant Doctor Sheppard enters and says, "Janet, you've done well, but we should proceed with the Cesarean," words she accedes to.

This time escort her hospital bed into the operating room and observe near the end, grasping her free hand, the other taped with ports and an IV.

Janet had fought for this right, denied four years earlier. Then, once home, she had co-founded the Cesarean Parents of Mercer County. They worked to establish awareness and compassion for the issues confronting birth couples and achieved concessions from Mercer Hospital administrators and doctors to have fathers present and more. Now allowed in, I appreciate their inroads.

Bliss arrives under the sign of the Crab as with a radiant smile Janet cradles our newborn on her chest.

"You did it, Jan." She's exhausted and elated as all of us hear Kate Amelia's cries. She's born a healthy weight, has a good Apgar score, with a bald head and searching blue eyes.

While in mild shock mixed with pleasure that we have another child, kiss Jan's forehead, "You did tremendous. Beautiful." Both blessed and happy, we share glee and relief.

They release her and Kate from Obstetrics, and I pick them up with Jesse in his car seat. He's happy with the introduction to his sister. Once home, our friends and families greet our daughter with elan.

Jan's mom exclaims, "A granddaughter and a rich man's family!" since we have a boy and a girl. We're exalted. We've prepped Jesse by reading illustrated children's books of animal young appearing, as he's watched his Mommy's tummy grow immense on her petite 4'11" frame.

Janet mends the next two weeks after the major surgery, besides ministering to us. While she tries to rest, I spend time with Jesse, clean, work around the house and yard, and try not to encumber her. Like walking on eggshells, recognize she's the pincushion, me a needle if not careful.

Don't stick that on her, Rod. She's got enough to do.

74

One noontime while nursing, she runs into the kitchen cradling Kate.

"Rod, Rod, her lips are blue! She was nursing, then stopped."

She stopped breathing!?

"What!? What should we do?"

Jan plunks her on her shoulder, and with vigorous rubs and pats, also jounces up and down.

What's going on? What can I do?

Our stressed new daughter takes in breaths. *Thank you.*

"Quick, Rod, grab her diaper bag!" Snatch the carryall and we bolt out the door. I drive fast but not super-fast to Emergency at Mercer, Jesse in his car seat, Janet in the back cooing to Kate. After a rushed intake, they roll her into Intensive Neonatal Care.

Depart with Jesse and drive four miles to Janet's mom's, and after a quick explanation, speed back to the hospital.

Jan fills me in. "I asked the doctor if she'll be all right, but they won't have a diagnosis for a while. We have to... wait. I'm worried." Her trepidations are real as we try to glean the best out of the very worst. *Dear God, I hope our baby's all right. Hurry doctors!*

The petite specialist joins us in the hall. "I want to put her on intravenous feeding because it's serious."

Reticent and reluctant, we agree, trusting her judgement. We watch through the glass as a nurse gingerly sticks a butterfly needle into Kate's tiny heel to attach the clear liquid IV.

"Waugh, waugh, waugh," she wails, and Jan's face agonizes.

"Rod, our poor Kate, and how will I be able to nurse her?"

She inquires into options with the doctor and staff. The hospital provides a bed in a metal-and-glass enclosed room next to our daughter's so Jan can stay, pump her milk, and feed Kate.

Our baby is ill from an unknown cause with a high fever.

We pray, "Thy Name is my healing, O my God, and remembrance of Thee is my remedy."[16] At home, prayers and food dishes flood in from friends. Some sit with Jesse as I visit the hospital.

After two worrisome days, she's diagnosed with a severe infection and nurses monitor her progress every hour. The doctor treats her with an aggressive regimen of antibiotics. After five more days and steady improvement in her vital signs, she's declared healthy, released, and everyone's relieved and grateful.

Insha'allah, by the Will of God, she will be fine.

We look upon Kate's recovery with grateful hearts.

During 1981's Governor's race, Republican candidate Thomas H. Kean broadcasts campaign promises to foster job creation, clean up toxic waste, reduce crime, and preserve home rule, the life-or-death craving of every New Jersey municipality no matter how small. He challenges powerful south Jersey Democrat Jim Florio, expected to win.

The election is a nail biter. In a surprise, it's "KEAN UPSETS FLORIO" on the newsstands. He wins the contest by less than two-thousand votes out of two-million-three-hundred-thousand cast.

The Democrats thought they had it.

Republicans exult. Tom Kean is sworn in on January nineteenth. As an Independent registered voter and state employee, it's always the same: some Governors make things better, some worse, and always, always, bring change. For us in the trenches the major fear is layoffs. The major hope is more authority and a raise.

By April familiar agency directors, chiefs of staff, deputies, and policymakers, some friends, are let go and new functionaries replace them.

We sigh and Alice and I call agencies to search out strange new contacts, explaining to the new appointees how we work, hoping for agreement. We set up more rollouts of IBM-compatible Telex equipment for the growing SNA network. The State's online accounting system for all funds and monies, AAS, mandated for all agency fiscal offices, is the driving force behind why all agency fiscal staffs sign on to CRT displays and use them.

To Alice and me, it's twice as ironic that Chris held the Project Manager position at BDP when heading the COBOL programming implementation for AAS just a few years earlier and is now in charge of deployments.

Now, thousands of displays and printers are delivered to far-flung offices so they can use them for daily fiscal functions.

Absorbed in commitments. Manic dreams and thoughts, Princeton House and Fair Oaks confinements, doctors, and apathetic feelings are past imaginings as buckle down, strap in, and try to thwart daily work and new father pressures.

Thanks to Fate, baby lives,
training approved, new Gov sworn in,
greased wheels spin

2.3 ACTING LIKE AN ADULT

"Rod, considering your excellent contributions we're changing your title to DP Programmer two with a four-thousand-dollar salary increase."

Taken aback. "Ah, thanks, Chris. I, appreciate your confidence. Whatever I can do to get everything done, I will. Ah, I'd also like to recommend Alice for a raise, she's the linchpin to our 3270 rollouts."

"Appreciate that, Rod, and will look into it. Alice is very competent."

Had neither asked nor expected this promotion. The ego boost is temporary and doesn't lift a negative malaise. Snap at Alice. Curt when agency staff call and inquire about their projects. Don't jump when Chris calls my name nor return agency phone calls. Delegate more and take on more. Consult less. Smoke more. Can't get enough done. Can't get enough. Drink more coffees. Can't get done.

In the house, show displeasure at Janet's gentle pill and other reminders, denigrate her cooking, or question her choices. "Hell no," or "Shit," pepper my speech as raise my voice at her. Careless, thoughtless words, and inattentiveness, like sharp, stinging arrows, pierce her upbeat attitude.

She says, "I feel belittled, even betrayed. Can't you be nice?"

Only playing beside Jesse or Kate defers an agitated, brooding spirit cruising for conflict.

After a short row she chides, "Rod, don't you think this could be the bipolar acting out?"

Daily discontent grows until, in half-hearted agreement, Jan calls Greenspring's office for us to meet with Doctor Argueta.

My astute Guatemalan psychiatrist doubles medications and recommends bi-weekly sessions with local Psychologist Mark Wilenski to calm my mind and mend our contentious relationship. His office is in a two-story apartment complex off Parkside Avenue, in Ewing Township, our home turf, where first met Jan at Ewing High after a homesick return from California in April 1967.

Mark is super casual in looks and clothes, with his worn jeans, and bushy graying hair and beard. He's good-humored, and opens with, "The goal is to improve communication. I want you to chuck all your old baggage and start fresh. Don't discount your feelings and be aware each of you is human and can get hurt easily."

Attend sessions like obedient children, but tensions and stiffness run high, and love lost is high too. Frosty silence reigns, Janet's oft-used sign of frustration. When she bangs pots or slams doors, she's aggravated. She's clanged and groused for some time.

Remain mum. It only engenders, "Rod, why won't you talk to me?"

Hurts and slights between us have built cage walls. Remarks like, "Seriously?" and "No need to raise your voice," end our heated exchanges.

Mark is adept and teases out our simmering emotions and misplaced unrealistic projections like a snake charmer whose beguiling and rhythmic flute playing raises the cobra out of its thick-woven basket. He's relentless, varied in approach, yet kind. He doesn't wag a finger or tongue at us. He maintains civility and levity. His verbal and written exercises challenge our ideas of marital togetherness.

"Here's paper and pen. Answer the question 'I want for myself.' Then we'll go over it."

As we read them aloud, few agree:

Jan: To be happy and loved

Me: Peace and quiet

Jan: Open communication

Me: To be left alone

Jan: Talking with adults

Me: To be trusted

Jan: To be appreciated and heard

We strain our words between silences. Janet's more forthright, "He acts like I'm not here." Say little and don't register her pain and rejection.

These months, tighter state government policies and procedures issue forth faster than Simon says, "Do this," or "Don't do that."

The new Republican administration tightens DPTC approvals, the first stop in BDP's quest for purchase order and waiver signoffs. Its staffers Ed Maute and Barney Bloom balk at Alice and my requests and nitpick them, which aggravates more because they hadn't before. Must kowtow to their picayune questions before carrying our big-ticket procurements to the Purchase Bureau.

Once there, Jack Hoyer and Johnny Wasko, the Purchase Bureau Buyers we're assigned to, both say, "No more Blanket Waivers Rod. They must show competition," another hindrance and roadblock.

Soliciting written vendor quotations from the competition, a tricky proposition, adds to the crunch of other tasks. Now must scrutinize each BDP request, dot every i, and cross every tee.

"I don't have time for this bullshit." It's pressure not needed nor wanted but redouble efforts without resorting to overtime.

As weeks fly by and Janet and I re-acclimate to each other, daily interactions settle down. Routines are comfortable again no catfights, thanks to Mark's monthly sessions.

Janet joins California-based Discovery Toys as a Hostess. We had discussed it before Janet signed the application form. Their business model is home sales of educational games, books, and toys for young ages.

"It's a great idea, Jan. It's a brilliant match for your talents." Pleased she wants to try it.

We laugh, learn, and test the DT toys with Jesse and Kate.

"Bawl!" Kate fondles the blue octagon plastic ball with slots for yellow shapes that fit into its sides. Jesse prefers the peg handled wooden Ravensburger jigsaw puzzles made in Germany, whose colorful pieces and slots he matches in minutes.

Janet buys plastic folding cartons, which she packs with toys and books, and I lug them to her car for evening product demonstrations.

Her first Sales Flyer declares:

Discovery Toys thinks you're special . . (so do I !!!) . . as a customer . . as a hostess . . as someone who cares about others

She schedules party demonstrations with potential hostesses and tries to recruit them. Hear her say, "Hours are flexible, you do it in the comfort of your home, and you earn a percentage of sales." That seals the deal. Her enthusiasm is contagious as she convinces them over the phone to invite relatives, coworkers, friends, and neighbors.

It keeps her mobile and meeting new people, which she lives for. I bond closer with Jesse and Kate in the evening hours when she's out.

In a cheerful mood, volunteer again to coordinate twenty marchers and banners for the annual Hamilton Township Memorial Day Parade, a two-mile march up Nottingham Way and past our prior Dutch Colonial abode.

Hopped up for the festivities on that Monday, carry two joined banners a foot over our heads, nine-feet long and four-feet high.

It's a common Bahá'í theme. As we march, citizens and families gather, gawk, clap, wave, and nod their heads at the universal message.

Acquaintances and strangers yell, "Way to go," "Couldn't agree more!" while Janet, Jesse and Kate, Grandmum and Grandad, and friends, wait for us in lawn chairs at our annual spot. As our small corps of paradors approach, they smile and shout encouragement in pride.

Spud pops into the street and snaps photos for the papers.

We gather around the TV set a week later to watch the parade unfold on the local Hamilton cable channel and see what we missed.

One afternoon a letter arrives from the National Teaching Committee of the NSA.

"Jan, look, it's my appointment to the New Jersey District Teaching Committee." Our DTC goal is to, "…encourage believers throughout New Jersey to build up their communities and proclaim the Faith."

Wind north on my motorcycle on the Garden State Parkway with its ultra-skinny lanes mobbed with speeding, lane-hopping drivers to the Wilhelm Property.

"I have got to invest in a much louder horn."

There, a rustic log cabin greets me, surrounded by eighty-foot-tall pines. It and the stucco house next to it comprise an open oasis in the middle of hundreds of small home dwellings in Teaneck.

At DTC meetings, the six of us pray, consult, and brainstorm.

"How can we get the name Bahá'í Faith in the public eye? How do we fuel proclamation activities given our limited resources?" Thousand-dollar questions and we don't have thousands of dollars or ideas to answer them.

American's fear of foreign-sounding things is a barrier, although scads of Bahá'í books in English are available that make it clear we have peaceful goals and altruistic intensions.

But suspicion, even distaste of things non-Christian, is prevalent, even though the divine stations and missions of Jesus Christ and all major prophets are also our sacred beliefs.

"Eighty-five percent of Americans are Christian. Somehow we must do better at making the case that Christ returned—like He said He would."

Believe, as colleagues do, that our hopes for a better world are gradually coming about according to God's plan in His way.

"Unity is the foundation, and the goal, which means everyone has to be part of the solution if it's to come sooner," Lionel says.

Like the old saying.

'You're part of the solution or part of the problem.'

All things need a name
to become known by
Time to proclaim the Glory

Christ said, "I'll return."
Now to prove He did
to a doubting populace

2.4 RED SCARE

Kate fills the red, yellow, blue, and green Discovery Toys nesting cups with her bathwater, then dumps them out to see the water splash.

"Rod, look at this rash on Kate's back. I wonder what it is?"

"It doesn't look good. It covers her chest and back. Should we call the doctor?"

"I think I will, I've never seen it before."

Kate's cranky too, which is unlike her.

Monday, we drive her to our pediatrician who says, "It's just the summer heat. It'll pass."

The next day it hasn't. Alarmed. But not sure how to handle it. At the office, mention it to Chris. Her eyes look up and left for a moment.

"That sounds like Lyme disease, Rod. They've had reported cases near Block Island where we go sailing. It's from a deer tick, I think."

That night at dinner, "Jan, let me tell you what Chris said." We write to the Connecticut Health Department and receive a brochure and letter from the Office of Epidemiology. The rash hasn't gone away, is redder, looks like a bullseye, and Kate has a fever.

Return to the pediatrician. As Janet wrings her hands, she recites our litany of worries and observations. We show the brochure. He pulls down a medical textbook, flips to a page, reads it, then orders a blood test.

The test comes back and confirms his suspicion. We administer ten days of Penicillin, and it clears up. It's the first documented case of Lyme's in Mercer County.

Its 1983. Learn that people bit by the bug can develop joint pains, memory problems, severe headaches, and debilitating tiredness.

She dodges bullet
heading toward her red bullseye
Pinprick tick routed

Chris summons us into her office one July day. It's been four years working for her, a little less for Alice. The Jersey economy is expanding under Governor Kean, unemployment is low, citizens are upbeat, and Fiscal Year '84 tax coffers are in positive territory.

She announces, "BDP is now the Management and Financial Data Center, or MFDC. We've also changed our unit's name to Resource Development. We will announce other changes." Both names fit since Treasury controls all state finances, cash in and cash out, and we cover procurement, planning, research, equipment implementation and more.

What will other changes be?

Not long afterward, Chris calls me into her corner office.

"Rodney, I want to show you my appreciation. You're instrumental to our progress, so I've promoted you to a DP Analyst position."

Not expecting this.

"Gee, thank you, Chris." *Guess we're doing better than okay.* "I'll continue as hard as I can, you know that. Anything else I should do?"

"I want you to join the Quality Circle sessions and learn what you can. Also, maintain the pace on the waivers. We'll be expanding more SNA terminal deployments to more agencies too. Training is growing and I'll need your help there as well."

The jump to Analyst is $31,000—darn good for not having a college degree. Ten times the three-thousand-dollar annual salary I earned at the Trenton Psychiatric Hospital in 1969 as a geriatric food service worker. That year too, found myself hanging out my two-story apartment window after an acid high while Vanilla Fudge played "Lord in the Country" on my record player.

Janet, pleased with the income, cooks cheese raviolis and her homemade sauce, Dad's recipe, for dinner, a favorite of mine although she eats none. She's a meat and potatoes type gal.

True to her word, assigned to Project Manager Robin Gersternacker in charge of training MFDC's mainframe computer operators and COBOL programmer interns. "Rod, we need copies of these Deltak instruction modules for classes by Wednesday. Can you see Pete at the Taxation Print Shop and ask if he can run them off, please?"

"Sure, will do Robin." At first, handle all physical copy runs and collating needed for students, but within a month Robin asks me to train three computer operators in JES2, IBM control language for job, data, and task execution functions on the mainframes.

Impress upon them, "Without JES2, our two expensive IBM 3081-D16 mainframes would be heavier and deader than the Titanic's ship anchor. Without JES2 you can't re-IPL from the console if the machine crashes. Then you've got thousands of users with blank CICS and AAS screens."

Also, convince MFDC's Assistant Supervisor Charlie Burrows to allow me to take the IQ test potential programmers take. Finish it in the allotted time and score 132 and glad to be at least average. Know one thing, I don't know it all.

Janet later shares hers: 131. Except Jan is a creative talent and eclectic bibliophile while only science fiction or movie thrillers perk my interest, like 1956's *Forbidden Planet* with its Krell civilization and 1951's *The Day the Earth Stood Still* with superior detached acting by Michael Rennie. His command uttered by Patricia Neal to the indestructible Gort, "Klaatu barrada nikto," gives the world one chance to reform before it's annihilated for incessant infighting.

The movie ends not knowing the world's response.

Ask Jan one night, "Do we still need to meet with Mark, or have we settled our major differences?"

"Well, you've improved and I'm comfortable with that."

Enter our last session together and say, "Mark, you've helped us and we're appreciative, and we thank you for your insights." He's gracious.

Jan writes the last thirty-dollar check dated October 9, 1984.

All his takeaways are practical.

"You have to banish unrealistic expectations. It'll take practice, but you can do it." We both accept that we can't read minds, so if we want something done, spell it out. I can't assume Janet can guess what I like or don't. She can't assume just because the grass is tall that like a robot, I'll put on my yard clothes and start the lawnmower.

She had said to Mark, "I mean, he must notice it, right? I expect him to cut the grass when it needs it or put garbage out on Wednesday and Saturday." But I never notice until she remarks on it. Then hop on our sit-down Murray for an hour or lug out the garbage cans.

On the flip side, Mark has repeated, "Rodney, share more. Share what you want for yourself and for Janet, what you're experiencing. It doesn't have to be a lot."

After this, Janet leaves a list of tasks on the kitchen counter. Don't mind one bit. Most are short and doable, like filling her gas tank when low.

"Ahh, feels good to draw a line through this one."

It's also clear, always clear between us, "What happens in the past stays in the past." It's unproductive to dredge up old hurts or dwell on past grievances, which only breed rancor. We assimilate the lesson, remember the okay and good times, and leap over the bad. We joke more. When on a roll make her cry tears of laughter.

Tender moments occur as we lie under the covers with the lights off. Try hard to listen to her hopes and wants, although clueless when her words include hidden meanings meant for me to pick up.

"Let's promise not to go to sleep mad." We adhere to the promise.

In stupefaction of her unshakeable love and steadfast support, amazed at her fidelity. Feel no need to test it with spurious behavior, impractical dreams, or unrealistic wishes.

If only I reciprocated in natural, organic ways without prodding.
If only I put others before myself, and her before others.

Must resurrect key
to heart's hidden lockbox
and twist to Open

2.5 SHAKEUP OR SHAKEDOWN?

"Uh oh. What now?" Questions spread like wildfires through drought-stricken western brush and forests in the state data processing community as we read Governor Kean's Executive Order in November 1984. It declares, "...all state data centers will merge under single management."

Shock, surprise, and doomsday scenarios rock status quos. As the Treasury Data Center since our 1960s inception, like other departments, had operated an independent shop.

"What does it mean?" is on everyone's lips except a few insiders.

EO-84 mandates consolidation of the five major state data centers Human Services, Labor, Transportation, and Law & Public Safety, with our Management & Financial Data Center exempt "until a later time." Further, EO-84 establishes a brand-new organization, the Office of Telecommunications and Information Systems[17] responsible for Data Processing policies and departmental budgets, mainframe processors and software realignments, and hundreds of personnel.

"What's this mean for me?" is the $64,000 question on everyone's lips. Potential personnel moves or layoffs upset all. Tell Alice, "We're lucky to be in Treasury though. After the Governor's Office, we're the most powerful department."

Everyone's abuzz. "OTIS?" "What's the deal?" "Who'll be in charge?"

Anxiety levels gurgle up like angry, ugly, blood-stained apparitions in the movie *Thirteen Ghosts* with threats of layoffs, position changes, or title downgrades in the hands of a new faceless bureaucracy.

The shocking surprise is that the entity is also responsible to establish uniform policies statewide for "information processing," a new buzzword for computer equipment, software, and facilities. "Information" replaces "Data" overnight. But as an old computer operator, it's still GIGO—Garbage In, Garbage Out—if not careful. *Will OTIS know the difference?*

This is a power grab akin to Purchase Bureau's absolute authority over all state procurements, or the Office of Management and Budget's control over all state purse strings and positions. There is no choice.

OTIS also splinters entrenched DP fiefdoms with their demanding parochial personalities and archaic equipment, like Pensions. Consolidation of disparate services begins too. Scuttlebutt reveals hundreds of programmers, project managers, analysts, system programmers, operators, tech support, and administrative staff are being reassigned.

It's grim and chaotic except for the elite few appointed to top positions in the new OTIS hierarchy. But the most impactful pronouncement for Alice and I hits home when we unpack the new Circular Letter together:

"...all agency requests to procure information processing goods and services must first be approved by OTIS."

"Holy crap, Al, they get first crack at all procurements too. Another damn approval level."

Gov's pen inks OTIS
Status quos shatter
Individuals scamper

January 1985 marks the assimilation of MFDC into OTIS. Chris transfers to OTIS headquarters without notice. I'm not asked.

"What?"

Maybe Lew Jensen, Chris's assistant director, will take her place. Like many state employees now adrift in a sea change of uncertainty, wonder who I'll be reporting to.

Then, without warning, Lew transfers to 850 Bear Tavern Road in West Trenton. Named Director of the Garden State Network, he'll oversee the physical schema to build T1 data transmission lines for linking the state's data centers. AT&T's T1 lines at 1.544 Megabits are the fastest communication means possible for the required data exchange rates.

Now, it's all about "The Network."

OTIS also announces plans to construct from scratch one massive central data center, the Hub, on the grounds of the West Trenton State Police Headquarters.

Soon after Lew departs, Alice takes a position with the OTIS Planning Unit. *Ouch, damn!* It's run by Hank Murray, who was once in charge of DPTC, now abolished and subsumed by OTIS. Confident Alice will thrive since she's so competent.

But me? My career is down the tubes like an abandoned ten-year-old drifting on a sloshing water slide into the Black Lagoon or the Unemployment Office. Uncertainty permeates. Employees jump like leaping sailors from a burning container ship of hand grenades as explosions go "Boom, boom, boom!" Genuine talent hightails it in lifeboats to OTIS if lucky.

What will happen? Back to Operations? With Chris and Lew gone, who'll be in charge? Will we even keep the same functions? Will OTIS assume my responsibilities? Am I superfluous?

For the rank-and-file it's a murky thundercloud of false hopes and gloomy fortune-telling what-ifs. Each day, more bodies transfer as if struck by lightning to the new organization. Many who yearn to don't.

Anxieties high
Uncertainties run rampant
Stable careers shot

No sense crafting Requests for Proposals or evaluating bid responses since those functions are now with OTIS. Without Alice's help, still compile the IP waiver for MFDC installed equipment and software and coordinate the dumb terminal rollouts, occupying most hours.

At least don't buy *The Trentonian* and read it at my desk all day.

"There's no one to rely on; no one to go to for protection." A once-promising professional career path vanished. The solid track under my running shoes and the painted white lane lines guiding each upward move for the past fourteen years, obliterated.

A career not just stalled but buried under tons of benign neglect.

Bemoan the fact I haven't received that magic call, "Rod, would you be interested in coming to OTIS?"

Does this mean oblivion?

A useless sailor
on a fickle ship of state
Jump overboard now?

2.6 A MODICUM OF STABILITY

A mental straitjacket clings and drips with sweat from dour speculation. *What's next at MFDC? How do I get back to normal?*

Janet pilots our family around the rocky outcrops of an unforeseen future like VP running mate Geraldine Ferraro navigates around those shocked at the thought of a woman in the second-highest office. Janet does it for the four of us with loving attention to details with unquenchable enthusiasm and intelligent pragmatism so nothing falls through cracks.

In her petite and lively frame, she exhibits the combined all-seeing expertise of Carol Martin and live-in housekeeper Alice Nelson from *The Brady Bunch* with our calico cat Whiskers masquerading as Tiger the dog. Her creativity makes any hurdle shorter than the Empire State Building too small to fret over. When stuck dumb, all I need to do is hint at a question and she has five concrete ideas.

Yet, like Edgar Bergen's mute dummy, Charlie McCarthy, don't talk or share or outright ask unless faced with zero alternatives. Taurus-like, refuse to take advantage of her natural talents.

Self-reliant down to the dregs of a vanishing cup, can't pinpoint why.

Try to get my mind off BDP, PB, OMB, MFDC, and OTIS. Relegate dire doubts about job prospects to a mental file drawer called "Career—On hold." Can't let circumstances weigh down an already tenuous spirit. Spend off-work hours in flurries of Bahá'í proclamation activities, like arranging with NJ Transit to display 14 x 30-inch cardstock ads that show a white Dove of Peace on a sky-blue background. Will place them on the inside of buses of Trenton routes.

Present a series of public talks at *The Times* Community Room along with other speakers, after in-person and telephone handholding by their community news and religion editor Frank Tyger, a super friendly and solicitous guy. The Assembly even runs ads.

Also lead an evening public discussion at the Hamilton Township Neighborhood Service Center on Wilfred Avenue, which our community has used often and who's bigger than life Director, John O. "Poppy" Wilson, welcomes our rentals. A few days later, run into Spud.

"Hey, Sir Rodness."

"Yep, what's up Spudley?" He's a close bud, witty jokester, storyteller, parade float builder, and our PI Rep and media guru. He looks like Angel from *The Rockford Files* with his kinky black hair and beard.

"I sent a photo of you into the *Times*, but don't know if they'll print it."

"That's cool, either way."

Had spoken on "Extremes of Poverty and Wealth in America," U.S. economics, and the four trillion dollars in federal debt. It was appropriate, considering the poorer neighborhood where the center is located. It was ironic too, especially since the audience was only middle-income Bahá'ís.

At the end of the week Janet says, "Rod, your photo's in the paper!"
Ah, thanks Spud.
In it I point at chicken-scratch on a flip chart under a curt caption with my name. Recall my first photo in *The Times* as a pimply thirteen-year-old Boy Scout in uniform brandishing a pool cue at the Catholic Youth Center next door to Sacred Heart Church and grammar school in Trenton. This photo neither impresses nor engenders pride as that first one did. Shooting pool was more fun and as educational as learning knots. But then asked, "Will you be Godfather to your Spanish Troop Leader?"
Surprised and flattered, nodded "Yes." Memorized The Lord's Prayer in Latin and recited it alongside the baptismal fountain. "Pater noster, qui es in caelis; sanctificetur nomen tuum...."
A few coworkers comment on *The Times* photo. "What's Bahá'í? Never heard of it." Offer them the elevator pitch.

"We believe there's only one God who sent divine messengers from time to time, each with promises of love and peace. A new messenger for modern times, Bahá'u'lláh, came to teach universal cooperation, equality, justice, and unity."

Most people ask no further, comfortable under their own cloaks of beliefs, which is fine. It's enough they asked. If they inquire further, invite them over for coffee and conversation, or offer pamphlets or books. Often, the brief spiritual truths in Bahá'u'lláh's book *The Hidden Words* are the first to attract serious interest because they're so universal.

Hours spent in the office are languorous, but evenings and weekends are hectic with Bahá'í obligations, household chores, groundskeeping, looking after the kids while Jan's out doing Discovery Toys demonstrations, and treasurer duties for the Assembly and community.

Observe and interact with Kate, who's pleasant and happy, a lot like her brother, yet with a unique and bubbly personality.

"Dad, Whiskers is attacking me!" Our cat chases and paws at Kate like when she traipses through the house like she's a mouse toy on a string.

"Whiskers, stop it! Leave Kate alone," and chuckle, then pick up our calico cat and move her to another room. Jesse, absorbed in art and creative projects along with video games, is also an excellent reader and has built up a DC comics collection. We hit the trade shows at local fire stations on weekends and comb through white boxes lined with comics standing in plastic-sleeves.

Both benefit from Jan's instruction. Neither watch TV because our only sets are in our bedroom and kitchen.

Concentrate on mundane tasks but search inward for new perspectives. *What's my overall purpose? Goals? What will happen at work? When will the world get it right?*

Such thoughts raise doubts. Don't share them with Jan, despite Mark's past enlightenments. Tears, fears, and joys, locked in an emotional battle, fail to settle down no matter how keenly try to generate a normal response.

Like a rod of iron struck with a hammer on an anvil, emotions only spark through sporadic pounding by a concealed blacksmith in a too-often apathetic heart. He pounds my psyche when he feels like it, never when asked or expected.

Love of Janet, kids, friends, and family only captivate waking thoughts as afterthoughts. Few ecstatic surges, no exuberances, and only minor buoyed interests perk my ears or turn my head. No natural warmth penetrates my chilled exterior. The saturation of blood and brain from medicinal chemicals cycle moderation or ennui without cessation.

Feel dull-witted and slow. "But you can't blame the drugs. It's you, shithead."

No time to dwell on where emotions hide. No time to unearth them from their secreted cubbyhole, locked up long ago as a lost teenager looking for life's purpose. No time to be afraid of reentering that psychotic, misguided manic state. Must fight off negative thoughts that strive to consume what's left of discernable spirit, lackluster as it is.

Remember though, man is not a body with a spirit, but a spirit with a body. Be grateful you have the Faith, Janet, the kids, and a job.

Mumble, "Just keep away from the hospitals, Rod, they're spirit killers."

Can't appreciate that in reality they are spirit revivers.

As depressed introspections
and self-doubts control,
a vision ascends

2.7 THE VISION

"Ahh, peaceful."

Thoughts, blank, as sit on our concrete front steps inhaling a Kool on an odd, windless March night. But the missing gusts may be a subtle message, as when watching the climactic scenes of *Dune* when the Fremen riding giant sandworms and their messiah Paul Atreides win the jihad and the Empire. Odd though, the soundtrack is now missing, and my eyes, too absorbed in the action on the big movie screen, fail to notice.

"Maybe this is the ingathering."

Blackened neighborhood windows glow with faint glimmers in front of drawn white blinds. Not even the flashes of headlights from busy Route 524 flash by my neighbor's glass front door at this time of the morning. The yellow shine of streetlamps in the sleeping development is the only illumination. A handful of stars and planets not obscured by light pollution twinkle their pinpoints. Off to the right, scalloped clouds skim across the face of the ever observant and ageless moon with its own message.

Eyes close. See what it sees.

Act 2 closes on stage as if I am both a chief player and perched in the first row enthralled in the opening of Act 3…

Attired in a thick ankle-length white robe, trimmed with brown-pelted ermine and gold flecks, survey the Mountain of God as it looms high above. A humble mood pours through relaxed sinews.

Begin to mount a hundred steps upward toward the shining Shrine of the Báb. It stands majestic, garbed in white, with a gold-clad tiled dome on the midmost heart of Mount Carmel, the City of God, come down from the clouds, a celestial Kaaba.

A long queue of kings, queens, and potentates trail behind, to the foot of the holy mountain.

Clear skies shimmer and the sun shines in supernal glory… marble terraces with iron balustrades amid breathtaking gardens surround us… the lush greenery belies the hidden underground pipes that feed and water their roots… pools of cool liquid in bone cisterns sparkle like Venetian crystal.

Triumphal music plays from every side.

Leaders from each nation who follow behind me recognize their follies and have sworn allegiance to universal spiritual truths and human rights.

They are here to dedicate themselves to the care of Earth and its creatures.

They will protect and preserve human dignity through just and fair laws.

They will see that service and cooperation reign, animosities and violence cease, and civilization flourish throughout the planet.

This is the Day billions of souls have sung and prayed for, sighed and longed for, sacrificed and died for.

At last, just government and sane religion, the two most powerful forces for unity on the planet, will safeguard the interests of humanity.

Billions of breaths release pent-up tensions in a collective "Whoosh." Their thankful faces turn in joy toward the Fashioner of the Universe. All acknowledge we are one race, and our survival depends on each other.

The revealed Word of God, universal in the past, universal in the future, provides the constitution of the world.

The triumphal music rises...

This is that Great Day of God prophesied in all the Scriptures and Holy Books.

This is that Day of God when His Kingdom and Power come in great glory.

This is the beginning of the Most Great Peace....

Stand mesmerized, memorizing the imaginary life-size images.[18]

This is that timeless and motionless otherworld, experienced on that wild October night standing naked, free of this world's encumbrances, in the clearing of the surrounding silent pines at the Sand Company under piercing moonlight.

A whisper of a song begins. Hear firm fingers strum a guitar and raise a plaint in haunting, soulful, hopeful tones, now realized...

Last night I had the strangest dream
I ever dreamed before...

Open eyes and refocus on the dark home across the street and the family cars lined in front. The neighborhood is hushed except for the dull roar of speeding vehicles a mile away rolling 65 or 70 on the Turnpike's divided four-lane highway. *We are speeding headlong toward unity.*

Wish with my being it appears soon, as walk to the car to seek 7/Eleven coffee.

How soon before
the Promised Day arrives?
We need it. We all need it.

2.8 STICKING A NEW POSITION

Phone her again.

"Chris, I'd like to be part of OTIS too. Can you use any help?"

"We'll see Rod, we'll see."

At least she doesn't say "No" outright. Adrift, yearn for direction and careful not to whine. At least the new MFDC Director Blair Shirk is a congenial fella.

Changes and announcements fly, like the outsider from AT&T appointed to head OTIS, a Ph.D., Doctor Ridgway. Volatile and formidable Bob Meybohm, director at the SAC Data Center is named as one of three OTIS Administrators reporting to him. A new face, Ronald Maxson, who has the look of Prince Valiant with his black hair, is another. No one can keep up with the new talking heads.

As school starts in September, Jesse, age eight, hands us a Hamilton YMCA Flyer. Janet reads it, announcing the Indian Guides Program[19] with the slogan **Father and Son, Pals Forever**.

"Rod, this looks interesting. Maybe you and Jesse can try it."

It sounds like a novel way to spend time with him, so talk with Jesse, sign us up, pay the annual fee, and convene a meeting in our living room.

Four fathers and their eight-year-old sons compose our fledgling tribe. No one volunteers so assume Chief duties as host. We share our backgrounds while the boys horseplay.

Hand out printed Y guidebooks, quiet down, and recite the listed AIMS in unison:

- To be clean in body and pure in heart
- To be friends forever with my dad
- To love the sacred circle of my family
- To listen while others speak
- To love my neighbor as myself
- To respect the traditions and beliefs of all people
- To seek and preserve the beauty of Our Creator's work in forest, field, and stream

These native-culture beliefs reach deep and Bahá'í tenets mirror them.

Russ Kivler, a lawyer whose office has an eight-foot white marble eagle out front, suggests our name, Blackfoot, and all heads nod. We brainstorm a symbol, choosing the mighty buffalo, and set up a schedule and divvy up tasks for future tribal meetings that promise to be collegial and fun.

"What d'ya think, Jess?"

"I like it, Dad. Can't wait for more!"

Persistent phone calls to Chris pay off. *Yes!*

After five months of limbo, Blair and OMB approve my transfer to her unit at OTIS in their leased offices at 850 Bear Tavern Road, a fifteen-minute commute on Interstate 295. Tell coworkers and agency contacts and receive a few envious stares and comments. *OTIS here I come. What will you have me do?* Possibilities outweigh trepidations.

Feel like an Olympic gymnast twirling on the high bar at top speed as I release at the perfect apex and stick the landing with both feet planted squarely on the landing mat. *Grateful, Chris, again.*

On the appointed day, shown into the first floor hopping with excitement. I'm led to a huge gray metal desk, 1960s vintage, resembling a beached hippo. There's another antique monster-sized desk eight feet away. No phone, terminal, or PC sits atop either of them. There're no shelves for storage, nothing but gray walls and carpet. Both hippos sit alone, forlorn amid the tomb-like space in the middle of the floor-length room except for some half-cubicles twenty feet away.

"Sigh." *Will I find fulfillment, or is this a blind alley?*

No bustling staff pass by given all the havoc OTIS is wreaking throughout the agencies. No phones ringing. Only silence. The action is on the second floor where the Administrators and Directors hold court.

What have I gotten into?

Meet with Chris as she sits in her cramped walled office with a door, window, furniture, phone, and IBM PC. She uses WordPerfect for word processing, Lotus 123 for spreadsheets, and produces hard to read printouts on her dot matrix printer. Her spartan accommodations are little better than mine. Dare not complain.

Things pick up.

Receive a push-button phone and Tech Support sets up my imaged IBM PC clone running Windows 1.0 bought from DS Squared, who has the new, the first, state contract for Microcomputers. Some days starved for an assignment; others can't type fast enough with two fingers. Learning the quirks and functions of Windows, WordPerfect, Lotus, and MS-DOS occupy excessive downtime.

On the job it's a struggle to look busy with anything semi-productive. Our task is to review OTIS Requests for Proposals or RFPs, whether for big mainframe processors or other IP hardware, but pickings are slim. Chris takes the first crack and I scoop up the crumbs. Meanwhile, she writes policies and procedures for the nascent OTIS conglomerate and doesn't ask my opinion. I wish she would.

A month later, Bob Longman arrives fresh from the Labor Department. At one time an Expediter from Perkin Elmer Data Systems Group before that, he's eager to learn. Try to show him a chipper attitude.

Chris says, "You'll be senior, Rod."

He sets down at the other beached hippo.

One morning the desk phone rings. It could be anyone.

"Technical Services, Rod speaking," a name Chris made up for us. We are also an information reference desk.

"What's Treasury's mainframe, and how many MIPS is it running?"

MIPS—millions of instructions per second.

"Treasury has an IBM Model 3084-QC8," *That I had helped write the waiver for so we could buy it.*

"It has a one-hundred and twenty-eight-megabyte core processor and forty-eight channels, running MVS 370 XA Operating System. I'll call you with the number. Anything else?" Write the person's name, number, and MIPS with a question mark on the pad.

Hang up and call the Treasury IBM Customer Engineer for the rating, young, tall, and handsome Mac. We kibitz and talk shop, old buds. Janet also knows him because he used to rent our second-floor apartment on Nottingham Way, our first mortgaged house. He shuffled through a bevy of girlfriends, and we heard their lovemaking in the bedroom above ours. We ignored it and refrained from confronting him, although, doubt he'd be embarrassed. Mac's black Chevy custom van had also been fitted out and soundproofed as a moving bedroom.

Call the requester later the same day.

"The MIPS turns out to be less than a handful, about four or five."

"That's all?"

"About that, yes."

The machine had cost eight million dollars.

Ponder if this is all we'll do, or if more assignments will bare their teeth and bite my interest.

Fathers and sons bond
Adrift career salvaged?
Tasks seem obscure and moot

2.9 THE FIRST SPILL

"Vroom—Screech—Lurch!"

Whaat?!

Struggle to regain wits as the sound of brakes that only one vehicle makes fades behind me. Sprawled on the rough asphalt, look up and twist head back.

Oh hell!

The NJ Transit bus has halted on its way to Trenton. It looms within eight feet of where I lay. The bike had slid out from under. An oil slick covers the middle of the lane. *Gotta expect things like this.*

Not scared but surprised at the sudden slip and fall. No one exits the bus, but curious or alarmed spectators in stopped cars roll down their windows and gawk. *At least the bus driver isn't blowing his obnoxious horn.*

Pick up the bike, mount, press the electric start, press gear down, and twist the throttle handle back to speed up. Glad the bike's not damaged.

On weekends ride the Honda CB360 on county roads and spend time, aimless and free, leaning into curves, speeding on straightaways, and passing. Revel in the torque of the compact engine between my legs that jumps when I twist the throttle.

If I crash My Guardian Angels will save Me.

Accept daily events in stride, with nothing except Jesse and Kate's demands for my time budging my dial from "Subdued" on an unnotched barometer of emotions. Neither rambunctious joy nor abject sorrow insinuates themselves.

At one fifteen-minute visit every month in a casual aside, Doctor Argueta shares he owns a small coffee plantation in Guatemala, then switches and probes my "dulling of emotions."

"Consider it as bipolar's modus operandi, Doc, nothing to concern myself about, a necessary byproduct of medications."

A nasty tongue is ever-present, however, to match mercurial impulses that strike willy-nilly at the office.

"Bob, you've got to finish this report. I wanted it on my desk yesterday."

"I'm waiting for IBM's last update, Rod."

"Well, call them and move 'em off their butts. If you have to, drive to their office on West State Street and pick it up."

At home, "Rod, did you talk to your mom about her July Fourth picnic? What time does it start?"

"Yeah, I will, maybe later."

"Well, I asked you two days ago."

"Okay, I get it!"

No problem finding energy though, from the second eyes snap awake when the alarm radio sounds at seven until bedtime at ten or eleven.

When Janet asks, "How was work?" respond, "Nothing we couldn't handle."

No highs, no lows, but temper outbursts cause Janet to cower at my raised voice. A perennial limbo with only fleeting visits to cavorting heavens or chain-whipped hells. Like a well-worn groove, a needle on a 33LP record that captivates in music and lyrics until it skips, and they jar the heart. Then shrill vibrato or pounding sounds echo when shouldn't until the hypomania subsides.

The new year's April turns out sunny and mild as it should. Good riding weather for stretches between rain showers. Cherish the time alone when thoughts enter and leave without firing up emotions or triggering guilt at not being perfect. Admire nature and its abundance.

Pull into Pullen's gas station on Quaker Bridge Road to fill up the bike.

Dave, the owner, an older second-cousin, has a red and white sign on his Honda motorcycle with a brown tank lined with black and white racing stripes. Sign reads, "For Sale $500."

It's a chrome beauty. Dave says, "Rodney, take it for a spin, why don't cha. Its 140 cc's bigger than your CB360. Here's the key."

Park my bike, jump on, start up, pull into traffic, and test it out. Responsive, in mint condition, its running boards for footrests provide a genteel ride with easy gear shifting. "What if I could own this?"

Minutes before hitting the bank to withdraw five hundred dollars, tell Dave, "I'd better consult with Janet. I'll be back."

Race home.

"Hon, the front and rear crash bars make it much safer, and it's a cruising bike, not a racer. Dave has kept it in excellent condition and it's a good deal money-wise. And it's much more comfortable to ride."

Jan concedes, bring a check, return, and pay Dave what he asked, no blood relative discount.

Place an ad in *The Times* classifieds and sell the CB360 for a hundred.

The buyer phones a week later. "I want my money back. Gear changes aren't as fluid as they should be. I think it's the transmission."

"If it is, I never had a problem that a little cable-tightening didn't fix." He had inspected it and ridden it hard on our neighborhood streets until satisfied. Had sold it "As is."

If could tighten
mental wires then could fix
volatile conduct too

2.10 A FAMILY THAT PLAYS TOGETHER

"Happy birthday, Katie!"

We and grandparents Mom, Dad, Doris, and Lyn exchange cheers and claps around Kate, who sits at the head of our dining room table as we celebrate her milestone June birthday. Kate's face tries to absorb all the hubbub, smiles, and claps. Janet serves homemade chocolate-chip cookies, Carvel ice cream cake with five candles which I light, and fruit salad. Glad to watch Kate's own smiles.

She opens her presents surprised at the fuss, and of course, there are games. The four of us like to play Clue, Life, and Monopoly, and when we do, horse around, laugh, and tell jokes. Our basement shelves are full of games like Twister and Perfection and jigsaw puzzles.

Kate is in a mild stupor from all the attention, and we all share stories and food over coffee and tea before saying goodbyes.

Jan is a quick wit and we all like to play games on each other. Jesse takes after her.

"What has hands but doesn't clap? Give up?"

"A clock."

"What goes up but never comes down?"

"Your age?"

"What begins with T, ends with T, and has T in it?" Stumped, Jesse, Kate, and I raise eyebrows.

"A Teapot!" Jan says, and this is her favorite since she adores objects like teatime hand towels, tea cozies, and unique teapots like the one we picked up at a Japanese store in New Hope, Pennsylvania, a village of small boutique shops that subsists on tourists.

Every morning she boils water then sips her Red Rose Decaf tea as she scans *The Times* page by page searching for past students, people, or neighbors she recognizes. Hamilton news is secondary. Know better than to disturb her sacrosanct teatime. It's a trait inherited from her British war bride mother.

Listen and feign interest if she shares what she finds, since although I care what she thinks, care little about provocative headlines and other tales of woe or success. They're always full of dreads, doubts, deaths, and downfalls; or awards, achievements, accolades, and accomplishments.

The brutalities are despicable, but some attainments are magnificent. And the wheel turns, and another daily cycle begins or ends in one minute of fame. Neither surprised by the bad nor bowled over by the little good that's conveyed.

But *The Times,* and its focus on local community coverage is more positive than most. Hold firm that greater goodness exists because more decent people exist just by looking at neighbors around us. Jerks, misfits, and politicians get the attention, but they are the minority of normal, average people. In fact, they're not normal at all but for a few.

Every day my belief proves true at local stores when strangers hold doors open or smile, clerks smile, drivers let my car into their line of traffic, or folks say "Please," and "Thank you." If Truthfulness is the foundation of all virtues, Courtesy is the prince that builds a home upon it. [20]

Simple family joys
bring togetherness
that cements bonds of love

See ads for the Commodore 64 and excited, purchase one with monochrome monitor, keyboard, joystick, and an eight-inch floppy disk drive for one-hundred fifty-nine bucks. Set it up in the basement, and half the fun is pecking around discovering how to operate it. We also buy three boxed games with scant instructions.

In *Barbie*, Kate, enraptured, sits on my lap as we shop for clothes for a date with Ken. On the screen she tries on outfits at one store, but before we pick the right ensemble, the phone ding-a-lings and Ken, in an upbeat tone that grates, says, "Barbie, plans have changed!" Her pink car drives up out front and off we scoot to another fashion store to try on a colorful new combination, like an evening dress for a different activity. Kate basks in the constant travel to dress shops, despite Ken's incessant interruptions.

You SOB, when are you going to stop jerking our chain?!

Kate and I seldom make it to the tennis courts for a game, or to the fancy ball. Ken never shows his face. Want to kick him.

Together with Jesse's dexterity and prowess, he and I confront the perils faced by the intrepid *Fellowship of the Ring* band. The "Da Da Dum, Da Da Dum," music from the C64's speaker casts spells of doom that echo in the hollows and caverns of evil Moria. It accompanies wild chases, zinging arrows, ominous traps, and dead ends until, in a last-ditch miracle move, we extricate the Fellowship from bloodthirsty Orcs.

"High five Jess!" marks each success and "Next time," each failure.

My favorite is *Impossible Mission*, where a secret agent in a blue suit tries to retrieve computer codes that will prevent an evil genius from corrupting national computers. But our hero, confronted by a maze of tiered rooms inhabited by protective robots, must be sly and precise. We take turns pushing and popping the joystick so he can leap from ledge to ledge to avoid brushing electrified metallic guardians protecting the codes.

"ZZTTT!"

"ARGHH!" he screams and body flailing, plummets down a deep shaft after brushing one. *Crap, we only needed three more!*

We spend hours on it.

Or we configure Jesse's parcel of Autobot Transformers or build Lego contraptions from the hundreds of shapes and colored pieces in his bins.

Comfortable and relaxed, completed chores result in satisfied kudos from Jan around the house. Draw lines through items on my weekend list once finished.

~~Clean bathrooms, Vacuum, make beds~~
~~Weed gardens and mow lawn~~

Just another Saturday, in our secluded development, as the song lyrics might go if I could actually sing.

In the backyard, construct a wooden 4 x 6 x 8-foot frame and platform out of 2 by 4s for a playhouse next to one of our sixty-foot Norway maples. The kids and their friends hang out in it.

"Take one thing at a time" is my go-to mantra, or "Don't even go there" my safe fallback when bombarded with impulses to scream at those who don't understand me or why I do a thing.

Downtime is evading reality by reading *The Hunt for Red October*, *Time*, or *The American Bahá'í* magazine without becoming invested.

But nagging questions excavate all-too-familiar rebellion.

What if I just took off? Why exist? What difference can I make?

We deserve joy
Duties and obligations
should not kill our spirit

2.11 CRASH AND LEARN

HRDI OFFERS SUPERVISORY AND MANAGEMENT PROGRAM

The new posting this morning on the office break room Bulletin Board is half-hidden behind Promotional Announcements.

> A three-year supervisory and management training course to obtain certification as a State Supervisor and/or Manager that builds on skills and abilities necessary for an evolving workplace.

Classes are one day per week, out on College Road in Plainsboro. *May as well learn what I'm supposed to be doing.*

Hurry back, coffee in hand. Track down an application. Qualify as a supervisor, albeit for one person. That night mention the course to Janet and she says, "Go for it."

The next morning complete the application and ask Chris for approval. She signs it and I run it upstairs to Human Resources.

After a week, they approve it. Thrilled to join a classroom environment of diverse peers starting in September. *This will help if I ever get more staff and responsibilities.*

Late one July morning, head northwest down the two-lane Quaker Bridge Road toward Rich and Liz's for the Martyrdom of the Báb Holy Day commemoration, *a different kind of mourning.* The CB500 is cushy and ready to hurry past the slow drivers under the green light when a faded turquoise early model Ford Fairlane switches into my lane.

Catch up to her fast, with vehicles in the left lane next to me.

Speedometer reads 40.

With no blinker on, she brakes and slows to 10 mph to make a right turn.

"Holy crap!"

Throttle off with the right hand and grab handbrake, snap left side clutch handle, downshift with left foot, press brake pedal with the right, backoff throttle with right hand, and twist and swing the bike down on its right side.

"Bang!" The careening cycle smacks the hot macadam hard.

"Skreee...." Skid sideways toward the Ford's rear-end.

Shit. Damn! How could she not see me?

Hug the bike's frame with both legs.

"Skreee...." Scrape the asphalt toward the big Ford in slow motion.

Its wide chrome bumper fills my view.

Slide stops. Traffic screeches and halts as well.

"Unghh."

Lift and scramble up and off the bike. Shaky, comb body with both hands feeling for bone breaks.

No damage, bike fine, climb aboard, hit the electric start, and resume trip. The twin crash bars had protected body parts. The bouffant black-haired woman in the Ford is oblivious and finishes her turn onto Sloan.

When Janet finds torn and bloodied jeans or hears complaints about how blind drivers are, she states, "Rod, you have to be more careful."

However, this time she says, "Rod, you have two children now, don't you think you should cut down the risks?" Always tolerant, she hasn't laid on guilt or begrudged the time spent riding it or polishing chrome. She doesn't nag to get rid of it.

But we have one strict policy when it involves the bike—neither child will ever ride it—not even in our driveway.

The eight-year-old son of an ex-schoolmate of Janet's had done that. Their motorcycle friend had driven the boy on his lap, careful to ride up and down their driveway as the parents watched, enjoying their son's glee. But the boy twisted the throttle back, the bike zoomed forward, and crashed into their concrete porch.

Their poor son, thrown off, landed in a crumpled mess and broke his neck. An awful, incomprehensible accident.

Cycling isn't just fun or a thrill. It's more like piloting an F-16 fighter jet in a dogfight with seen and unseen enemy attackers. Nerves, eyesight, and body reactions all interact and must not slacken. It's not like sitting in a car protected by shields of prefab steel enjoying Surround Sound.

Caution, wits, and eyeballs vital
or lax cyclists
appear in obits

Start September HRDI classes in Supervision full of enthusiasm and determined to excel. Maneuver the twelve miles there on back roads; anything to avoid the U.S. 1/Princeton parking lot at rush hour. In class, the four-inch-thick blue binder full of handouts and exercises looks daunting, but the twelve of us have over a year to absorb it.

Our instructor states, "This course is Pass/Fail but I expect your best." It's a perfect parallel for mucking through each day somewhat pleased.

Jess and I, in Indian Guides again, only this time more eager, anticipate January's glorious Winter Weekend five months away. Expect repeat thrills of fun-filled frolicking at Camp Mason in the pristine forested mountains of the Delaware River Gap in northwestern New Jersey. The interaction with nation tribes of fathers and sons should be another unique bonding experience and terrific enjoyment.

2.12 DEALMAKERS

"Rod, would you stop by my office for a few minutes?"

"Sure, Dick, I'll be right there."

Dick Reichle is the no-nonsense yet congenial Manager of OTIS Fiscal and Procurement. His unit handles the gamut of OTIS spending for pencils to copy paper to furniture to computers, software, and all other purchasing categories including services. *What's goin' on?*

Enter and sit.

"Rod, I've spoken with Chet. We've talked to Chris, and we'd like you to supervise procurements. You'll report directly to me."

Whoa. A big switch. I'll be leaving Chris.

"Bob will continue under you, and Cindy Jablonski and Lynda Bolling will also join your team. What do you think?"

"Ah, I'd like that." *What am I supposed to think? Seems like a done deal. Chris must be in on this. Or she had no choice? But what will she do without us? My God, never expected this.*

"Cindy is exceptional, adept, and considerate. Lynda's just as qualified and hard-working too. Bob and I get along well and he's reliable. This is a fantastic opportunity, thanks. Any rules I should be aware of, Dick?"

"You know what we do, right? Just keep everything kosher. You'll also be the point man for the IP annual continuation waiver for all state agencies, not just OTIS. Think you can handle that?"

"Okay, sure, I managed MFDC's and know the drill. Anything else?

"Isn't that enough? But if you run into problems, see me."

"Of course. When do I start?"

"Wednesday sound good?"

"Absolutely. I'll do my best." *And with a lot more to cover.*

"Oh, and you can move into Bill's old office. *An office with a door. And nice furniture. A long way from my beached hippo's desk.* "

"That's terrific, thanks, Dick. Appreciate the opportunity."

Now supervise three, not just one. This position is a gift from the state capos and godfathers, *an appointment for proven loyalty?* Not an offer to mull over, and dare not say "No thank you." When bosses ask a question or state a direction, it's best to jump. It's not a negotiation.

Circle desk calendar, January 6, 1987.

"Just learn what he wants, Rod." But don't know the man fully yet. "Do what you do only now your responsible for a sheaf of OTIS smaller DPA procurements, more RFPs, and all fifty agencies for the IP waiver. Hah. Child's play. Right?"

This should be challenging. It'll be fun. I'm sure Chris had no choice either. What will she be doing?

Meet with Chris and express awkward gratitude for how she's helped me. She wishes the best, with no advice or comments on the circumstances. *Guess she'll craft OTIS policies and procedures?*

Our group convenes and Bob, Lynda, and Cindy are sharp, knowledgeable, honest, perform well, and don't invoke temperamental ire.

Dick didn't mention a promotion or salary increase, but that's how people move in state government.

One day in one position, the next transferred, and nary a promise of promotion. If lucky, they grant a permanent title, which may take years. Everyone recognizes how the system works, like it or not. Not worth fretting over or trying to guess the larger picture. Some people, that's all they do, speculate on everyone's moves and what they might mean. Never went down that path, never saw where any of that helped. *Whenever the bosses agree, it's a done deal. Accept it.*

Learned though, it's best not to burn bridges. Dictates can change.

Dick and his right-hand man, Jim O'Connor, negotiate big-ticket OTIS purchases with giant vendors like IBM, Honeywell, AT&T, Computer Associates, DEC, and others. Now, observe their negotiations firsthand.

Dick, a seasoned manipulator, starts friendly and convivial with vendor reps but has a master playbook in his head. Jim, a wizened and cunning Irishman, interrogates their price offers with "What discount did you give Pennsylvania?"

Together the two of them comprise a professional wrestling tag team. Dick's name in the ring could be "Salesman's Remorse," because of the chagrined faces he elicits at his rhetorical questions and ultimatums. Jim is "The Irish Wolfhound" because he sniffs out every crack in their polished exteriors and canned presentations. Like veterans of a hundred matches, they gauge the minutest flaws in their opponent's tactics, counterattack, wring concessions, and pin their dark-suited shoulders to the mat, showing no mercy.

For us, it's a matter of legally buying something requested by someone inside OTIS. It's serious business, with taxpayer dollars on the line. Dick and Jim don't just dicker price, but also terms and conditions on delivery, payment terms, indemnification, free training, technical support, and more. Their pow-wows with slick corporate white men in their high-priced suits are behind closed doors for a reason.

Relish the contest to squeeze real dollar savings out of these monolithic vendors with their hefty product and maintenance price tags. Learn techniques like "The Sandwich," "The Salami," and "something for something." Sharp waiver negotiations help us obtain big dollar savings that look good to Purchase Bureau, OMB, OTIS management, and the State Treasurer's office, which we leverage for even more credibility.

Also, learn in a flash that whether negotiating for a waivered purchase, crafting a Request for Proposals and bidding, or requiring a contract action of any kind, to push through procurement roadblocks as if behind the

103

wheel of a ten-ton Caterpillar loader. First, be prepared for the objection, second lift it up, move it off the table, and deposit it on the dust heap of non-starters.

And when we can't?

Saying "No" and showing the vendor out is the ultimate power against their full-court presses. Yet nine out of ten times discounts are more favorable after we leave the negotiating table "friends."

It's like Dick has said:

"It's easier to ask for forgiveness than it is for permission."

We either make the deals with a bit of smugness or with no comment despite the sweat and preparation we put into each ahead of time.

"Prepare ahead, or prepare to lose."

And it's a revolving door of preparations and deals.

Someone is always asking us to buy something.

Negotiations
used to be pat, civil
Now, gritty and muddy

2.13 ADDITION(AL) STRESS

"Bang, bang... bang, bang, bang." The sounds of two hammers pounding nails are incessant, and my head hurts from decisions.

It's a beautiful New Jersey Garden State spring with a pot-pourri of flowering trees, shrubs, flowers, and brilliant white Bradford Pears. Jesse's nine-and-a-half and Kate will be six in June.

Janet had said, "Rod, Jesse, and Kate need their own bedrooms."

Can't disagree. The house is constricting despite an unfinished basement.

First, we look at homes in Hamilton for something we can afford. They're too small, need work, or are too expensive. That leaves an addition. We agree it will be a master bedroom and bath.

On a recommendation, meet with strapping, yellow-haired Bob Plummer, and his calloused, wrinkled dad. Bob offers a better floor plan than mine, so sign a contract to build on the back of our thirty-two-year-old rancher, from where our bedroom is now.

First, Bob uses a backhoe and excavates a 6 x 18 x 18-foot square area, then they haul in wet cement by wheelbarrow for the footings. When dry, masons lay cinder block sides.

Bob and his dad install sills, floor joists, and thick plywood floors for future carpets, then frame the walls and cutouts for the sliding door and three Anderson Windows. The ceiling joists for the new roof go on and they nail 4 x 8-foot sheathing on joists and exterior walls, then staple on house wrap and shingle the roof to match the existing.

We're amazed at how much the two of them do unaided.

Each day questions arise, especially when interior work begins. A hallway goes in. Walls for a closet and new bath go up in our new bedroom. Bob's dad builds a closet in our old bedroom for Kate.

"Do you want sliding or bifold doors?"

The electrician visits. "What kind of light fixtures do you want? And where?" When he returns, I help install wall outlets. Then Bob and his dad insulate the interior walls and ceiling and screw the 4 x 8-foot sheetrock panels on.

It's decision after decision, minor, large, routine, or immediate.

Mike and Dave from our excellent heating service ENCON connect a sleek ring of baseboard pipes with modern white covers along perimeter walls where they join the floors. "Where do you want the release valves?"

Two subcontracted plumbers, both young and chatty, run copper or PVC for water lines to the new toilet, sink, and shower they connect into the extended cast iron sewer line. Bob installs the two bath cabinets I had constructed from IKEA kits, then the shower stall ordered from Beebee

Supply. When all done, I cut out and fit a quarter-inch plywood floor and then lay patterned adhesive-vinyl tiles on top and caulk the edges.

It's a constant do, do, do.

We say, "Yes, that's good," or "How about here," or "We'll use that brand," or "I'll do that." Trying to stay one step ahead and not delay the schedule is like guessing the winning Pick 3 lottery number. Every day brings questions.

One-night stay up past midnight and stain the raw pine trim boards and coving chestnut brown so the Plummers' can install it the next morning.

Make a hundred decisions and the addition is complete. A learning process for sure, replete with hasty gut-level choices.

Like my work at OTIS.

Harsh Hamilton Township inspectors perform their duties for foundation, framing, electrical, and plumbing, and issue a Certificate of Occupancy dated June 16, 1987.

From our Home Equity account, we pay Plummer Construction ten thousand dollars balance due for exemplary work.

The dash isn't over. Apply two coats of paint on raw surfaces, repaint the kids rooms, set up furniture, and transfer clothes and furnishings. Select and buy a beige carpet for the new master bedroom and hall, and Home Depot installers do that. We buy an IKEA pinewood bedroom set with a foam mattress and sell our 1940s mahogany one for five hundred dollars.

When final and ready, the kids, comfortable and ensconced in their new room decors, show off their personalities and invite friends over as we also enjoy our master suite. It's a new abode.

The only thing I have left to do is scrape, caulk, and paint the garage, breezeway, house, and the addition's exterior wood shingles pale yellow with Sears Weatherbeater. All fifteen-hundred-square-feet.

Better than money,
hire those you trust and do
what you can yourself

2.14 IT SEEMS ABSURD

"Hi Jason, how's it going?"

"Pretty good, Rod, can't complain. Here's today's mail."

"Thanks, buddy, enjoy your rounds."

"Yeah, at least in this air conditioning I don't have to fry."

"Agreed, it's ninety out there. What would we do without AC."

"Man, got that right. See you tomorrow."

"You too."

Pick out the oversized pink Interoffice envelope and rip it open. A half-slip of paper has name and SS number on it.

Management Information Systems Specialist 3
Salary Increase to $37,491.00
Effective 7/15/87

"Nice! My permanent appointment from the Promotional Application. Filed for it four months ago, almost forgot." That Announcement had appeared on the break room Bulletin Board and filed for it the next day.

Although not possessing a bachelor's degree to qualify, education, had met Civil Service requirements. Mercer County Community College night courses like Business Organization and Management, English Comp II, Program Logic, World Lit, Technical Writing, and Business Law, all 4.0s and three credits each, had helped. Civil Service classes on Effective Writing, Problem Solving and Decision Making, and a weeklong AMA course in Manhattan on Fundamentals of Finance and Accounting added credibility. Those and experience counted.

"Super. At least this new title encompasses actual work I do."

Take Jan to Scotto's in Dover Park Plaza, our favorite pizzeria, to celebrate. Order three thin crust slices with sweet Italian sausage and fountain Cokes with crushed ice, her's diet.

"This must be from my promotion to procurement supervisor. I'll have to thank Dick."

"You better. Always show gratitude even though you did the work."

Another unexpected promotion.

View such events as if embodied in flesh and blood in the fictional protagonist Meursault, in Albert Camus' *The Stranger,* a seminal book admired since I authored a report on it for Mister Cowie's senior English class. Got an A on the paper but a D in that class and Chemistry yet graduated Ewing High despite skipping over thirty days I should have been in classes. Didn't even attend Senior Prom. Out with upperclassman Stanley Tashlik flirting and drinking with two girls never seen again.

Camus' novel left an impression, only never knew why. In it, the 1940s French character Meursault sets out along an Algiers beachfront with a gun, almost heat-stroked and blinded by the sun. Clumsy and lost, he shoots an Arab dead with no motive. Meursault is jailed, tried, and convicted, more for his indifferent attitude towards the recent death of his mother than for his murderous act. In jail he feels no guilt, no self-recrimination, neither despair nor hope, just acceptance. In the end, that acceptance of absurdity creates meaning.

Like him, never quite sure what is free will versus what's ordained, what to curse the universe for, what to thank it for.

Regardless it's been said, "No one outruns their fate."

They guillotined Meursault for the murder.

Didn't ask outright for the title or increase and care little about Dick's motivations but assume he requires the expertise. *Recognition for increased responsibilities? Who can tell? Thirty percent of the time in state government, a warm body and keeping the machine running are enough.*

"You're welcome, Rod. You do an excellent job. That's what we want," is what Dick said when thanking him, so keep that uppermost. Also, try not to treat Cindy, Lynda, and Bob as underlings but as coworkers and equals. Try to be friendly and courteous, but it comes with an edge. Can turn tough and cold like the prosecutor and the judge in *The Stranger*.

The insidious and hypnotic draw of hypomania. Unaware, slide into mental quicksand and once sucked down don't realize rapid thoughts are smothered in perfectionist traits until rationality wallows in a yawning pit of delusion. Then autocratic grandiose beliefs discharge power over the universe, staff, family, events, everything. *As if I'm in charge. As if. Thank God and Bahá'u'lláh, Janet reminds me I'm not.*

As a state employee, just another functionary. One position number among thirty thousand. Must adhere to the pedantic will of an entrenched bureaucracy mired in statutes, Circular Letters, Executive Orders, and Administrative Codes. New or revised procurement rules and regulations appear without warning.

Bureaucrats either are or can be as blind as the universe.

But "I exist," we tell them.

Each time they and the universe reply, "That fact, in me, does not create an obligation."

Too often, despite our compelling and rational arguments to move a Purchase Bureau Buyer off their morass of overloaded assignments to seal a beneficial deal, state bureaucracy ignores prudent logic. Even though every PB contact from clerks to Buyers to the Director want to be helpful, they're beset with emergencies and fires that take precedence.

And every sales agent we meet creates urgency with the ultimatum, "This offer only stands if you sign before the end of our quarter." This common ploy is transparent but effective as the company-drawn line in the sand. But it's our job to pluck those discounts from their greedy coffers in whatever ways we can, without crossing our own lines.

But Purchase Bureau Buyers are immune to our pressure; it's not their money and they must work on something else. They tell us, "You have to wait for…" and we must wait, powerless. We must quell our frustration with them because if we complain animosity results. We don't want their rancor since we depend on their goodwill or our entreaties to move procurements through the time-intensive steps will fail.

It's Catch-22: "Don't bite the hand that approves you or you'll be begging for scraps." Yet, that's all we get until the stars align.

We can't tell them how to do their job although we'd like to; everyone hates that. All we want is to push the deal through in time to obtain tens of thousands of dollars in cash savings.

Strike deals when hot,
not when cold or dead, waiting
for the next day's lackey

From top to bottom the overarching concern is appearance. The last thing any official wants is negative newspaper headlines.

STATE EMPLOYEE'S HANDS CAUGHT IN THE TILL
TREASURY AWARDS 2 MILLION IN NO-BID CONTRACT
DIRECTOR APPROVES ILLEGAL CONTRACT

I understand but am stymied. The people in these positions want to help but have their hands tied. Time is always against them, us. When they do help, and they try, we praise them to the sky.

Yet when manic and grandiose ideas cram my head with dreams of authority and power, want to proclaim, "Do it this way" and "Do it now" in huge bold Futura Black font headline on the face of the moon.

Then, in my manic state, My universe is a personal, all-knowing, subservient Muse. Problems have solutions. Creative solutions, like Janet has in spades, drip like droplets from hundreds of melting icicles in my brain. If only people, many people, could see them the way I do, no barriers would block progress and success.

Two steps forward and one back sucks. *Who has time for that?*

When under pressure, it's unfortunate when I treat staff, coworkers, and agency personnel in curt, no-nonsense tones that don't brook dissent. Lack of impulse control over my cruel words is like a gun barrel jammed to my head by ego and self. Instead of a solid head on caring shoulders, it's a donkey's ass. And my feelings are removed from the fray as if the telltale heart were encased in stone.

It's no way to show leadership or friendship.

2.15 ANOTHER DEPARTURE

"Rodney, ah, it's your brother. He's, in the hospital." Can't see Mom's face on the phone but visualize agony as hear trembles in her voice.

"Huh? Stephen? With what? Why?" *He's so young.*

"The doctors aren't sure. They're monitoring his condition." More pain. *What could be wrong? He was healthy.*

"What hospital is he in?"

"Saint Francis. They said they may have to move him, into Intensive Care. I'm, worried."

"Try not to worry, Mom. The doctors will do their best. We can say prayers too."

"That's all I've been doing."

"Can he have visitors?"

"Maybe soon." *I gotta get over there.*

Visit him again as he sits half-upright in his bed in Intensive Care, cordoned off in a clear-plastic isolation tent. Brushed chestnut brown hair, almost black, high cheekbones, once ready smile with thin lips and straight white teeth, healthy just weeks earlier. He never even smoked.

Look closer. Disheveled, frail, and gaunt in a thin pale blue hospital gown—he's a sallow-skinned skeleton. None of us are sure what has caused his obvious suffering to rise to this precipitous level. *Why is he so sick? What happened, what's wrong?*

He's unable to speak, with a shunt in his skull, IV in his arm, transparent oxygen tube in his nostrils, and a feeding tube scheduled for his stomach the next day. *They'll fix him up.*

He's breathing hard, face drawn, eyelids raised in terror, mouth open, and black pupils dilated in unmistakable distress. *What do I do? What can I do?*

"Nurse. Nurse!" She appears.

"Umm, can he have some warm soup? I think he'd like it."

"Let me check Mr. Richards." *Why is he so ill?*

She reenters with thin rubber gloves and a light-blue mask on, carrying an orange, thick plastic bowl and matching plastic-coated spoon. She places them on his tray.

"Please put these gloves on and wear this mask." They match hers. Comply. *Why all the protection? Is he infectious?*

The bowl she hands me is lukewarm. No steam.

She zips up the translucent plastic shell of the side closest, then leaves. Part the plastic shroud and move in close. Spoon out split pea soup between his halting gasps and swallows. Wipe the dribbles from his lower lip with the spoon edge or a napkin.

Poor Stephen, what is it? Will you recover?

The next night, Sunday, August thirty, meet Mom and Dad, stepsister Carleen, and stepbrothers Charlie and Ralph Junior in the hospital lobby. We reach Stephen, who sleeps, and so we leave. We amble in subdued silence to Papa's Tomato Pies two blocks away. Somber, no one will project the outcome of his condition. Someone remarks on the tastiness of the thin-crust pizzas and cozy atmosphere in the dim light of the traditional interior. When done, Dad pays the bill, and we chip in on the tip.

As we return, Ralphie stops in the gift shop on the first floor and buys a handheld statue of the Blessed Mother for Stephen's room, since we all appreciate that he admires such things. He's always been devout.

As we exit the elevator on our way to ICU, the statue slips out of Ralphie's fingers, and the plaster-of-Paris gift hits the linoleum floor. The head splits off and rolls a short distance....

Stephen's door is shut, and the thick blue-green window curtain drawn. A nurse says, "Please wait for the doctor." We move into the waiting room and huddle, expectant. Five minutes later he enters, takes Mom aside, and whispers.

Oh No. She takes two steps forward and stops in front of me. *Do I dare look up?*

She peers down, sorrow and pain etched on her face. Wrap her waist, hug her with closed eyes. *Where are my tears? Stephen!*

Complete shock rocks us.

Shit. Wasn't with you. Did you leave to avoid our anguish? That'd be like you. This is crappy. Be strong for Mom.

Carleen sobs and Chaz and Ralphie tear up, anguished, as they hug and comfort Mom. She's cemented and standing in place, shaking for her lost son, our lost brother.

Dad stands nearby, at a loss too. Mom, however, is tough Irish and has dealt with adversity. Her face unreadable, her lips and eyes turned down, wrenched for the boy she raised single-handedly from baby to adulthood. *Loving years, an endless number of tears can never bring back. Future years, an endless number of tears will never see.*

Fifteen minutes later enter a green windowless room and shut the door. There are neither chairs nor adornments on the walls. A waist-high gurney commands the center of the space. A long wide white sheet drapes Stephen's body, only his head exposed. The two of us, together again, like we were as children, he asleep in his bed, me sneaking in late.

Can't feel your earthly presence. Lightheaded, unsure, hands, muscles, head vibrate.

111

"Brother, I'm, I'm sorry. Can you forgive what I've done to you? I loved you... and never showed it."

Only thirty-five. *Did you die from my indifference?*

"I wish... I had hugged you at the family get-togethers... I wish..."

The Prayer for the Departed issues from parched lips. "O my Lord!" Mouth each syllable as tremble for the progress of his pure soul. "Purify them from trespasses, dispel their sorrows, and change their darkness into light. Cause them to enter the garden of happiness, cleanse them with the most pure water...."[13] Stop, can't finish.

"Stephen, I'm here for you, but too late, an onlooker, just like at Dad's service." Uncover his hand. Hold it. Thin, stark, skeletal. Clear flat ribbons of whitish veins. Stare at the grimace of death on the young sunken face, with dried white spittle formed into bubbles that cling to the sides of a rock-hard gaping mouth, jaw jutting out.

You died gasping for air.

"I deserted you. Not one phone call to you after leaving home at eighteen. My estranged and private brother. How did you live? What made you happy? I should know the answers. Only interested now."

If I am capable of shame, it's time to feel it.

Chastened, leave. Join the family in a moaning procession.

Hold mass at Immaculate Conception Church in Ewing. The priest mispronounces Stephen's name each time as Stefan, and because the funeral directors haven't arranged for any organ playing or singing, the silence is embarrassing. Cousin Cheri King, gowned in black with her trademark family black hair, rises behind me without prompting.

"Amazing grace... How sweet the sound... That saved a wretch like me... I once was lost, but now I am found...." Her clear soprano voice undulates sweetness and sentimentality through the hollow chamber. *All sinners, yet saved when our last breaths appear without warning, we hope.* Grateful for her courage and kindness.

When time for remembrances, rise, and speak from the podium. Decry his short lifespan, 1952 to 1987. Praise his spirit and how we are all proud of him. Eyes water, hold back welled-up tears, and apologize.

A week after Stephen passes, hear "How are you feeling, Rod?"

"Fine hon. Okay." *Does she think I'm going to flip out like after Dad's death? Is that what she thinks?*

Take stock. No anxiety or racing thoughts this time, mania's first signs.

Cautious, recite the expectant invocation, "Is there any Remover of difficulties save God?"[21] Always the first inner reassurance that crops up at a sign of trouble. Or when in need of hope. Can't let emotions overrun a teeter-tottering brain.

Some evenings leave work and drive Hamilton Avenue to Cedar Lane, turn into St. Mary's cemetery, pull to the curb, and beeline it to Stephen's grave. Don't hear a bird call or a car pass on the street.

Stand at the granite headstone with Mom's and Dad's names on it too and recite the short Prayer for the Departed. A prayer, a meditation, a five-minute visit, a slight gesture that doesn't assuage Catholic guilt.

His tomb, under Mom's reserved plot, fits. Always intimate and close, someday they'll be conjoined in spirit in the eternal realm.

No one asks about the actual cause of death. Stephen's doctor had not spoken it aloud to us—only to Mom.

Later, she confides, "When I saw Ralphie drop the Blessed Mother, I knew it was a sign."

Brother's unnamed killer
hurts deeper than expected
Grieve for Mom's loss

2.16 "DOCTOR, DOCTOR!"

It's the start of our last year in YMCA Indian Guides as Jesse begins fifth grade at Yardville Elementary. We welcome another set of Richardses, Joe and his son Josh, as they join us at our open house. As chief again, convene the new tribe in our living room. Invoke the Great Spirit as we point heavenward then at each other.

"And now may the Great Spirit of all Great Spirits, be with you, you, and you, for now, and evermore."

Josh is great, unruly brown hair, gangly and excitable. He and Jess meld in the natural curiosity and interests of ten-year-olds. Joe, a brooding Vietnam veteran, wears his Army M-65 green field jacket like a Jersey bear wears its heavy black fur. Our Blackfoot tribe consists only of the four of us.

"Knock, knock, knock."

Rouse drowsy body up from the living room couch. It's Saturday morning and Janet and Kate are running errands in the October chill. Hear zings, swishes, and bells from Jess manipulating Link in *The Legend of Zelda* on his Nintendo in his room.

Who's this?

Unlock the door, Joe steps in.

"Ah, Hi Joe, what's up? I was just taking a nap."

"Rod, did you forget the Nation was at Veteran's Lake for tepee-building this morning? As Shaman you were supposed to start it off. Did you forget that too?" He's angry, red-faced.

"Oh shit. I did. I fuzzed out and forgot. I can't believe it. I'm sorry, Joe. I mean it."

He snorts and paces. "Well, believe it." His arms wave.

"Josh and I waited, but you didn't show. It was impossible to build a mock tepee in the howling wind. And you were supposed to bring the twine."

Ouch. Stupidass.

Feel like Klaus Barbie on trial for World War II war crimes.

Put palms up. "Joe, I apologize, really. It won't happen again, promise. I'm sorry." It's a tough sell. No valid excuse, and our bond, once trusting, now seems shattered.

Jesse's unaware of Joe's visit and the nation's activity as he plays Legos and Nintendo, although it's not his job to remember.

As soon as Joe leaves, *You missed another obligation you shouldn't have. Do you care about anything?*

So? Messed up. Not the end of the world. But here you are, a doctor for your nation but not for yourself. Shithead. Try not to disappoint him a second time.

This is familiar. Fail to pay attention and remember anything Jan tells me. Can't count all the times. Not ashamed when should be.

Like Joe, it must be how Janet feels when I ignore what she says or when fail to remember a commitment. Or don't respond as she expects—or at all. *If I had a dollar for everything I forgot to do or did something not right, I'd be Sam Walton.*

Yet women seem to remember for themselves and their mates, including kids, work, school, everything. Janet's always five steps ahead. *What's my problem? Why can't I listen and retain what she's said?*

"Rod, I told you I was going shopping."

"I told you yesterday we have Feast tonight."

"Rod, you can't. We're supposed to be at your mom's on Sunday."

Aloof and removed, hear her reminders as if two arm lengths away. Only concentrate on what's before my face, not yesterday's living or tomorrow's dying.

The only exception is on the job. Able to concentrate and meet deadlines as if the progress of state government depends on strength of will and knife-edged ability. There, focused and alert, a closet perfectionist.

As a Bahá'í, friendly, level-headed, support community activities, and appear virtuous. Except for the damn cigarettes. "Is it time for a smoke, yet?" insinuates and superimposes itself on conscious thoughts.

In public relegated to secluded spots, like behind our office building with other diehards since the state ban went into effect. When walk anywhere, always cup it when passing kids. Dad had demonstrated how to tee butts, an old military trick. Snap off the lit tobacco end, obliterate it with a stomp, and stick the dirty filter in rear pants pocket.

Until forget to dispose of one and Janet finds it in the dryer.

"Rod, this is disgusting. You can't do that." *Must remember not to. Except there are too many musts to remember.*

Must try harder to swing memory's door wide and let the lightbulb go on, do it right, and be done with it. Tired of walking through doors like the one on the Twilight Zone's eerie opening sequence, whereby an ironic twist spells doom. *Must suspend the awful belief I can't save myself.*

"Junior, get with the program," Dad always said.

Your Shaman of the Y's Iroquois Nation for Great Spirit's sake. Can't you doctor your thoughts and reactions?

Shaman or doctor
can never play a wise part
if dumb and absent

115

2.17 THE DREAMS, OH, THE DREAMS

Stand in a vast ballroom of sepia hues and earthy tones...
 Gold flock wallpaper in red, green, and tan floral print
materializes on high walls. Rectangular mirrors like billboards, in
thick curly-cued gilded frames, take shape.
 Peer closer...
 Diminutive in a floor-length adobe-tinted abba and short, white-
fez, with glistening white beard and hair, the figure of 'Abdu'l-
Bahá hovers fifteen feet away. Sagacious, generous, loving, and
forthright, one foot in the spiritual realm, the other on the
practical path, His arms open wide in a fatherly "Welcome."
 Rush to them...
 He wraps my torso in a warm hug for His prodigal son returned,
He the Master, me the lost one, the absent one, the missing one.
 Embrace in joy and thankfulness; found, loved, missed.
 Inhale the jasmine fragrance of His sweetness and meekness.
 He releases, turns, and points...
 Hundreds of imprinted brocade couches in Queen Anne tufted
styles fill the grand hall in turquoise, gray, beige, violet, white, and
brown. They squat on oak or mahogany ferrule-bottomed legs,
fronts, backs, and arms studded with small brass rounded tacks
tapped into their edges to hold the linens tight.
 Above the height of the couches, partway across the cavernous
space, observe one person, a man, slope-shouldered, deep brown
hair, sitting facing away.
 Cannot discern his features, but it's clear he waits.
 Begin approach across the expanse, weave through the aisles,
no sounds issuing from footfalls. As near, see his delicate hands
folded on his lap as he stares aside.
 Join him on the spacious sofa. Sit down close. He turns full-face...
  ... it's Stephen.
 His mouth and eyes widen into a beatific smile...
 He glows with inner peace and outer delight...
 A beloved, friendly sight we gather within outstretched arms
as tears stream...
 Surges of endless joy and forgiveness overwhelm senses....

With mist-filled eyes, open them to the shadowed contours of our bedroom. Bemused, content, and prayerful, lift the bedcovers then tiptoe to the bathroom. Switch on the light.

Remember standing amid that dark watchful brood of pines as shouted and screamed at humanity's follies even as medications have performed their chemical persuasions, morning, day, evening, and night. Despite the disease, function well enough to hold a job and maintain a family.

Have mood stabilizers made me ignore what's going on? Should I just accept whatever happens?

To hell with that.

Clean up, dress, and leave.

It's before other cars or delivery trucks traffic the road. Pull into 7/Eleven's empty lot and park. Inside, plunk three dollars on the busy crowded counter of packages and ads.

"Salem one-hundreds, please."

Receive the light green pack, matches, and change, without words. Light up outside. It lasts three minutes instead of only six drags and has a lighter taste. *Damned if I'm gonna pay the same price for shorter cigarettes.*

Have got to make changes, and not just pennies, nickels, and dimes.

And more than a new cigarette brand.

Dreams:
insights into soul's niches
Ignore, as you will
But don't forget

117

2.18 TROUBLES

It's windy, freezing weather, colder than it should be. Four inches of snow blankets our sidewalks and driveway, so shovel.

Bend, push, bend and lift, twist, toss. Walk back.

Bend, push, bend and lift, twist, toss. Walk back.

Pause, wipe nose with tissue.

Bend, push, bend and lift, twist, …

"Ouch!" Sharp daggers wrack low back. Struggle to stand upright amid shooting spasms.

"Ouch, ouch, ouch." Hobble indoors. *Burdened by the weight of my sins?*

"Jan, ah, it's my back again, I've got to see Tina."

She calls Doctor Balletto, then finishes clearing the driveway.

Incapacitated, call out sick to work. The sharpest low back pains recede after three visits under Tina's gifted manipulations and her Actuator. A few days of fastidious posture allow semi-normal functioning if walk as an old man with an imaginary cane. Contorting like a pretzel in and out of the driver's seat to use the car is the worst.

Will see Tina again next month for scheduled spinal adjustment and words of wisdom and encouragement.

At one time was a chiropractic skeptic. Now a firm believer.

OTIS is frenetic and there are no respites for weary fingers on the keyboard, thumbing through twenty-page reports, or dialing phone contacts. Write ten pages of specifications for an upgrade to the soon-to-be Hub's IBM mainframe processor. Review Section One's boilerplate:

1.0 Purpose and Intent

This Request for Proposal (RFP) is issued by the Purchase Bureau, Division of Purchase & Property, Department of Treasury, on behalf of the Office of Telecommunications and Information Systems (OTIS). The purpose of this RFP is to solicit bid proposals for the mainframe computer equipment described herein.

IBM will bid, of course, Amdahl the outlier, up-and-coming Hitachi most likely, Honeywell, hope not. Later, will inform Purchase Bureau of the estimated value, five million dollars, a romp in Big Blue's park. These multi-million-dollar bids are like targets in a Jersey boardwalk shooting gallery: shoot one CPU duck down, and another pops up.

This big iron bid requires research and overtime, so on Saturdays drive the cold slushy commute on Interstate 295. No one else in the office to distract me. Put on a pot of coffee and drink most of it from my well-worn cornflower-blue OTIS mug in between striking keys. Smoke on the hour and leave at noon, careful to empty and turn off the pot.

One Saturday visit Mom. Two months have passed since his premature death. We've been talking about Stephen at the kitchen table.

She opens up.

"In early August, after calling his apartment phone many times, I had a premonition. I told Ralph, 'Something's wrong with Stephen.' I convinced him to drive us there. The row house was dark with its shades pulled.

"He pounded on the brownstone door, 'Stephen, Stephen, please open the door!' I was adamant we get inside. We called Uncle Tony, who has a key to drive over and unlock it.

"After entering and peering through the dim interior, I spotted him and cried out, 'Stephen!' He had his light blue robe on and clung onto the railing halfway down the stairway. He looked in a stupor, pale, eyes red, sunken cheeks; wobbly. He seemed about to fall.

"I rushed over and ordered, 'We're taking him to Saint Francis, now.'

"I only wish I knew much sooner he was ill."

"Mom don't blame yourself. You found him and got help. God had other plans."

"He's in heaven."

"He is, Mom, he is."

After dedicated effort and triple-checking RFP wording and requirements, meet the December sixteenth deadline for the IBM mainframe upgrade.

At home, uncommunicative.

Leave the house after dinner and return late, with few words to Jan. Continue avoiding her until one night find her note on the kitchen counter.

> I feel very unwanted. Instead of 5 nights alone watching TV—I can now number it 6. I'm sorry I'm so boring and such poor company. What else do you want me to say? I presume your staying out very late was intentional, so I'd have something to worry about. Wherever you were—don't people have to get up and work? Another thrilling week begun...

Reply on the same yellow pad.

> I told you where I was. Can't you just understand that I wanted to be out for its own sake? Went to Bob's, we had a snowball fight, played Backgammon etc. Was that so bad? Why do you insist that it's a reflection on you? I don't love you less because I'm away from you.

The next day we speak choice words.

That night when arrive home, find her written response.

> Oh, for me it's out of sight, out of mind—I certainly don't mind you going out if you could be considerate about it—like "Do you mind...?" or "Would you like to come...?" or "What would you like to do?"—for

119

a change. Must have been fun—you, Bob, and Backgammon? I'm so confused and sad.

Print at the bottom of the page.

Wake me before you leave so I can hug you, OK?

In the morning, enter the kitchen while Janet boils her water for tea.

"Rod, are you feeling all right? You've been on edge lately, you're out late every night. Are you getting enough sleep?"

"Yes. Fine. Don't worry."

I've explained myself—that should be enough.

Decision making is difficult, even simple ones at the office, like which vendor out of three written quotations to pick and why. Short-tempered, touchy, curse at staff for the slightest delay.

Janet asks one night, "Where have you been so long?"

"Bob's. Can't I go to my friend's?" Storm out of the kitchen. *I need a smoke.*

Ruminate on earth-shattering ideas and plans to improve life on the planet, how to stop violence and injustice, and telling governments to retract their repressive policies. Convinced, "If others follow these, order and peace will result."

Taking meds is haphazard. If forget to take them, push them down in the kitchen garbage bag so she doesn't find out.

"Yeah, I took 'em," when asked.

The doc had told us, "Missing multiple doses is guaranteed mania if not caught in time." *But I'm not abnormal. Not. Damned if I'm a mental case. Hah! I don't care!*

Does anyone want to think, "I'm mentally ill?" Does anyone want to second guess every wayward thought? Question every emotion or lack of emotion? Every word and every action?

Don't think about it, Rod.

With effort, calm down. Get lucky once PB Director Lana Sims issues the public award to IBM in March. Had no formal protests from vendors who lost, so had been straightforward. *That's a relief.*

Tech staff and managers pat my back.

But then, a new jumpiness, wake earlier, erratic thoughts, cold indifference, stay out later, can't concentrate, moody, micromanage staff, raise voice.

But, one night, "Hon, I'm, ah, not feeling well… maybe we ought to see the doctor?"

"Rod, what's wrong?"

"Racing thinking… can't… control… thinking."

"That would explain a lot. Have you missed any pills?"

"Ah, not sure."

She dials Doctor Argueta. He says, "Have him come in tomorrow."
Visit his office the next afternoon to please Janet.

"Double up on lithium and antipsychotics. I want you to make an appointment for a week from today. Janet, call earlier if no improvement."

The next few days it's difficult to focus without veering down tangents. Strenuous effort required to corral feral thoughts and evils that need righting, or to remember to empty house garbage bins. Disconnected, distant, a disinterested observer. Truer, a Gatling gun whose crank spits lead judgments into burning consciousness, errant brain cells, and inner spirit, creating even more anxious thoughts.

This must be mania.

Doctor Argueta and Janet chat often as flesh, blood, and chemistry acclimate to extra doses of meds with no side effects. Janet observes every word and movement and ensures pills are downed on time. Cut out socializing and Bahá'í activities, read more, and quash self-righteous judgments as we watch TV in bed. Let routines settle in like riding a bicycle around the neighborhood again after a ten-year hiatus.

Swallow two Trazodone tablets at bedtime to lengthen sleep.

Yet hear whispered intonations from bodiless voices when dream. *Why don't you end it? You can't take this! You're done. What else can you do? Who cares?*

Hear a soothing familiar voice, *"Hold it together, Rod."*

Avoid the death of soul from mental corruption. Dodge two-hundred rounds per minute straight out of treacherous mind fields.

Neither Janet nor I speak about what could have happened—a month-long hospitalization—and incredible stress on her.

Don't admit to throwing away meds to her or anyone else.

My tornados
wrap me in fear
of what I may become
without her

3.0 EPISODE THREE

3.1 POLITICAL CORRECTNESS ASIDE

Sit with Mom at her kitchen table.

"I can't believe you're thirty-eight, Rodney dear."

"Yeah, Mom, and do you believe Janet and I married seventeen years ago next month?"

"Oh, I'm so proud of you and your family. You've done well, but you know that. Do you want coffee?"

"No thanks, Mom, just had one."

Unfold *The Times* to today's headline. U.S. Surgeon General C. Everett Koop reports that the addictive properties of nicotine are like heroin and cocaine. *Doubt they'd ever outlaw nicotine like they do illegal drug use. Heh! That'll be the day.*

Stephen interrupts. Shunt paper aside. She sits, coffee in hand.

"Mom, tell me, what did Stephen die of?" Look at her eyes.

Pause. She focuses on her folded hands. *Ashamed?*

"That terrible disease."

"What was it?"

"I don't want you to tell the others."

"I promise I won't." We haven't known what took him. Jan has guessed.

"HIV—AIDS."

Ouch. More reports have surfaced in the news. There are no treatments. *Ahh. Isolation makes sense now.*

She closes her eyes. Rise and hug her. We squeeze hands.

That night in bed share our talk with Janet. It confirms her suspicion.

Feel sorry and sad. *Brother, in your doomed battle for an idyllic lifestyle, did you find some happiness?*

Pause. Recall teenage experiences with adult males. *Where would I be except for an inborn libido and the woman lying next to me?*

"Jan, you know I love you, right?"

"What do you think, Rod?"

> *Numberless loves*
> *are happiest when lovers*
> *still live—for each other*

Sail upon a sea of serendipity after my birthday, as warmer weather attracts bicyclists, runners, strollers, and walkers to the clean sidewalks and roads of the neighborhood and throughout the township. Hear motorcycles and the distinctive sounds of their exhausts on Route 524 behind the house as dig out dandelion roots, trim seven-foot-tall lilac bushes, and clip low-hanging Norway maple branches on non-rainy days.

Promote the Faith through offers of informal discussions in our home, hoping to attract those seeking spiritual yet practical solutions to life's problems. Yet few prospects join. *Is it my approach? Too subtle?*

Suzen Owen had attended activities and often hosted them at her and husband Larry's house for years. He was a Bahá'í from the early 1970s. She knew the Writings and exhibited qualities anyone could ask for in a believer, yet she didn't declare belief for years.

Someone asked, "Suzen, was there a reason you waited so long?"

"I didn't think I could live up to its standards. I'm still not sure but think I can."

The rest of us said, "But Suzen, we're normal too! No one's perfect. We're not saints, we make mistakes all the time. And you are exemplary. So pleased you figured it out."

It's an individual path. It's not our purview to tell someone what and how and when to believe. It's a process of search and discovery. Religion isn't a state of deaf, dumb, and blind adherence. Everything is a learning and choosing process.

Offer the Message
as a gift and don't push
or scare seekers away

I first heard about the Faith while sharing a seven-bedroom house on Berkeley Avenue in Trenton with five guys and Margaret. Our 1969 Christmas card featured each of us in a Charles Schulz Peanut's cartoon fashion, titled Charenton, in facetious honor of the French insane asylum.

That summer night, sitting in the library room, Mick Jagger shouted the words to "Street Fighting Man" from the thirty-three LP as I waited for Janet to arrive. A visitor named Ted Ehmann came by to see one of the guys. We chatted, and he mentioned he was a Bahá'í.

My soul ached for a spiritual anchor. Recent readings from the *Book of Tao* and *I Ching* on my mind asked questions. Janet arrived.

"Hon, this is Teddy, and he has some pretty interesting things to say about a Movement he's in. I'd like to hear more. We can still get to Briehler's for ice cream, okay?"

We took Teddy with us to the Olden Avenue hangout.

Like the lyrics and the year, it was an era ripe for change.

Janet became interested too.

The Ancients knew truth
and unveiled its Changeless Name
Pure hearts unearth it

June. Prime riding season. Perfect weather to sell.

Will miss riding on sunny invigorating days, whether in spring, summer, or fall, heeding impulses to tour central Jersey and its sweeping fields, active farms, swale meadows, and forests. Visualize the color-filled popping flowers like the ubiquitous lavender wisteria vines choking eighty-foot-tall trees and their overpowering scent, the lime-green fresh growth, the fullness, the pines, ash, maples, and willows whose branches list in the wind as the bike lists through the pushing air and over the asphalt lanes. Felt free along with hand waves to cyclists headed in opposite directions, or even next to me.

On such days the car is no consolation prize and longings remain.

Clean, polish, and fondle the Honda one last time. It shines as bright as my heart whines like its 500cc engine used to. Ask for three-hundred dollars in a *Times* classified ad. Meet with a middle-aged man who resembles country and pop singer John Denver. When he returns from his test drive and says, "It sure rides smooth." Figure it's a lock.

The bike is in excellent condition, and its running boards and unique shift linkage are a bonus. The front and rear chrome crash bars seal the deal. We agree on two-seventy-five cash after compromising on his two-forty offer. Negotiation tactics have taught that the best deals come about when both parties feel they've each gained something.

It's a fun bike, easy to ride, and safe—for someone else now.

Lock daily thoughts of the bike into an inner compartment, "What had to be, had to be." Instead, considering risks, spend evenings safe with Janet and the kids, secure from intrusions.

The free-wheeling release from tasteless TV shows or reading fast-paced pages of Robert Ludlum novels is behind me.

Mind's wheels scream, "Run free!"
away from society's banshees
Drug helmet intervenes

Discovery Toys announces its 1988 annual summer conference at Disney World in Orlando. Janet says, "Rod, I'd like to go. We can go as a family. I'll make the arrangements."

"Hey, that'd be great! I'm all for it. We can start planning." Remember wanting to do this since forever.

Dick approves my summer vacation request for our week away. Excited like I was as a happy six-year-old finding a cowboy hat, holster, and cap gun under our tree Christmas morning in 1956.

When time, Janet operates the Toyota south down Interstate 95 toward our one-thousand-mile goal like a professional truck driver, without flaws.

Turning off and stopped at a red traffic signal on Main Street in a small Georgia town, the older male crewcut driver and female passenger with angry faces in the car alongside us call out to our open windows.

"Dirty hippies! Go back where you came from!"

I turn, face deadpan, and ignore them. Hair and beard aren't that long, and Janet's red mane is bushy but modest. The kids don't notice the slur.

The four of us stay at a Disney hotel. The first day we explore the Magic Kingdom attractions until jaded and exhausted. The next morning escort Jesse and Kate to our midsize hotel pool and soon they prefer to cavort and splash in the water under a canopy rather than walk and wait in long lines.

The curved pool with orange and purple fish painted on its blue walls is their mesmerizing babysitter. Janet hobnobs in the conference sessions and soaks up the party sales lines.

That evening, Janet asks, "Want to attend a keynote address with me tomorrow morning?"

"Okay. What's it about?"

"It'll be a surprise to both of us."

...Next morning, we hand over the kids to Child Care Services and sit in the great auditorium packed with yakking women and a few males. Rosa, an umber-skinned red-haired middle-aged firecracker and inspirational speaker, takes the stage. She describes greeting her husband at their front door as he arrives from work.

"Welcome home honey!"

Then she says, "Of course I was naked and wrapped in cellophane!"

"Haha!" "Go, girl!" "Great idea!" echoes from the ballroom full of hundreds of cat-calling and whistling women.

It's a tad awkward for us few dozen husbands, but we receive some smiles and sly looks. Rosa further inspires the crowd with her positive 'Go for it' and take no prisoners persona.

The surprise highlight is the next morning's Character Breakfast with Goofy, Minnie, and Mickey. Janet had reserved our spots when she booked the trip. The kids, us too, are googly eyed when the three costumed icons join our booth and pat, cuddle, and fawn over them.

Such innocent smiles! Even those carved into the costumed face masks.

That night we tour Epcot Center and Janet dawdles in the little British store and photographs the red classic telephone booth on the lake. But seven-year-old Kate becomes sick with a fever, nausea, earache, sore throat, and vomiting. We rush her to the Buena Vista Walk-in Medical Center and her temperature is 102.4 degrees. After Tylenol and 250-milligram doses of amoxicillin she clears up for the trip home.

It's a reminder that all that seems well and fine can transform on a dime.

Wishes become real
down the road if patient
Some match expectations

Back in Hamilton, the Assembly receives the call we've hoped for.

"Chris can meet with your group Tuesday, September thirteenth, from ten to ten-twenty. Can you be here then?" says Representative Chris Smith's aide.

"Of course. We'll be brief."

Our Assembly has convened a delegation to visit him at his Hamilton office at the request of our national External Affairs Office, charged with contacting prominent personages.

On the appointed day, with Mehri Roayai and Wilson Ngashu, listen as Scott McNear reads our prepared statement of thanks for upholding the right to worship without fear of repression in Iran. Mehri recites the appalling conditions there now. Wonder how Chris will respond, but he's on record for upholding human rights.

"The United States Bahá'í Community is concerned at the recrudescence of unjust imprisonments and executions of Bahá'ís there because of our beliefs, although the Faith espouses non-violence, non-involvement in politics, and loyalty to just government."

Chris responds, "I'm aware of the plight of your brethren in Iran, and it's unfortunate. I have sponsored congressional resolutions condemning human rights abuses against them and others and will continue to do so."

Observe and listen. He's personable, attentive, and concerned. Like his rolled-up sleeve persona. We thank him for his time, agree must preserve all human rights, and shake hands. Then Spud takes a group photo for the paper.

Out walking the yard, draw in cigarette smoke, as self-doubt haunts and lingers. *Who am I? What should I be doing?*

Aw, hell. Just get with the program. Stop the bullshit.

One thing's sure. Cooped up in a treatment facility for a month helps no one and hurts Janet. Neither does it answer nagging questions. *Just cling to sanity. Hold on to reality. Look at Jan. Packed with self-reliance.*

For freedom from the eruptions of bipolar disease, or eruptions of religious fanaticism, must espouse the safety provided by medications and the outcries from the international community. Safety comes from self-awareness and self-control. Healthy people want a secure and natural order, and they work toward one.

What do I want?

> *Find all remedies for relief*
> *from oppression*
> *Use them until well*

3.2 MILESTONE?

"Dad, how do you like my Flash?"

"Wow looks just like him. Nice. And he's almost three-feet tall!"

"Yup. I had just enough red Legos." Flash's arms, legs and chest are muscled with the yellow lightning prominent.

Jesse, consumed reading DC comic books, drawing, and with art, also builds a sixteen-inch-tall Batman drawn from his tubs of Legos. He manipulates his Nintendo stars Mega Man and Super Mario like a pro, and when I try, offers tips. He's a whiz at school and has faithful friends like Marc Vogtman who lives around the corner and who is easy to talk with.

Jesse has graduated from Indian Guides, so join the Y's Indian Princess program with Kate right after she goes back to school. It's the same set-up and principles as the Guides only for dads and daughters. She's a fast learner. We begin a new tribe and agree on the same name, Blackfoot. Mike and Andrea, Jules and his daughter, Brian and his daughter, round out our octet. After two meetings we've gelled.

"Mike, can you pass the glue gun?"

"Sure, for you, five bucks."

"Ha-ha. You'd sell me my own glue gun?"

"Only because I like you."

Position and attach the Guide's circular patch, FATHER/DAUGHTER— FRIENDS FOREVER to Kate's leather vest, then one to mine. At each meeting there's a craft project conceived by the host father. The atmosphere is casual suburban and in conversations learn my cohorts idolize Hamilton's perennial and congenial Republican Mayor Jack Rafferty and his tenacious hold on taxes.

"But when they justify a new school, we should vote for the budget, right? We can't have schools unfit for kids." That receives grumbles and no firm commitments.

At our casual meetings, pick up blow-by-blow accounts of the Philadelphia Eagles' prowess, or miscues, and the merits of Head Coach Buddy Ryan. Soon, follow fevered sports banter with interest. Having played guard on Tustin High's B football team, and watched twenty Super Bowls, capable of conversing in the lingo. It's near un-American not to.

On a sunny crisp Wednesday morning, drive to downtown Trenton and scoop up a metered parking spot on West State Street by the State Museum. No easy feat within a five-hundred yards of the State House.

Light up, cross the lawn to the State Auditorium, and sit on the concrete retailing wall. Watch a few women and mostly men in business attire enter.

Finish cigarette, lounge, then scoot inside at nine. The hubbub grows louder until the program begins. *What a haul to get here.*

The buzz and excitement are palpable from the over one hundred state managers gathered from almost as many agencies.

Forty-five minutes later, the person at the podium calls "Rodney Richards, OTIS." Cross the stage in my best charcoal suit.

A well-dressed woman from HRDI hands over a parchment certificat

The State of New Jersey and Rutgers State
University

Rodney Richards

Certified Public Manager

November 15, 1989

Move to a smiling Governor Jim Florio, elected a year ago, as we shake right hands.

Congratulations."

"Thank you, sir, appreciate it. Good luck to you," and mean it.

"Yes, and to you too." Hope he means it. He must be pleased after his loss to Tom Kean eight years earlier.

Onstage representatives continue to hand out certificates and empathize with what recipients have endured. One, it was a commuting challenge through Princeton's and Plainsboro's abominable traffic to attend all-day classes once a week. Only the back roads through Grover's Mill, the site of War of the Worlds, helped. Can hear Orson Welles' exited voice describe the action. Two, it took three years to finish.

First, passed the HRDI Supervisory course, then the Manager's version, both challenging and intense. *Damn proud. A Certified Public Manager, one of the state's first.*

After the staged ceremony, drive to the office and glide through the rest of the day a little self-inflated. Stop at K-Mart on the way home and purchase a two-dollar wood and glass frame.

After framing it, Janet takes a photo as I pose. The designation only cost two-hundred and fifty dollars out of pocket, chickenfeed, payable to Rutgers. *Heck, worth the ugly commute.*

Carry it in the next morning and hang it on my office wall. The CPM course conveyed powerful knowledge. One important sound bite is The Five Organizational Powers—Legitimate, Expert, Coercive, Referent, and Reward. Each feature on any job. Legitimate state contract managers like me exercise these powers to cajole agency staffs to respond to our requests.

In State government, only legitimate power carries absolute weight. For that, lean on those in charge and rely on wits and intimate knowledge of procurement to gain their trust. Not everyone can walk into the State

Treasurer's Office under the Capital Dome and walk out with a signed multi-million-dollar deal. We do.

Capturing their approvals is like building a house of cards with each one placed in sequence. If one card, low or high, can't hold up the others and they fall, setting them up again is iffy. That failure is the kiss of a black widow's bite to agency clerks and managers who rely on us to construct an unassailable case for approval by the fiscal year deadline.

Glance at the CPM Certificate weeks later, hanging across from my desk.

"Humph. Haven't heard of any promotions or uses for this. Is it another well-intentioned state endeavor relegated to obscurity?"

Note the long thin frame I had hung near it.

Dogbert zings "Bah" to Dilbert in a colored three-panel facsimile of a Scott Adams cartoon. "Hmmm"

If only I could say "Bah" to the mewling vendors. *The hoops we must jump through to pay them!*

Don't mind fair-minded scrutiny from Purchase Bureau, but some of it is uncalled for. The system expects us to be like trained dogs on the Ed Sullivan Show who earn tasty nuggets when they do it right yet get chastised when not perfect.

But it's rare to receive a nugget; it's more "Ho-hum" and on to the next procurement. Which is even more pressure. Sometimes, our ceaseless efforts to streamline the process fail and delays result. The only succor comes from removing bureaucratic objections to our well-documented submissions when the planets align.

The poet Robert Burns comes to mind:

"The best laid schemes o' Mice an' Men Gang aft agley"

Man plans and God laughs.

Big shots must say "Yes"
or procurement targets fail
Failures get walked back

3.3 SNOW COVERS DEEP

"Okay, Kate, your turn. I'll give you a push," and down the well-worn hill she goes, passing those climbing to the top pulling sleds.

Kate and other dads and daughters, and I, delight in the free-for-all and roughing it for three days, even though our cabin has a full kitchen and a refrigerator to cool the beers for late night storytelling and jokes. The girls retire to bunks in the next room and fall asleep without shouting reminders.

For a sixty-dollar fee for meals and cabin lodging, excited by our tribe's January trek to Camp Mason in eight-inch snow-covered Blairstown for our annual Indian Princesses Winter Weekend, situated in the Kittatinny Valley amongst mountains and rocky hills. The remote area breathes memories of romping good times in its clean, invigorating, rustic atmosphere with Jesse and prior tribal mates.

The girls and dads, by tribe, take turns performing Saturday night skits in the Canteen as watchers drink hot cocoa, share snacks, and gab. Simple sketches engender laughs or impart American Indian folklore, like the heroism of Sitting Bull even as a young man, protecting his people and their sacred lands. Our tribe tells of the life-saving search across the plains for iinii (buffalo).

Our unity, strengthened by easy camaraderie without dramatic or upsetting scenes between the girls, and with the invigorating enjoyment of the almost knee-deep snow, fortifies our unity. We trek through the bare woods, following gurgling streams and explore as the girls babble too. No one gets lost, and no cuts or bruises mar the fun.

On the way home ask, "How d'you like the weekend?"

"Thanks Daddy, I loved it!"

"I loved it too, and you." The easy familiarity of our special time rejuvenates waves of fondness and deep-set love. She, my child, is so much more than a pal.

> *Girls, boys, women, men,*
> *at heart, a guide or princess*
> *One worldwide human tribe*

Borriing. Give me work any day.

Communicate well with Jan, no tits-for-tats, but of late, pay scarce attention to Bahá'í, family, and social activities taking place.

But at my desk and PC, empowered as a Master shaping Destiny despite being bound by a plethora of New Jersey state laws, regulations, and an ancient Greek labyrinth of procedural steps where multiple Minotaurs block success. It's near impossible to rush and push our procurements through, which elicits a satisfying "Yes!" when we do. Maintain excellent terms with agency heads and clerks through contact by phone, fax, email, or interoffice memo, like cultivating tender Jersey tomato plants and bell peppers in our garden with regular watering and weeding.

With help from Mike Shifman, my close buddy and assigned PB Buyer, announce to all state agencies on Purchase Bureau letterhead:

> "The Annual Statewide meeting for the Fiscal Year 1990 Information Processing Waiver will be held Wednesday, February 21, at the Purchase Bureau Bid Room, 33 West State Street, Trenton, starting at 1 p.m. Submitting agencies should send a representative to this important meeting."

Mike will introduce and monitor the in-person session as usual. He is so inundated and overwhelmed by paperwork that his office looks like Louisiana after a Gulf of Mexico hurricane. He welcomes my lead, and I appreciate his trust and friendship.

On the twenty-first, run the gathering like strict Sister Agnes used to run eighth-grade class and detail what the waiver will cover, what it doesn't, documents needed, and deadlines. Answer questions from the forty-six state agency personnel in attendance.

Succeed only when
preparations ensure
no unanswered questions

Show up as expected to local Bahá'í events only because Janet acts as social director. Drag body along as she tries to spur interest. Wear bored indifference like a winter peacoat. Don't even hear her speak.

"Rod! I told you that!" or "Want to know what the doctor said?"

"Did you notice anything different?"

"What?"

"I had my hair cut short," or, when away for the weekend, "Do you see anything different?"

"No."

"The new color in the kitchen!" It was lime green. Lucky to remember to buy her a card the day before her birthday. One time forgot. It was a knife stab to her tender heart with a twist.

We use the backside of our daily Far Side Calendar to jot quick notes and to list chores and appointments after we chuckle over Gary Larson's arcane sense of humor. But too often still don't communicate.

"Where were you?

"Dunkin."

"Duh, I can see that. But don't you think you could have told me or left a note?" Chastened and abashed. *Does she care that much?*

Feel no such attachment, not like that. Out of sight, out of mind. Janet, the kids, Mom, Dad, or siblings, assume they're safe. Cared when dated Janet in high school. Cared when she severed our relationship after an intense argument over plastic sofa covers.

Adamant, "We're going to have them."

She vehement, "Are you serious? No, we aren't."

Furious and stymied, storm out.

Phone her daily the after regaining compassion. Her mom says, "She doesn't want to speak to you, Rodney."

Search for an olive branch. Look through books in the house. Walk to the Ewing Library across the street and ask the librarian for romantic suggestions. Uncover Shakespeare's Sonnet Number Forty.

> Take all my loves, my love, yea, take them all:
> What hast thou then more than thou hadst before?
> No love, my love, that thou mayst true love call—
> All mine was thine before thou hadst this more.
> Then if for my love thou my love receivest,
> I cannot blame thee for my love thou usest;
> But yet be blamed if thou this self deceivest
> By willful taste of what thyself refusest.
> I do forgive thy robb'ry, gentle thief,
> Although thou steal thee all my poverty;
> And yet love knows it is a greater grief
> To bear love's wrong than hate's known injury.
>> Lascivious grace, in whom all ill well shows,
>> Kill me with spites, yet we must not be foes.

Realize when cool down that grabbing her upper arms in a vise and leaving bruises on her pale freckled skin was wrong, wrong, wrong. Tried to say it would be a greater wrong to let our love fail.

We'd dated only a year by then, the summer of 1968. Only after a month, and mailing her the sonnet and a yearbook photo, did she relent. We speak, and she accepts my abject apologies. *Oh, so happy!*

Admit I love and need her, want only to be near her, care only for her. Just because my parents had clear slipcovers on their sofa and chairs doesn't mean we need them too.

Was it the bipolar erupting, even then? Or male Taurean stupidity?

> *Love's tender kisses*
> *layered like deep mountain snow*
> *hide ruts of cruel hurts*

3.4 ROCK-AND-ROLL WITH THE PUNCH

Dick calls his team into the conference room.

"Effective immediately, fiscal and procurement operations for all Treasury divisions will be under the Division of Administration headed by Jack Flynn." Note the raised eyebrows.

Overnight, our unit flies into disarray, gossip mounts. No doubt other units feel lost too. "Who's Jack Flynn?" "Will we stay here or move?" "Are our positions safe?" What changes will there be?"

It means Treasury fiscal and procurement staffs and functions for OTIS, Pensions, Taxation, Investments, Lottery, Building and Construction, Purchase and Property, and others are one entity. No longer separate. No warning, no specifics, a fait accompli.

It's May 1990. *What a birthday present.*

Dick is privy to details but is close-lipped. But we government troops take orders whether brilliant, stupid, or wasteful, unless egregious. We don't hear the rationales or politics behind decisions made.

Years in government teach that surprises lurk behind each front office pronouncement or *Star-Ledger* headline. Either go with the flow or slink behind a desk and stare at *The Trentonian's* page six bikini-clad pinup all day. Rattled, we roll forward on square wheels.

The seven of us relocate our belongings to leased space shared with the Division of Pensions at 50 West State Street on the eighth floor amid the cluster of state office buildings in downtown Trenton. The state is a big tenant of the fourteen-story 267,000 square foot building. Doored offices line the outside perimeter for privacy and views of Trenton while connected cubicles like cardboard boxes without lids fill the interior. Forty fiscal and procurement personnel from other Treasury divisions transfer in. Tech support installs networked PCs, and Maggie Dorato and her ace team installs multi-line telephones.

We do, and don't, expect upheavals. We should be used to them but never quite are. First, every two, four, or eight years with a new governor, legislators, commissioners, new treasurer, and division directors. Second, as they assume power and enact or alter laws and policies or abolish them. We mold to the whims of the new powerbrokers, duties added, switched, or eliminated. Bodies and titles are moveable, replaceable, or dispensable. Everything is on a 'need to know' basis until summoned into a corner office or receive a pink Interoffice envelope.

It's a helluva way to run a business. Especially the public's business. These disruptive cycles with new people and their ideas result in instability until their dictates are tested and pan out or blow up. Add the budget process every year and its guaranteed chaos. The politics behind it suck.

But I know, "No one is irreplaceable." That had been the first thing Joe Marino said when he hired me. Just twenty-years-old then, recall experiencing that sobering truth now.

We're chagrined when Lynda transfers to the Printing Control Office as part of Purchase & Property and Cyndi transfers to the Pensions Fiscal Manager Office, but I'm pleased we add a competent young man to the unit, Anthony Gibbons, streetwise and polite, and Anne Asaro, an old pro at all functions, from the Human Services fiscal office.

Now only a block from the Statehouse, it means speedy, walkable access to the Treasurer's Office in the gold-domed Capitol building. It's also a short jaywalk away to OMB and Purchase Bureau across the street at 33 West State on different floors. I save time and can hand-carry our waivers on foot to them, except those I drive to the OTIS Administrator in West Trenton. The irony's profound having left it.

Remark to Bob Longman, "We'll see if centralized administration is beneficial," and privately repeat "Insha'allah," God willing, in private, hopeful the quality of my work and reputation passes muster and can avoid the worst.

As bodies materialize and dematerialize, hear, "We don't do it that way." And then, "Well, we do it that way now," our mixture of government soldiers grinds down sharp conflicting procedures between overlapping functions, staff quirks, and ingrained methods.

After a few months, the gemstone is polished, and Administration's operations mesh like a computer using integrated circuits to execute transactions in milliseconds not minutes. Don't glimpse *Trentonian* newspapers laying open on peoples' desks, the public's oft-cited complaint against lazy state employees. Neither overhear gossipers in the break room nor dirty jokes at the water cooler. Office talk is polite, racism and sexism nonexistent, and people remain on task.

None of the new Fiscal Manager team leaders micromanage or berate their staff that I hear of.

Contrary to some of the public's hurtful beliefs, we don't "sit on our asses all day." Government is an ocean liner; you can't turn the ship of state around quickly. It takes constant effort from everyone to fulfill operational demands. But if the public knew what happens when the Governor's Office calls, they'd be impressed with the rapid cuts to red tape. Everyone jumps like a private when the general walks by.

Then the ship of state is an inboard speedboat.

Then staff and crew move with even more alacrity. Then, using their name, barriers fall like pawns to a queen while the king oversees her captures in a complex game.

In the unified atmosphere of Treasury Administration, feel in control when all I need to do is ask and support is instant, exact, and complete.

Ships of State don't cruise
They toss, turn, and twist
while citizens stand in line

One day alone with Mom talk about Treasury's reorganization. She's keen to listen since she works at the Commerce Department supporting Urban Enterprise Zones in cities across the state. Our discussion turns to Stephen. Three years have passed since he died.

"I should have invited him."

"Who, Mom?"

"Joe. I should have invited him to Stephen's service."

I had liked Stephen's self-deprecating partner, but don't respond. Mom hadn't come to terms with their intimate relationship, although Joe had been a guest at some family dinners.

We had just heard that Joe had died of AIDS. He and Stephen had many go-happy years living together in New Hope, Pennsylvania, and all I knew was that they'd shared an apartment off Main Street. He must have frequented its streets daily since he didn't drive.

Shudder.

Death and change—constants
We respond with grave moans,
indifference, or loud shouts

There's alarm, concern, or hope in world-shaking events.

In January 1991 Operation Desert Storm troops, tanks, and jet fighters begin to liberate Kuwait from Iraqi incursion. On March 3rd, Rodney King is beaten by Los Angeles policemen and its captured on video. A local station broadcasts it, it goes national, and causes public furors. Street protesters decry the brutality and grab empathy for my namesake and millions of people of color until flaring into riots. My sensibilities ache for him and those treated without human respect and dignity.

Later the same month, Germany regains formal independence from the Allied powers, and the Civil War-era western *Dances with Wolves* wins Oscars for Best Director and Best Picture. I am thrilled for its actors, storyline, and sensitivity.

In July, the U.S. and Soviet Union sign the START 1 treaty setting limits on nuclear weapons. Yet they each retain thousands in their arsenals, and we are no safer.

In September the Soviet Union dissolves, and the world wonders and shivers at what it may become.

Arms races, wars, racism
Will world catastrophes abolish them?

3.5 PRELUDE

Spectacular.

View endless clouds and blue sky from the cramped, stuffy coach seat on a Continental jet flying to New York for the extended weekend. Sneak another peek down.

"Ah, sir, those thin pointy lakes. Do they have a name?" The man next to me wearing a white shirt and plain green tie is in my seat. Jealous since we boarded, he sits against the window.

"They're called Finger Lakes because they're long and look like crooked fingers," he admits with a grunt.

Asked him earlier, "Why are you going to Rochester?"

"Business." Grunt. *Isn't Kodak there?*

Steal more glimpses past him of miniature landscapes below and flat brown or green fields, threaded by tiny black ribbons with crawling cars that glare from sunlight off their hoods and roofs. As the white-shirted man tosses sideways glances, turn front and flip the Spring Issue airline magazine pages to the crossword puzzle.

Like the Trenton *Times* this one is crackable and fill in squares.

It's three-hundred-and-fifty miles to a weekend training session with twenty-five cohorts. Our team of Janet, Barb, Ev, and me will oversee the Sheraton Meadowlands Hotel and Conference Center in North Jersey. Thrilled for the jet ride, thrilled as a Bahá'í World Congress volunteer, and thrilled with this training. *It will be magical.*

The first, held in London's Albert Hall in 1963 with only seven-thousand attendees, was historic. At this second, a fourfold increase of fellow believers will overrun the mammoth Jacob K. Javits Center in Manhattan in November. *Monumental. Firsts are unique, seconds mean growth.*

Arrive at Rochester airport and find Michael Winger-Bearskin and his VW Bug waiting. Amiable, he drives to his friend Bob Rosenfeld's suburban home. He talks about their consulting company, Idea Connections Systems, and their methods to stimulate innovation.

It's fifty-nine degrees and sunny with billowing cumulus clouds above the hint of white and pink dogwood flowers, clumps of yellow daffodils, purple crocuses, white or pink azaleas, cherry trees with pink blossoms, and white-flowering apple trees that pass by. A picture of rebirth for my eyes and freshness for my nose, with growth and diversity after winter's perennial drabness. *Even the air invigorates.*

Once there, hear "Michigan," "Colorado," "Florida," "Texas," and more places from around the country, California, the farthest. I know her. Gry Kvalheim will be stationed at Congress headquarters, the Hyatt Regency in Manhattan, and is in charge of transportation for the thirty thousand visitors expected. Had greeted her a few times at her son Grant's house in Princeton. He and his artistic wife Wendy, stalwart and gracious hosts for Bahá'í activities at their spacious home, with children Dana, Miles, and Lauren, are a model of generosity.

Janet and my volunteer packets had read, "Your teams will accommodate thousands of co-religionists at their chosen New York City hotels during the four-day Congress." *Hope today we learn about hotel management, transportation, event, and people coordination.*

Will share what I learn with Janet and the rest of the team back home.

Our venue, the Sheraton Meadowlands, lies ten miles from the City with four-hundred-twenty-seven guest rooms, two ballrooms, meeting rooms, and the amenities of a four-star hotel. In East Rutherford, across the Hudson River, it's less expensive than the metro hotels like the Hyatt. *Wow, have never dealt with people on this scale before.*

We'll need policies and procedures on hotel and guest management.

Bob Rosenfeld calls order. "Our purpose this weekend is to learn how to be spiritual and caring service." *Huh? Thought this would help with hotel and guest management. Spiritual and caring? I should know what service means after twenty-one years. What about our jobs?*

He hands out the one-hundred-page manual titled *Lighting the Lamp of Service.* It shows nothing on Venue Management in the Table of Contents. *Others here say they have similar concerns.*

But it's as clear as the crystal serving bowls on the Rosenfeld's dining room table filled with Delicious red apples that the weekend will contain none of it. Instead, we pair up and do trust-building exercises, as in falling backward into each other's arms.

Fifteen minutes later it's, "Hurry Rod, hurry!"

Take baby steps and scrunch down, crawl around, and fumble through blanketed chairs under the large dining room table. Fingers touch the heels of the person crawling in front.

Partner directs, "Left, left!" Then, "Right!" "Almost there!" *Hell, which way's out? What's she expect? I'm blindfolded, for God's sake!*

Later we study and recite a prayer of humility revealed by 'Abdu'l-Bahá and discuss the importance of self-sacrifice. Memorize it as best we can. Service to the loved ones of God mentioned in the prayer is the weekend's theme. To put people's needs before ours is the goal—a life goal—treat each human being with respect, honesty, and kindness.

And to love for love's sake. Not my best attribute.

Venue teams will deal with hundreds of Bahá'ís from dozens of countries, so a living example and flexible heart and mind are what's expected rather than understanding how hotels operate. *I guess.*

After the long weekend, greet Janet at Newark Airport Arrivals.

"Learned a lot, but not what I expected."

In a few days, welcome Ev and Barb into our living room. Debrief them and Janet on the Rochester trip.

"It was so different. Here's the manual, every page about service, courtesy, and kindness. No logistical info at all." Try hard to convey the sense of spirit and helpfulness which is to be our guide—not our heads—but our hearts.

Ev goes through it and shares key points. They grasp it in a flash. *Perhaps being nurturing women helps?*

Experienced, organized, and astute, they know and exhibit all these spiritual principles. Close personal friends since the seventies, they're also focused, educated, practical, and reasonable. They share the same natural thoughtful and caring instincts.

I may be a fifth wheel in the trunk, under the mat, but darn sure helpful if a functioning body is needed.

"I'll just follow your lead. You've got it together." *No sense rockin' the banana boat."*

We phone a dozen volunteers needed as guides, registrars, readers, music venue helpers, and ushers. Reach a solid core that will assist. *There may be problems, this will be enormous. But no need to worry. The women will handle it. They're beyond qualified.*

"Along for the ride, and it's going to be a once-in-a-lifetime event."

November seems far off.

Lovely quotations uplift
but a letdown
Not one management tip

3.6 NOT FOR THE WEAK

Retype "Vendor will" or "Product will" as populate MS-Word pages with passive voice and dry RFP technical specifications that would put any average reader to sleep like Rip Van Winkle.

The only thunderous bowling balls that would wake anyone up are the million-dollar bids submitted by vendors in response. Three is good, six is great, more is rare. One is trouble.

With bureaucratic, innocuous words in mind, the blank page is no deterrent for my flying fingers. This bid for UCCEL Corp's computer off-the-shelf software, or COTSS, is needed to improve performance of the HUB's IBM mainframe because current CPU usage has been in the seventy percentiles. Everyone's aware tables have switched since the 1970s when equipment was king. Application software is king now, as equipment costs plummet and compatible models proliferate.

Software costs are skyrocketing.

No personal pronouns appear on any page. Hammer out phrases from the seat of my pants, without an outline, describing what users have said they want and from my research in DATAPRO's information pages. MS-Word's copy and paste is priceless for boilerplate sections.

Say "Come back later," as wave away knocks on my office door.

It's cold impersonal writing slanted toward cold predatory companies trying to obtain the state's business by hook, crook, or a wheedling foot in the door. Not all vendor reps nor every company are con artists, arrogant or greedy, but they wear slick veneers like the disguised wolf in Grandma's bed enticing Little Red Riding Hood with "Why don't you come closer, my dear?"

And company sales reps—no matter how solicitous or helpful—appear as alluring Sirens and gods from the Golden Age of Greek mythology when first they meet with our team, with their smiling faces, glib offers, product silver linings, technical jargon, and vows to solve our problems.

"We can increase your productivity and provide state-of-the-art software and hardware solutions," or "There's nothing like our product on the market," and "Our technical support is unparalleled." Each product or service they tout is a golden fleece with healing powers.

We listen, wary, on our tippy toes, shields up wearing our most solicitous mask to match theirs, especially for salespeople with cockamamie ideas to save the state money sent to us by state legislators. In every case, before we even hear their appeals and pitches, know what they're going to say.

"Just sign this agreement," or "Try it on trial," or "Select our bid."

Some, we stop taking their calls.

Some, we collaborate, and they support us well enough.

Some, we do business, and they do great.

Some, we accept, but they struggle. We try to show patience.

None are perfect. But we expect performance in return for payment and file a complaint with PB contract management when they don't.

We are gatekeepers.

…And we are enablers when the stars align for purchase.

Only one vendor out of dozens is an expert at gaming the system. Slick Dennis Calabrese of outlier Honeywell, the underdog winner against behemoth IBM in 1974 in a court battle. He wrangles his talons into the halls of power and through the thicket of procurement rules as if he is a state official himself. With consummate salesmanship and tactics, he manipulates Human Services information processing purchases step by step, and converts them into checks drawn on the State Treasury. Dealing with him is a contest of wits to at least keep sole-source at bay. But DHS greases his efforts when they back his schemes one hundred percent.

Every vulture
wants to prey on our carcass
while yet still alive

These weeks try being sociable with staff.

"Tony, how's your new son?"

"Annie how are Sal's landscapes selling?" but detached from the asking, taciturn and private. Don't socialize, have no friends to confide in, and only talk business with minimal chit-chat. Can't quell the indwelling or the pressure. *We've got to increase the pace. Three more waiver requests. I'll take Labor, but who do I assign Corrections and DEP to?*

We're inundated. Under the gun, terse and abrupt with coworkers.

Concentrate upon compiling and reviewing the FY93 statewide IP Waiver requests from thirty-eight agencies with forty-seven vendors and hundreds of products and services. Page by page we check agency and vendor compliance with PB dictates, and some, whether agency or vendor, try to fool the system and cut corners so must expose their tricks.

After laboring through and personally resolving finer points, all waiver reviews are complete, and we sigh.

"Yahoo!, we did it gang. Annie, Tony, Bob, outstanding work."

Staff has again produced a continuation IP waiver worthy of submission to Purchase Bureau. Or, what we think they will accept. It's always a crap shoot. But they know just as we do that if the state does not make these payments, some agency IP functions would falter, or worse, halt.

"Okay, let' see here." Double-check vendor spellings first, then the formulas for the Vendor and Agency Totals column.

Review each line of the attached three-page Excel spreadsheet. Each entry means their documents are in order, both the agency's forms and the vendor quotations.

141

Hewlett-Packard	$ 63,491
IBM Corp	$ 1,698,743
Unisys	$ 54,782
Sun Microsystems	$ 72,916
NCR	$ 61,543
AT&T	$ 785,924
Memorex Telex	$ 475,964
Applied Data Research	$ 89,267
Computer Associates	$ 414,798
Hitachi Data Systems	$ 579,568
Honeywell Bull	$ 886,439
Digital Equipment Corp	$ 344,576

...scan through the rest.

"Wish I could control mood swings like these numbers." Half the grand total that we've stitched together belongs to OTIS. Some individual OTIS or agency request packages are fifteen pages thick. The entire assortment comprises three four-ring binders and we need a copy too.

"I shudda bought stock in XEROX."

Use the only IBM Selectric in the office. Type "Rod Richards" and phone number on the PB-129 Waiver Form as Contact, initial it, type in "Date needed July 1, 1992." then the other fields and the total "$19,694,481.45".

"Phase one, done. Onto Approvals."

Each new Waiver season starts in October, builds to a simmer, turns into a pressure cooker, and becomes a nail-biter until, and after, we submit it.

First, must tie off the waiver checkpoints laid out by PB Circular Letter, then obtain Jack Flynn's signature as de facto department head. OTIS is next for technical, followed by OMB. Then Purchase Bureau checks legal and regulatory. Then walk it to the State Treasurer's office, then back to PB. Meanwhile, unbridled expectations from waiting agencies are like delicate lightbulb-filled letters ready to drop in Times Square.

One hiccup or snag and HAPPY NEW FISCAL YEAR in bright lights will falter, flicker, or fail, and we'll hear a loud "Boo!" or "Boo Hoo." Only after Purchase Bureau's final approval can agencies receive my notifications. If lucky, that's the second week of July.

Then, write each their memo using an annual MS-Word template:

To Department (Division) of _____,
The Fiscal Year ____ Information Processing Waiver is complete.
Your request(s) are approved as follows:
   (List vendors and amounts)
Your authorized Waiver Number is _____.
   DO NOT EXCEED THIS AUTHORIZED AMOUNT.
Rodney Richards, Manager
Contract Administration Unit

That's the pièce of paper de résistance. When they receive it, cheers billow and agencies issue purchase orders and process vendor payments.

Government procurement is not for the faint-hearted nor the weak-minded. Each step might burn and crash with a glitchy question or a fault-finding phone call. On the other end, in May, vendors pound their chests for signed agreements or renewals, and their money.

Purchase order or payment delays cause vendor uproars and agency agita.

But when successful, the ship of state sails on unruffled waters for the new fiscal year, twelve months July through June.

Few pats on the back
although filled agency coffers
with hard-won cash

3.7 LAYOFF GLOOM

Newspaper headlines and newscasters scream.

Consumer, business confidence falling

The recession hits New Jersey and the country like a tsunami hitting the Pacific Rim. Jersey's economy tanks like a hot-air balloon with the gas flame that kept it afloat blown out by a cyclone. The State Budget is a shambles and revenue searchers are frantic to maintain agency operations despite frozen spending accounts. The few available funds left hide like stripped fish carcasses buried six feet deep in Arctic tundra with only a spoon to dig them out.

Rumors abound. Radio, newspapers, TV reports, and pundits cry doom.

Belt-tightening is no option for 8.4 percent of New Jerseyans who are unemployed. Those working minimum wage, if not laid off, earn less than five dollars per hour.

The Early Retirement Incentive package of 1992, offered to seasoned state employees, will help decrease payroll outlays in the short term. Chris Reid, ex-mentor and understanding boss, retires from OTIS. Administration Director Jack Flynn retires, so does Dick. They know what's coming and take advantage of the rare opportunity to exit unscathed. Hundreds leave without fanfare or seething with acrimony.

Strong rumblings say it's not enough.

Desperate, Governor Florio and the legislature raise State Sales Taxes from six to seven percent, and Gross Income Tax rises from 3.5 to 7 percent, filling a three-billion-dollar budget gap.

RIF notices in ubiquitous pink interoffice envelopes get sent to all forty-some-thousand State employees. The atmosphere, like a pall of yellow-brown mustard gas that burns careers, is toxic. More exit.

And I listen. "Rod, can you believe it? After six years. All I've given them. And I had all threes on my PARs."

"I know Diane, it isn't fair. I will miss our work together. What you put together was always topnotch. It's their loss." No one can foretell how it might end, or when the economy will pick up.

An unknown new Director in his thirties, Chuck Chianese, who oversaw operations at State Use Industries, appears on the scene to fill Jack Flynn's spot. According to Circular Letter fiat, when buying shelves or furniture, every agency must check for those items at State Use first. State prison inmates make the items.

"Well, he must have experience in fiscal and procurement," I tell staff.

144

In our first face-to-face, Chuck states, "Keep your name and our name out of the papers. Do an honest job. And don't gossip and backbite—I don't like that."

That's easy; don't do it. The Faith taught me well.

Not sure where else this will go.

"Dick's retired, but I need someone there. I'm checking into you as his replacement. In the meantime, you can move into his old office."

"Ah, thanks for the confidence, Chuck, and I'll keep the operation running. We'll do our best."

Unsure whether to be pleased at the private office and management possibilities or devastated if a layoff hits my new desk.

Answer phone one morning before leaving for lunch.

"Rod, this is Debbie from Human Resources. Can you be at your desk tomorrow at ten o'clock? I have to go over personnel plans with you."

"Of course, Deb, whatever you need."

"Good. Tomorrow at ten then." *What's this about? It could be about me or the staff. It could be the Reduction in Force Notice or something about my salary. Has Chuck come through? If that's it, he moves fast.*

This is novel; never received such a call before. Debbie Westwood is known for her pragmatic, no-nonsense style though.

Eat a BLT at Towne House and say a prayer for assistance.

Arrive home later, tell Jan.

"Well, don't think the worse, you have no idea what she'll say. Whatever you do, don't say or do anything rash."

The next morning, study my desk plaque: "You can't improve what you can't measure," a quote from W. Edwards Deming, the father of continuous improvement. *How will we improve this?* The bad economy. Twenty-seven hundred employees slated for layoffs. That also means thousands of "bumps"—lower staff pushed out of their position by those with higher seniority in Civil Service. Controlled chaos amidst rampant insecurity.

Watch says five to ten. Tap pen on a blank yellow pad. Minutes drag. *I must be safe. I have a permanent title. I have seniority, don't I?*

Flinch at the "Bringg…bringg…."

"Contract Administration, Rod speaking."

"Rodney, this is Deb from Personnel."

"Yeah, Deb. What's up?"

"I'm calling because there are no positions for you in your current Management Information Systems Specialist three title. An employee at OMB has seniority and bumped you back to your last permanent title of DP I/O Control Specialist one." *Uh oh. Shit. Uh oh.*

"What's that mean?"

145

"It means that you return to your old title and will have to relocate to OTIS Operations at the HUB Data Center in West Trenton." *What!?*

"You can't be serious. I left that job in 1980."

"There's no other option if you want to stay in State government."

"No other option? What about my salary?"

"Your salary will decrease. I'm sorry, there's no way around it."

"Oh." *Will we have to cancel our World Congress trip? A helluva lot more.*

"Rodney, I need your decision. Do you want it? Or do you want to pursue employment elsewhere?" *Elsewhere? Hell. At least, Janet's teaching sixth-graders full-time. But our mortgage, bills....*

Intone, *"Is there any Remover of difficulties save God? Say: Praised be God! He is God! All are His servants and all abide by His bidding!"*[21] *Even if I haven't done that job in over a decade, resign? Can't retire yet, only forty-two. That's a forty percent penalty. I'll be out of a job and forced to find a new one. And in today's environment?*

"Rod?"

"Well, Deb, you give me no choice. Ah, I'll take it." *Have to.*

"Good. Hopefully, over time, it will work out. I'll be sending you the official notice. Do you understand?" *What choice is there?*

"Yes, Deb. Don't want to say 'Thanks,' but I'll still be here, I hope."

"I've got to make more phone calls, so we'll be in touch."

"Yeah, good luck with that. I don't envy you."

"We'll be in touch, Rod." *I hope not.*

This ordeal is like being a small blue rubber ball smacked between one wall to the next by a steel paddle. Feel like the ball and the wall at the moment of impact. Hadn't excelled at handball in Tustin High School, not now either. *Have I wasted the last twelve years? Well, I'm vested at least. If can avoid regressing to operations at the HUB, I'll bite the damn shotgun shell and swallow it. Things might turnaround.*

Gotta phone Janet. *Oh, can't—can't call her out of class.*

Think. I/O Control Specialists fix JCL so hundreds of batches and online application programs will run without a hiccup on the mainframe, and gotta keep them all running on tight schedules. Operations has changed though. I'll be behind.

Trudge outside. Light up. Meditate on major disruptions. Shudder. "All I did to get here, now this." A shotgun blast in the gut.

Back upstairs, hit the break room for coffee.

At five o'clock drag outside for a smoke in front of the parking garage. Feel like a condemned man on Death Row.

Once home, tell Jan the details.

"Don't worry. We'll make the best of it. Wait for the official notice, Rod, before leaping to catastrophe." Her positive attitude props up dejected emotions. *Hell, call me Rod Taylor in a one-way time machine.*

The Three Fates have spoken again.

146

Jason drops off mail a few days later. Look in In-basket and there's a pink interoffice envelope from Human Resources. Debbie Westwood's name is on it. *Uh oh.*

Open it. No letter, no memo, just a plain white half-slip with name and SS number.

10-14-92 RIF to DP I/O Control Specialist I (2) $37,722

Almost a twenty-k difference! A third cut from current gross. *What the…? How will we make up that?*

Show it to Jan later. She starts crafting a new budget. Hadn't had to before. Our commitment to the World Congress and those expenses stays.

As days pass, State employee morale sinks lower than a torpedoed ship in the middle of the Atlantic during the height of World War II. Only we employees have no armaments to fight back with. Layoffs, retirements, and RIF changes cause ripple effects throughout hundreds of agencies. *How will it affect our work? Agency contacts will change.*

That will delay procurements and waivers.

Walk on a bed of red-hot coals as wait for Deb's follow-up call with the date to report to OTIS. Chew fingernails that haven't felt yellowed incisors since age fifteen when they were white.

News outlets report over fifteen-hundred state employees have lost their jobs. DEP's hit the hardest, as always. In Admin, most are fortunate compared to Bob Longman and Jim O'Connor, both laid off. They only linger a week on-site. We don't have a party. Bob goes through a tough time, worried about losing his recently built house. Sympathize, but not in a position to help in any concrete way.

Thousands more displaced by bumping. *Like me.*

Weeks pass. No word from Debbie. No word from Chuck. No pink interoffice envelopes with unwelcome news, either. *Will I end up going back to Operations at the Hub?*

As de facto head of our unit, proceed as if unaffected since told no one my status, but cautious. Many of our contacts at the agencies remain intact, but some change. Some of those lost positions remain vacant and we're left in limbo. New purchases are a trickle, but that's expected.

One early morning the phone rings.

"Rod, it's time for your annual PAR. Please draft the standards and get back to me." It's Joann, Chuck's executive secretary.

Compose what might be acceptable for the Annual Performance Assessment Review. Deliver it to Joann the next day.

A week later, she summons me into Chuck's corner office. Sit across from him at his little round table, my PAR form open. Black hair, trim build, clean-shaven, no-nonsense, and handsome, he's sucked up smaller units like Human Resources into his burgeoning division. He's an excellent Director and we've hit it off, although haven't spoken to him since our one-on-one and send him status reports every Wednesday.

"Rodney, I gave you threes. You're doing an excellent job, keep it up."

"Thanks, Chuck, I intend to."

"About your title. I'll try to make up for the loss. Also, I want you to fill Dick's slot permanently. That'll take a while to go through. I'm also hoping you won't transfer to OTIS, so hang tight. Can you do that?"

"Ah, no problem, Chuck, whatever you can do. I'll be here for whatever you need. Thanks." *He likes what I do, great. Patience! It's out of my hands. OMB holds the aces since they control all budgeted state positions. At least Chuck's a king. Shouldn't have to worry about sliding backward...if he comes through.*

Chuck appears one day at my office doorway like Riccardo Muti of the Philadelphia Orchestra on stage, only he's now conducting a seventy-piece orchestra of talented staffers in his division. *Uh-oh, good news or bad?*

"Rod, we have to change the name of the unit. Purchase Bureau just formed the Contract Administration Unit or CAU, so we can't use that anymore. Can you think of something else?"

"Well, we handle statewide contracts. How about Statewide Contract Consolidation?"

"Hmm, like it. We'll go with it. Start using that."

"Will do Chuck."

"Good." He leaves as sharply as executing a hard tap with a baton on his music stand, signaling the end of the horn section.

Our permanence assured, confirm name change with Dave Ridolfino, Budget Manager for Treasury. Order new business cards with functional title, "Rodney Richards, Manager, SCC Unit." My Civil Service bump has turned into a tap too, for a time.

Not all others have. Horror stories circulate like vengeful ghouls on Mischief Night. A return to OTIS Operations would be a career-killing throwback, but at least the cash setback isn't. With Jan's frugal household management and her teacher's salary, it's not godawful. As long as both Chuck and Dave feel I'm an asset, there's hope.

Do whatever it takes. This is your livelihood. Janet and the kids depend on you.

Back on the train track,
not derailed—not yet
Only God knows where headed

3.8 BATMAN RIDES

(November 21, 1992, Saturday)

"Shame, Philly's WHYY has cut out. Car Talk was great today."

Force job pressures and the new waiver cycle into a mental file drawer labeled SCC to focus on the World Congress. The team will follow tomorrow. Expecting hugs updates greeting old friends and new.

"It'll be amazing. Can't wait."

It's early Saturday afternoon on the bustling and infamous New Jersey Turnpike with Exits lampooned as the stinky armpits of the Northeast Corridor. Traveling north in advance of the team to set up our office in the Sheraton Hotel next to Giants stadium. Dodge other vehicles as sing along with Motown hits on the Oldies but Goodies station.

Speed through the sixty-five miles and daydream of the next day's auspicious event. Respond to the radio voices as pass by familiar surroundings. Hit 75 just like the Indy 500 pace car, other cars behind, some going the 55-mph limit. Mile markers flash by.

Arrive and slip into a parking slot. Grab my carryon tote.

At the Sheraton's counter, ask for the manager. "Hi, I'm Rodney Richards, here as a venue coordinator for the Bahá'í World Congress."

He scans a list. "Yes, Mr. Richards, we have a room for you and your family."

"Great." Extend a credit card. Clerk records it.

"We have an office set up for you on the mezzanine. Would you like me to show you there now or after you've settled in?"

"Now please." *Why fidgety? Stop rubbing your fingertips!*

The hotel staff is courteous and the spacious facilities are tasteful in their beige tints. The Derby ballroom, reserved for registrations and socializing, holds two-hundred-and-fifty people, and the larger Diamond ballroom for morning devotions and evening entertainment accommodates six hundred.

Follow him to our headquarters on the wide second-floor balcony. Tucked in a corner behind a fat pillar is a 12 x 16-foot room with one wide table, six chairs, two draped credenzas along the long wall under the windows, two phones, and boxed supplies including five-foot-long cardboard containers. Open one large box, find free-standing directional signs. *Cool.*

OOPS, he's waiting. "Thanks so much, I think we have all our materials."

"Yes sir, good. If there's anything else you need, here's my card and number, or just ask the staff."

"No, thank Y-O-U."

Remember our team Checklist:

Follow the schedule
Coordinate events and volunteers
Setup devotions and entertainment
Handle registrations
Place signs out
Solve guest requests

All in the spirit and attitude of service.

"We do what's necessary to accommodate three-hundred-and-fifty to four-hundred guests expected to check-in Sunday," Evelyn had said.

We have Gry Kvalheim's cell number for emergencies, stationed at at the Hyatt, and so far, the planning and organization by Headquarters has been thorough.

Rearrange the tables and chairs in our make-shift office. Rip open and noodle inside the cardboard boxes stacked on the side. Layers of signs, documents, ID badges, neck-rope holders, nameplates, day passes, pens, and paper fill the containers. Shove all under the credenzas covered by clip-on light blue drapes since there's no door lock.

Exit to our guest room on the seventh floor. Standard, with white popcorn ceiling and white wood trim, tiny bath, bureau with TV, desk, and chair. Lift bag onto one of two queen beds. Unpack and throw clothes in two drawers, slam them shut. *Gotta get coffee.*

Take an elevator down and find the restaurant. Buy a large to go with cream and sugar. *Don't gripe about cost when there's no other choice. So, what if I'm paying extra for convenience. When in Rome....*

Bounce up the escalator to the second floor, and stroll toward our office as scan the broad, high atrium and lobby below. Inside, rummage through two boxes of signs. Construct the seven-foot-tall **WELCOME** banners and directional signs with a **Bahá'í World Congress** and nine-pointed star on them in dark blue and yellow.

Take a smoke break. *Tomorrow's gonna be wild with so many people here. Hope the week goes without chaotic upheavals. This is happening! The program should be phenomenal.*

After dinner in the restaurant, scurry to our room, plop down and select *Batman Returns* on the remote.

Call Jan at home and touch base.

"It looks like all our materials are here, so that's good. The hotel is huge, and we'll have plenty of room for attendees. You'll see tomorrow."

"Okay Rod, get some sleep. We'll be there by nine-thirty."

"Good, see you in the morning, luv ya, bye."

Watch Michael Keaton do a decent job for his first time in the title role. He projects more confidence in his bat suit than in a tux, and his voice changes lower and meaner. *Is that the point?* Jack Nicholson is psychotic after his fall into a chemical vat. *Hah, what a clown.* But to die laughing with a maniacal grin hits too close.

Scan movie offerings again. Select *Patriot Games* with Harrison Ford as canny CIA analyst Jack Ryan. It's full of vengeance and murder and can't resist rooting for Jack as he defends his life and his wife, excellent actress Anne Archer. *Sean Bean is brutal. What a coldhearted Irish anarchist SOB. Revenge is always served cold.*

After a wave-tossed climax, flip through hackneyed shows, then kill the TV.

At one o'clock, turn off lights, toss and turn, sleep in fits and starts.

Ride the Batman rollercoaster at Six Flags, hampered in a tight-fitting bat suit, alone but the Joker cackles from the seat behind. We're inverted, going round and round, up, then low, then twist and turn after turn. Hold back screams because the Joker wins if do. One scream and I'll fall out and plummet one hundred feet to the ground... and so will a dozen women and children.

(November 22, 1992, Sunday)

Rise by five. Thoughts intrude in waves. Emotions and power surge and wane, some pissant, some overwhelming. *Remember this? Forever long ago. Not happening. Keep control.*

Wide awake, wired, antsy. Forego shower, dress, leave. Find the restaurant.

"Dammit. Closed." Roam hotel for hot coffee, including service areas. Find employees' cafeteria, but coffee not ready.

"Shit! Bummer, bummer, bummer. I need my coffee! What the hell! Why don't you just have some fucking coffee for God's sake? What's so hard about this? I should buy a franchise, run it myself."

Climb the stairs from the basement to the second-floor Derby Ballroom and stumble upon a man in his fifties.

"Ah, hi, good morning, can I help you?"

"Eq-qua-door." Dressed in thick white woolen socks and tan sandals, the short stocky man wears a colorful red, orange, and black striped wool serape over his right shoulder that droops past his waist to his knees. Recognize his South American roots. It's hours before the bulk of guests arrive at noon. *Let me hug him, he's got to be Bahá'í.*

Embrace, share the spirit.

"Alláh-u-Abhá, Alláh-u-Abhá."

His voice husky, mine high-pitched.

"We are brothers."

Show him inside, "Please sit. Wait."

Jog to our office, find *The Bahá'ís Magazine,* and rush back. He rises. Hand it to him, flipping through glossy pictures of multi-hued people and children garbed in colorful clothing from many countries. Principles of the Faith and quotations adorn some pages. *At least he has something to do.*

He says, "Gracias," and bows. Return to our office and simmer. "Where are the damn girls?"

Drink two coffees followed by death sticks out front. Wait. "Why aren't they here yet? This is important!"

The team arrives after nine, and surprise, fifteen-year-old Jesse is with Janet. *I forgot! I hope he enjoys it.* He'll attend sessions with our friends the Yazhari's.

Janet asks, "Rod, what room are we in? Do you have my key?"

"Oh yeah, here Hon. Seventh floor. I'll go down and pick up my own."

They head to our room. Go pick up another key, then wait in our office. *Man, they're taking their time.*

Thirty minutes later they pour over materials and supplies I've laid out, while Jess hangs out with his multi-talented friend Laila. *This is taking way too long. I need to get out. A smoke will help.*

"Where's the registration lists?" Barb asks.

"I have them," Ev says.

"Oh, so that's why I didn't see them. Did National send them to you?"

"The Congress front office did. It's confidential."

After setup and consultation, plan to disperse and place signs in strategic spots and post directions to registration, morning devotions, entertainment, and the side door for bus loading the next morning.

Janet says, "I'll stay here." By this time, dozens of Bahá'ís and spouses have trickled in.

Ev says, "Rod, you want to be our floater? Can you help people with their questions or directions and check setup?"

"Sure Ev." *Remember, jack of all trades and master some. Just smile and welcome folks, show them where to go.*

Log out one-hundred-dollars in petty cash for emergencies. Out front, smoking, a cab pulls up. Three middle-aged, dark-haired women exit, pleading with the cabbie. *Why are they upset and waving their arms?*

They're practically sobbing. *What's going on?*

Approach the group. Look officious with a green-ribboned badge. Find out the cab ride from the airport had run up forty-five dollars.

"Too high. Told thirty dollars," one woman says. Her shrill tone is alarming. They seem to be from Italy.

"Ciao. Don't worry ladies, let me take care of this, please. You've come far. Welcome to America. Please go in and register and enjoy the friends." Wave them inside, and one kisses my cheek.

"Grazie, Ciao Bella."

Ladies leave, and a young bellhop helps carry their luggage.

Turn on the cabbie.

"What's wrong with you? Sonofabitch! How could you charge so much?" *Can't ... control ... anger.*

Cabbie takes it, head down, explains in between verbal assaults, "Its standard fare from JFK." *Oh, you better not give excuses!*

"Standard my ass. These are poor people here!"

Hand him a fifty and a five out of obligation, not out of thanks. Spurn his proffered receipt.

He speeds off.

Fume and smoke.

Address the bellhop who's returned, "What the fuck were you doing taking money from them for?"

An hour later, grab the black-haired young man by the arm, hand him a five, and apologize twice. Confide under breath, "I'm not doing well."

Say nothing to the team.

Shudda got a receipt from the cabbie.

Smokes, coffees, raise pulse
Anger boils ice-cold blood
Judgments skewed and cruel

3.9 A SPY IN BLACK

"Why are people following Me?" *Must be on guard.*

Visit the Derby Ballroom, where eight volunteers line up behind a row of narrow tables, processing a hundred pre-registered attendees. They check IDs and hand out session credentials and passes. The large space, jammed with people ranging from age fifteen to eighty-five, assaults my ears with voices as they stand in queues or mill about.

Miss nothing. Interrupt conversations with, "Welcome to your Congress."

Middle-aged woman approaches.

"Excuse me, I see you have a green ribbon on for Coordinator. Can you tell me when the buses will be here tomorrow morning?"

"Didn't you look at your packet? It's there."

"Well, I didn't ..."

"Eight-thirty sharp. Gather at the large sign in the lobby." Point downward.

"Oh, great, thanks!"

"Yeah, okay." *Idiot can't read.*

Roam the hotel and address quizzical looks and blank faces with, "What can I help you with?" or, "Yeah?"

> *Like a god, pooh-poohed*
> *innocent inquiries as*
> *insignificant*

Thoughts strike like baseball-sized hailstones pounding tin rooftops. *Who's in the office during lunch today? Should recheck registration. How many have registered? What about new arrivals? Do the girls need me?*

Torn. As coordinators, we had solicited two dozen volunteers for various tasks. As some arrive, show them their posts.

Move to the lobby, scan, move back to Registration, scan.

Hear, "James! I haven't seen you in ten years. How are you?" And "Jacques, Chere, so glad you made it. Tell me how Montreal is ...." Dozens, caught up in hugs and smiles, jabbering and laughing. Greet the Jersey Bahá'í contingent.

Soon it's SRO in the registration room; the scene is semi-controlled bedlam, except for patient weaving lines. It confirms the original idea that most guests would arrive and register Sunday afternoon and evening, before the Congress begins Monday, to end Thursday afternoon at five.

The next phase ensures our entertainers, organized and prepared, meet the seven o'clock program start time scheduled in the massive ballroom.

Roadies set up instruments, sound systems, and mics as the audience trickles in, then mobs fill its serried rows.

The emcee starts. Claps and hoots erupt. A few team members enjoy the music and singers as best we can while scanning for issues. The audience is friendly, cooperative. *Look at those dancers in the aisles!*

Over their screams and applause, shout to Ellen, a volunteer assistant, "They're enjoying the program!"

In between sets we handle requests for schedule information, event times, and directions. Our common refrain is, "Everything's in your packet, please check there first."

After a rushed day, lie in bed by eleven-thirty with Jan. Music has just ended downstairs. Jesse's tired, sleeping on the other queen bed. Janet soon falls asleep with her little snores. Count each wheeze ticking off the minutes left to live before nuclear disaster strikes when the digits on the bedside clock blow apart at midnight.

(November 23, 1992, Monday)

The bedtable clock shows 5:12 as eyes unclose from a dream…

A white Jeep has rear-ended my white sedan. Clamber out and stumble to the Jeep. See a youth dressed in a white tuxedo lounging in the driver's spot, draped over the seat and console as if drunk. The inside of the vehicle is white. He's clutching a bouquet of black-red roses. Looks like he's the groom on his way to his own wedding…

and fade out.

…Jeans, burgundy pullover and dark cotton socks lie on the chair, socks and loafer's underneath. *All here.* Carry clump to the bathroom and shut the door. Pee, dress in a hasty dash, brush teeth, hair. Turn out light.

Twist hallway door handle.

"Clunk." *Crap. The damn hotel door is so loud! Why do they make them so loud? Will it wake them? Oh well.*

In charge of dawn prayers in forty minutes. *Quick, where's Rich? He'll say a prayer, and Sharon, I can ask her.*

The search for early risers quickens until selecting a dozen readers for prayers and readings. Check PA microphone, "What d'ya think so far?" Appoint ushers throughout the rows lined for three hundred.

At seven-thirty, with Ev, Janet, Jesse, and Barb, select breakfast food from the generous restaurant buffet. Our friends Martha and Faramarz Yazhari and their daughter Laila pick up Jesse. Once in our office, we resolve a steady stream of final registrations, credentials, questions, and hotel issues.

Ten buses, scheduled to arrive at eight-thirty, will transport guests to Jacob Javits Center.

One middle eastern woman covered head to foot in a black burka approaches. She also wears a gruff demeanor and menacing countenance. Can only discern wide black eyebrows and large, piercing black eyes in the middle of her white sclera. Can't infer her expression behind the thick black veil that covers her lower face.

"Where my passes?"

Others had directed her to Us, to Me.

She repeats, stronger and louder, "Where my passes? Where list?" *Is this woman a Bahá'í?*

Severe garb doesn't disturb first impression, but her demanding attitude grates.

"Please follow Me." Escort her into our office. Hand her off to a smiling face. Then Jan, Barb, and Ev huddle and can't find her name on our registration lists. The question is whether to provide her with passes. All registrations were to be paid for by attendees themselves.

Despite the Faith's roots in Islam, hundreds of innocent Bahá'ís in Iran are harassed, beaten, imprisoned, and killed on a regular basis. Pogroms vilify them. The Shiah government had made innumerable attempts, some successful, to search them out by finagling membership lists. One reason National told us not to share them, even locally.

Feel shaken by this woman's belligerence. *Is she spying on us?*

Pick up a light plastic chair. *Smile wide, Rodney.*

"Please follow me." Show her to outside our office, put down the chair, offer her an arm as she sits.

"Ah, I'll be... right back... with the answer." She glares.

Ev dials headquarters. She explains, conveys the woman's contact information. Ev hangs up. "They'll call right away."

Minutes later, the phone rings.

"Sheraton, Bahá'í World Congress, Evelyn here... Yes... Umm... Okay... Got it."

Ev's jotted notes and gives a thumbs up. Retrieve the mystery woman from the hall. Barbara uses her best conciliatory tone and apologizes to her for the delay as she hands daily passes to her.

"Khoda-Hafez." She about faces and leaves. This is a good sign. *There could have been a scene. I knew Barb could assuage the woman as she's adept at handling our Assembly guests. Goodbye. Insha'allah. Will she return? Are we rid of her? What if she seeks me out? Stay down.*

Watch face shows eight-forty-five. Hear growing clamor downstairs. People ask, "Where's the bus?" *Houston, we have a problem!*

Morning buses scheduled to take Monday morning attendees eleven miles from here to Javits haven't shown up. Not one. *What are we going to do? Do we call the bus companies? How do we fix this?*

More people ask. *Shit, what do we do?*

Team scrambles and Ev calls Gry's emergency cell number. *Can she help?*

156

Gry answers Ev's call. Hear Ev explain. Pause.

Ev announces, "She'll take care of it. Rod, can you tell those waiting it'll be a few more minutes?"

Turn and scamper downstairs. A crowd mills around the assigned exit.

"The buses are on their way. Be patient, they're coming!"

Fifteen minutes of silent prayers for assistance and the first one arrives to hand clapping and shouts of glee. *Thanks, Gry.*

The second and third buses queue up. Guests load and depart.

Head back to our office. The team consults.

"Which of us will attend this afternoon?"

"I'd like to go."

They turn to Janet.

"Okay Rod but take your pills before you do."

Burst into a wide grin.

"Absolutely!"

Can't repress excitement
or mollify active demons
I'm going!

3.10 SOUL STIRRING

"These are made of molasses. Are they frozen too?" as watch the two hands on my watch crawl.

Morning hours pass as if a box turtle were crossing a country road with both lanes of traffic stopped.

At twelve, as agreed, join a joyous busload of thirty-five singing and chatting registrants headed to the Congress afternoon program, focused on the life and Message of Bahá'u'lláh. *Why so jittery?*

Mirror image morning and afternoon program sessions guarantee everyone will experience it. *What will it be like with fourteen thousand Bahá'ís under one roof?*

Disembark the shuttle bus into the overwhelming hubbub of excited and singsong voices outside. The many-storied Javits concourse is a talking, hugging, exclaiming swarm of buzzing bees, friendly hornets, and adorable yellowjackets as thousands thread its seventy-five-thousand square feet. Swarms enter the great hall with expectant hearts.

Hundreds of dozens of chair rows, placed at angles, line the immense floor and face raised stages. The choir stands on risers behind.

"King of Kings and Lord of Lords...Glory...Hallelujah!" rings out in rounds, rousing emotions.

Try to encompass the indigenous costumes, styles, and diversity of skin tones but impossibile. Dozens of pink and white mums and carnations offset the huge, darkened space, broken by overhead spotlights and hanging colored banners in large terra-cotta pots dotting the floor and stages. Rows of pots of red and yellow roses add to the sensory overload of wafting smells and sounds that flood eyes, ears, and nose. *I'm touching unity. This is mind blowin'; better than any acid trip.*

Brothers and sisters in native garbs from two-hundred countries invoke admiration. Sit and face the central stage as the orchestra plays. The five-hundred member Bahá'í Choir is a sea of smiling faces from twenty-four countries with blue or dark purple gowns and orange, turquoise, or light purple scarfs flowing to their feet. They stand in rows on risers, intermingled and majestic. *United as one resounding voice.*

Good friends Martha and daughter Laila are among them. *Where are they? Too many, don't see them.* Can visualize and hear Martha lead local Sunday school students and adults in "Its Nice to be a Bahá'í" and Red Grammar's "I Think You're Wonderful."[22] We'd respond in ragtag singsong accapella unison to Martha's allegro prompts.

The sopranos, countertenors, mezzo-sopranos, tenors, contraltos, baritones, and basses in front of me merge, yet contrasts between solos and choir bring chills. The thirty-piece orchestra undulates waves of stirring themes to ears and hearts. Relish the grand atmosphere of choreographed human voices and their vibrating tones.

More chilled hairs on arms rise.

The huge choir halts at a crescendo and in a roar our audience claps as New York City Mayor David Dinkins is introduced. He strides to the podium as chatters and asides become muffled. A hush fills the cavernous space as he addresses the huge assemblage with welcoming words and praises. Jumbotron screens bring sincerity to his smiling visage, as he says, "this is November twenty-third, 1992, Bahá'í World Congress Day."

Thunderous applause and smiles as hundreds, more, stand and clap.

Hand of the Cause of God Amatu'l-Bahá Rúhíyyih Khanum, legendary Bahá'í teacher, world traveler, and widow of Shoghi Effendi, offers her welcome message to the City of the Covenant chockful of encouragement from the Universal House of Justice in her cadenced Canadian crispness. She is an icon of wise stewardship. Listen, rapt, as she recounts vignettes from the Faith's slow spread when souls on fire broke through obscurity to establish presences in far-flung regions.

Then Djembe drummers on stage pound "Bada bada dum, da, bada bada dum, dum, dum, dum, da," conga drummers too, their pitch louder, softer, louder. Our announcer calls forth country representatives and they mount the largest stage single-file to admiration and applause. African dashikis and robes, orange, blue, and pink Indian saris, eagle feathers and leather regalia, Bavarian lederhosen, striped serapes, Texan Stetsons, chaps, and boots, colors and designs rich in culture and history parade in humble pride. *What a breadth of humanity!*

Reel from the import of proceedings, *Oh, the rarified atmosphere!*

Their multitudinous skin tones, shapes, and sizes ends. A hush falls.

Dash Crofts begins a lingering solo in his unique raspy voice with the choir reinforcing him. Had met Dash and Jimmy Seals in Bob's living room after one of their area concerts. As singers and musicians, with popular oft-heard tunes, their informal chats about Bahá'í with audiences after concerts added to their cachet. *We attended so many.*

"Gathered now at the mystic hour, in the Garden of Ridván…," he sings, clear as a church bell striking noon. Visualize that mystic hour, agonize, insides cry for how Bahá'u'lláh suffered. *To tell people about God.*

More music and voices touch, sear, and penetrate. Then, inhale a deep, stertorous, male British voice, so distinct, narrating the program through booming loudspeakers. The thirty-piece orchestra melds its notes into plucked heartstrings. Strains from a dozen violins fill the cavernous hall.

He intones, "Oh, Bahá'u'lláh, what hast Thou done?"

In tears, spellbound. The question pierces sinews and bones.

"Oh Bahá'u'lláh, what hast Thou done?" *Oh, My heart!*

Cry, try, can't, choke down tears. *Rod! Stop! Decorum, please.*

Can't stop, stifle wails. A blur across watery eyes crowds out dim surroundings. *Hide!*

Cover mouth. Rise, shaky, wander aisles, cross to one side near red velvet curtains. Sit for only a few minutes before moving, moving, must keep moving. *Can't sit still.*

Stabbed by import-laden words, as loving convincing speakers issue their refrain, "Just do your part. You're not alone. Just look around."

Inner and outer vibrations continue to rack mind and limbs as the choir sings *"God Is Sufficient Unto Me." Can't do this. I'm not capable, I'm a nobody. If believing were only enough!*

Final grand reverberating oratorio to Bahá'u'lláh fills the grand hall edge to edge. Drums and horns escalate, violin strings caress crying inconsolable heart. Cover face with palms, muffle guttural cries. *Rodney. Control. Not here.*

Must keep moving. Push off from the chair, move again.

"Oh Bahá'u'lláh, what hast Thou done?"

You released the Word of God, that's what. Capable of changing a gnat into an eagle. You renewed creation with fresh energy. Drink in that energy, drink up!

The music reaches its apex, then stops as stillness settles and lights dim. Spotlights rise.

This mind-shattering session ends, yet a new spirit has taken hold.

Straddle chair, stand. Walk. Legs hum. Lower head, avert eyes, pull arms down to sides, tighten and relax fists, follow masses of noisy throngs outdoors.

Wipe your eyes.

Dazed, search for yellow bus sign, **SHERATON**.

Soul roused as mind reels
spirit climbs the topmost rail
Body spent, speech fails

3.11 BATMAN ASCENDS

"Wasn't the parade of countries amazing?"

"Did you hear Rúhíyyih <u>Kh</u>anum describe the bounties of pioneering?"

"I feel so lucky being here."

As the bus pulls away, jump up and saunter down the center aisle. "Hello! My name's Rod from New Jersey. Where you from?"

The driver says, "Can you please sit sir?" *Oh, so happy!* Lose all senses, butterflies in stomach group together and soar away....

The thirty-six revelers exchange exclamations of excited wonderment. Li Po's poem surfaces. This return is even happier than that idyllic setting out across the calm river under the warming sun.

Arrive at the Sheraton, first off, stand next to the bus's open door, shake hands as spiritually charged revelers disembark. "Enjoy your time here!"

Float indoors. Get off at seventh floor. *Which way to go? Higher... they won't find Me.*

Open Exit door, bolt stairs two at a time, past floors, pass a friend, mumble "Hi, in a rush." Reach **Emergency Exit**. Shove bar and door, step out into the blinding sunlight. *Voila!*

Manhattan skyline gleams. Its spires pointing heavenward mesmerize. *Inviting... a short flight... miles to go before I die...*

REST

Plunk down on a gray metal flue, elbows on knees, cradle head. *Keep your eyes shut.*

Circular yellow shapes roam amidst a black backdrop. *Block out that Sun! Don't show your face.*

Raise head, "Can you help Me? How can I do Thy Will?" *Unworthy.*

"Hafta leave, can't take it." Moan louder, "How beautiful are people? How unique, like the city, its majesty, the brilliance of those reaching, reflective, rebellious towers... "

Open eyes and arms, "I beg you, Peace... Please... So sorry, don't know how to help... You... Myself... "

Cradle face.

"Don't know where to go..."

Loving arms grasp and hug quaking shoulders.

Janet's wispy voice coos, "Don't worry Rod, we caught it in time."

Fears, doubts, shortfalls swell...tears rain.

She coddles shaking shoulders, heaving chest, trembling legs.

She supports my weight, leads the way out and down to our room.

She makes a call. "Pat? It's Janet. Rodney's not feeling well. Can he stay there a few days?"

Assured yes, follow her down to our room, get my clothes, then to our Congress office. She consults the team, controlled—strong. We leave Jess in the Yazhari's care.

Jan concentrates on driving to my past youthful home.

"Someone saw you running up the stairs toward the roof and told us. We took a chance and looked for you there. You're safe Rod, everything will be fine. "

Can't stop shaking. Tap foot, fingers… try to listen to radio between rapid thoughts, images… wish for silence, hate silence.

She mouths reassuring words.

Is she reassuring herself?

Lie on den couch at Mom's. At least still have vacation days the rest of this week. Down extra sleeping pills, lithium, and antipsychotics. Sleep.

Wake, watch inane TV. Words and scenes flash like fifteen-second commercials, then blur away. For lunches Mom delivers home-cooked pasta soup with spinach and chickpeas, sandwiches of cold cuts, soda, and pills. Dinners are plates of ravioli or pasta and meatballs with sauce from Dad's tasty recipe.

Late Thursday afternoon Janet and Jess arrive from the Congress.

Don't dwell on this. Dodged a bombshell.

But next one, *next one?*

Jan has made an appointment with Dr. Argueta for Tuesday.

Dr. Argueta asks, as he always does, "How are you feeling?"

"Fine, no problems."

"Okay Rodney, stick out your tongue." He scans for white bumps on it, a sign of lithium toxicity. "Stick out your arms and hold your hands out straight."

Shakiness also a sure sign. Never shake. If do, trust he'll find another medicine. Consider these episodes anomalies, aberrations, flukes.

"Rodney, two weeks have passed since you felt off-kilter. How are your thoughts?"

"Fine, doc, nothing weird. I'm ready to return to work."

"It's certain that lack of sleep, racing thoughts, and over-excitement are your triggers. Are you sure you're feeling better?"

"Yes. Feel fine, normal."

"All right then, let's keep it that way."

If shake or falter
pills summon sane behavior
For how long this time?

3.12 IN A GOOD PLACE

"Everyone else is sacrificing. What can I contribute?" The Bahá'í world, focused on renewing its spiritual vigor on the hundredth anniversary of Bahá'u'lláh's ascension, offers personal resolutions in His name. *Obligated to at least sacrifice something. Money? What?*

After recuperation and in honor of this Holy Year, 1992, troubled. *Well, could I do it?*

Buy a box of Nicoderm thirty-day patches. Start with twenty-one-milligrams on upper arm, one a day, then in phases, down to fourteen-milligrams, then seven… then none. Able to not light up. Able to not buy a pack, an impossible dream. Don't think about foul breath, not smelling like an incinerator, or blackened lungs.

Avoiding cigarettes is easier than abstaining from coffee during the annual nineteen-day fasting period in March.

Associations are difficult to erase. A smoke every morning before entering the office, on hourly breaks, sometimes before and always after eating, and as leave for the day. All bite into automatic reflexes to light up.

Instead of breaks, visit with staff and confer. Have lunch more often at Casa Lido Restaurant, Checkers Bar & Grill, or Columbus Pizza as food becomes a minor substitute. Drink more coffee. Gain weight and balloon to one-hundred-eighty-two pounds on my medium five-foot eight-inch frame. Moving my right hand to lips and puffing those thin white cylinders linger like steam rising from a boiling kettle with no knob to turn it off.

Until the heat of addiction turns down and the steam dissipates, and thoughts of smoking are harmless memories, not impulses.

Janet, wary and pleased, doesn't comment, yet 38-inch-wide pants waist have no slack.

"Yes!" Liz has just called Janet inviting us to teach a week at Green Acre in July. My honey pot, my favorite faraway place despite the world's glorious choices, as happy as Winnie the Pooh in the Hundred Acre Wood when there.

In April, eager to meet with Barb and Janet at Barb and Bob's house to plan our annual week at Green Acre Bahá'í School in rural Eliot, Maine, the Vacationland of the northeast. Love the area, its history, its climate, its people, its food, even lodgings. It's across the border from touristy Portsmouth, New Hampshire, with its eclectic mix of gift and coffee shops, ice cream parlors, and antique stores which we tour each year.

The three of us instruct the adults in two sessions on weekdays, while Bob does his own thing during his. Green Acre had invited us back each year since 1980, and although it's a working vacation, when there, glory in the company of attendees and the setting.

Janet, Barb, and I brainstorm and agree we'll highlight seven Statements by the Universal House of Justice, including 1985's *Promise of World Peace* to the Peoples of the World, and 1988's *Individual Rights and Freedoms*. Janet, the creative one, designs our curriculums and hands-on activities to present singly by topic or in tandem.

With our scripts, handouts, and activities packed, Janet drives to Eliot with Jesse and Kate occupied in the back seat. Navigate using our worn AAA TripTik along our eight-hour trip as we traverse the Turnpike onto the Garden State Parkway, Route 287 over the six-lane Tappan Zee, then 684 and 84 to the Mass Pike, onto Route 495 skirting Boston, then 95 in New Hampshire to the first exit in Maine.

Dark tall green July summer trees, so opposite of short Jersey pines, and crisp air, embrace our hearts, minds, and bodies. After unpacking we greet regulars in the hundred-year-old Inn like our many Canadian friends, including young Sasha and his wife, Adair Luciani from Connecticut, and our quiet fan, Betty Egley who has a bungalow next to the campus.

Strait-laced Ray LaBelle, Administrator, and Liz, his perky blond wife and hostess, hug us at dinner and we sit and talk about our kids, GA changes, and our classroom needs. It's both spiritual renewal and a holiday return to the campus with its historic cottages and Bahá'í Hall, where we'll present our course to fifty adults.

Thrill to GA each summer because it's disconnected from civilization's decrepit TV fare and newspapers, the office, and home demands. This green oasis on the banks of the wide Piscataqua River, where poets like Emerson and spiritualists like Dharmapala visited, releases natural cravings to commune with one's inner spirit. *Thoreau would love this spot.*

Up early, meander the grounds in the mornings. Inhale the invigorating Maine air with its fresh clean scents, and stroll the bucolic grounds lost in literary meditations like poems.

Repeat the ultimate prayer of blessing, "Blessed is the spot, and the house, and the place, and the city, and the heart...."[23]

Our daily classes are a big hit during the week, and I close our last class with my contrived version of *Jeopardy!* based on what we've presented. It consternates some and delights most. Everyone, enamored of Bob's sessions and his non-stop jokes and puns for which he's famous, loves his speaking gifts which can move minds and hearts to joy or tears, mine too.

My favorite joke is his Lottery one.

"There was a poor man who lost his job and was having trouble feeding his family. He prayed to God for help. 'Dear God, Oh please. Dear God, help me win the Lottery.' The next day he looked through the newspaper but hadn't won. He prayed harder.

164

"The next day, he still hadn't won. This time he begged and begged. Harder and harder he begged to win the Lottery, calling on God to help erase his dire circumstances. He cried and sobbed.

"After many minutes passed, the heavens opened up and a booming voice spoke.

"'GIVE ME A BREAK. BUY A TICKET.'"

The crowd always cracked up.

The talent show on the last night is the climatic event. Campus adults, youth, children, and area believers gather in rustic Bahá'í Hall. Opening acts are a hit and gain wild applause.

When my turn, off to one side Bob announces, "Ladies and gentlemen, boys and girls, I present Arnold Schwarzenegger." Stride to the front, turn facing back for a moment and put on shades, turn around and grunt, "I'll be baack." Turn aside from the crowd and their snickers and applause and smile at silliness.

Bob then says, "Let me introduce actor Kirk Douglas." Remove the shades, scrunch face into a serious pose, clench teeth, touch index finger to bearded chin, and face front. Stoic and dramatic, say, "I took my brain, and washed it under the faucet," from 1951's *The Detective Story*.

Milder applause from those who don't get the reference. One more impersonation and take my seat with pats on the back.

The show has talent too: the eight-year-old violinist, the twelve-year-old pianist, recitations of memorized prayers, magic tricks by Dave Jenkins, songs that get the crowd jumping, and clever, funny skits from the teens with their homemade props and outlandish dressups.

Then the two MC youths introduce Bob. Liz accompanies him on piano, as he belts out a song with the gestures and emotions of a Broadway Musical artist and garners yells and kudos.

But he and I, the Two Amigos, are last on the program for a reason. Each year we compose lyrics mimicking the week's happenings to the tune of *Green Acres*, a 1960s sitcom on CBS. Liz plays the vibrato music on piano as we sing with gusto and exaggerated arm movements.

> Green Acre is the place to be
> Fuun livin' that's the life for me!
> On the banks of the Piscataqua
> We like it here just like 'Abdu'l-Bahá
>
> Ray and Liz keep us in happy cheers
> Host-ing guests from very far and near
> Adults and kids go off to daily classes
> And when all done, we pat our sore _____

Applause, or hoots and laughs, accompany each verse, and at the climax, the crowd erupts. The two of us bow and thank Liz.

Next morning, we pack up, clean our rooms, make fresh beds, eat breakfast in the dining hall, and attend devotions and singing in Bahá'í Hall. Goodbyes take half an hour, not the least between the kids and friends, and off we set, our "Jersey takes on the world" volleyball game.

Sad to depart, vow we'll attend the beautiful environs of Maine's countryside and the school every year as long as we are able.

Jess is at Steinert High School with its thousand students and bustling schedules, and Kate acclimates well to Reynolds Middle School.

We don't nag either of our children and are consistent with expectations of courteous and moral behavior. College-educated, Janet merges her motherly love and teacher disciplines into one natural process. Try to emulate her faultless lead and consult her when they ask tough life questions.

On weekdays Janet relishes teaching fifth graders at Mercerville Elementary School. She loves her students and their parents. Her flamboyant principal, Gary Bender, runs the school like a beloved day camp, and even plays kickball at recesses. He's created an open, caring environment, where students and teachers feel nurtured.

In private, Janet regales me with touching or funny stories about her class of twenty-five mountain lions. She also admires and respects her co-teachers, Diane Donovan, the veteran, and young Joan Petrowski, the meticulous one. They share passion for the profession and their students. They excel as counselors, confidantes, cheerleaders, encouragers, and psychologists, promoting healthy self-esteem and a love for learning.

Don't detect any by-products of my illness on Jesse or Kate, and Jan has gone to great lengths to mitigate any impacts on them. Can only hope they haven't seen the worst.

No abnormal incidents occur in our small family during the year worthy of worry.

Earth has continued to turn, as do the people spinning on it. South Africa, despite racial and social divides, adopts a majority-rules constitution with F. W. de Klerk and Nelson Mandela receiving the Nobel Peace Prize, which they deserve. All news outlets and NPR report the World Trade Center bombing in New York City, unthinkable because it's here at home, and the dreadful scary word "terrorist" enters the lexicon of average Americans.

Indelible positive achievements occur too, like the Israeli-Palestinian Oslo accords and hope for a peaceful Middle East, a prize, once achieved, greater than any Nobel. Steps toward the creation of the European Union, a promising unity of independent states with common regulations, make progress. Although always mixed, it's encouraging when humanity makes a step ahead. Pray for when it will only be forward yet knowing a sea change in attitudes is required.

166

That's what we and billions hope for and work toward. If only we could agree on how to get there, we'd be there already.

Evenings, Janet pursues her Master's degree at Trenton State College.

One morning a pink Interoffice Envelope joins others in my In-basket. It's from Human Resources.

"What's this about." Had buried the negative possibility of going back to OTIS. Remember AM station WTTM's wake up alarm song, "Pack up your troubles in your old kit bag, and smile, smile, smile."

Yeah, if ya can.

Rip it open, pull out the ominous-looking half-slip of white paper.

10-4-93   Supervising Contract Administrator $43,955

Darn if Chuck didn't come through. Wow. This is big time.

He must have clout. As Director of Treasury Department's premier centralized/decentralized organization, he talks to the Treasurer's Office daily. OMB and Civil Service had to approve this too.

This confirmation is fast considering how government moves. Most times it's so slow that six coats of paint have to dry before hanging a picture on an office wall. First, multiple officials must agree on which wall. Then, another picks a color of paint. Then, must overcome procurement hurdles to select painters to do the job. Then still, others decide where on the wall to hang the picture, high or low, what nail to use, ad nauseam.

And the title. Perfect.

It's a rare occurrence when title matches duties since thousands of state employees work in titles that bear little semblance to the work they perform. "The salary's still ten-thousand shy but making progress for sure." More excited about the new title than the increased pay. Janet will love both.

For lunch weeks later, enter the Spanish Deli[24] on Willow Street around the corner from my office.

"Hi Ana. Could I have a plate of hot pinto beans, raw onions, and salsa? And a Pepsi, please." Eat at one of four small tables. *Delicious.*

On the way out ask, "Oh, and how about a pack of Salem one-hundreds, box." Pay. Tear off the cellophane. Lift the lid, extract one, and light up in the foyer before pushing open the door to the nippy howling wind outside.

Something I haven't done in two years.

Take a hit. *God, it tastes awful.*

The urge to toss it flutters by like the windblown trash on Willow Street.

Within a month buy packs or cartons from Smokin' Joe's tobacco shop across the Delaware River in Morrisville. Manhandle the grated Calhoun Street Bridge to get there, and it's as narrow as running a gauntlet when large F-150 pickup trucks scare one silly as they approach in the opposite lane. Fear of crashing mirrors or scraped sides is palpable.

Remember Dad driving far right, Mom saying, "Ralph, be careful," but scraping the side of our 1960 Ford Galaxy as we crossed over to Pennsylvania on our way to Washington Crossing State Park. Age twelve, Stephen ten, we were out for a Sunday drive after mass.

But Joe's cash savings are worth the risk.

"Five-fifty a pack," Joe's clerk says, versus seven dollars and change in Jersey from its higher sales tax. My vice and murderer, rather, I am committing suicide—and legal to boot.

Janet doesn't complain when she pays the credit card bills for cartons but turns up her nose and moves six feet away unless I wash up after entering the house. If don't smoke near her, the kids, inside, or around others, it's tolerated. No other Bahá'ís smoke.

So always outside, off to the side. Not sneaking, although not ashamed. Embarrassment doesn't surface, although the smell permeates hair and clothes, even the hairs and skin on hands and arms.

Bahá'ís shouldn't smoke, but it's not forbidden.

And life and death move on.

Salem's bewitched
Two years free from nicotine,
addiction's back

168

4.0 FOURTH EPISODE

4.1 CAN'T THINK STRAIGHT

"Membership votes are in, and I'm pleased to announce Janet Richards of Mercerville School as the new President of Presidents for the Hamilton Township Board of PTA's," says the outgoing President at the annual dinner. Another feather in Janet's cap, it bolsters her coveted status as a Life Member bestowed by Yardville School PTA when she presided over their PTA. She's thrilled.

"Congratulations, hon!" Downplay proud response because she doesn't like attention. She's soon bestowed State and National Life Memberships.

Janet and her fifth-grade buddy and co-teacher Diane Donovan have attended Mercerville PTA meetings and support its endeavors like the School Store and fall mums' sales with their energy and time. Jan's not only on the Audit Committee but is also an invaluable aid to the treasurer.

After soul-searching, Jan bows out as longtime Managing Editor for *Brilliant Star* national Bahá'í children's magazine. She and the Editorial Board had transitioned it to a more upbeat publication from the decades-old *Child's Way* series. She flew to Kentucky for meetings, but each time suffered air sickness. Rita Leydon, its Art Director and our Swedish friend, creative talent in her art, thinking and cooking, had sat and cared for Jan on their flights. We had visited her and husband Chris, and sons Crispin and Lars often at their Lahaska, Pennsylvania farm, complete with sheep and early model foreign cars restored in painstaking original detail by Chris and his hand-crafting business.

Before Labor Day 1994, attend an orientation session for Hamilton Township Court mediators at the Hamilton Free Public Library, a thriving community center. In 1983 Janet had helped found its all-volunteer Friends of the Library which donated monies to its operations.

Seeing the short ad in *The Times,* she suggested, "You might be interested in this, Rod."

Go, and observe Blaine Greenfield, a dynamic expert Trenton mediator, describe what's required and the program components. Sitting next to Janice DiClaudio, a Harley owner, we chat and strike a friendship.

"Janice, I'm signing up. You? We could be on the same panel."

"I'd like that." After eighteen hours of training, put on Panel K and hear cases assigned by the judge every month. Mediation unclogs municipal courts and provides resolutions without fines in most cases.

At our sessions, we listen with open minds. Janice summarizes fine points and I write up each binding agreement between the parties. Our success rate is seventy percent.

Too soon, always too soon, temperatures plummet and white frost glistens atop dormant lawn grasses. Our Jersey Indian summer has died like a senior citizen in a nursing home, dreaming of the next family visit. At least the subsequent snow and mush aren't black with dirt, smog, and soot yet.

It's early Tuesday. Park my used white Saturn in the state lot and head for the office. Try to enjoy the first smoke as bundle down Willow Street. *Why aren't I happy? I'll die of lung cancer or lose my job or Janet will lose hers.*

Stop in the Towne House for the usual coffee with cream and sugar and say "Hi" to Mary and Hank, whom Mary calls Henrietta after their intense arguments over trivial points. Leave a quarter tip for Mary. Jaywalk across West State Street and enter our building lobby by eight o'clock as both female guards' glance up.

Forego usual morning wave.

On the elevator, one of six for the fourteen-story workplace, punch **8** and whisk upwards. Use keycard to enter Administration's doors and hightail it to the office. *Don't speak to me, I won't speak to you.*

Settle in and gulp the warm joe, turn on the PC and begin drafting the multi-pronged Request for Proposals that will go out to bid. With five categories, it's a beast. In between check emails, finish a status report, look up IBM's definitions for Systems Network Architecture, SDLC, ACF/VTAM, and TCP/IP for RFP use. Check twice.

Our SCC Team is also compiling FY95 Information Technology Continuation Waiver requests from all the agencies. Everyone calls it the IT Waiver, even Purchase Bureau. IP is passe.

Questions begin by nine-thirty. "Rod, what do I tell Human Services about their deficient request for Peter Martin software? Do I return it? I already asked them twice."

"For three-hundred-ninety-nine-thousand-dollars I think we have every right to an Ownership Disclosure Form. Tell them to tell the vendor that. Have 'em fax it if necessary."

Tony leaves. Three minutes go by. Another knock.

"Rod. Lou Marino isn't returning my calls."

"Annie, I'll call him later." Lou is the pushy Human Services CIO, Chief Information Officer, and runs a tight technical ship. *But thank goodness for Annie.* She's capable, leads during absences, and she's an excellent vendor contract negotiator. She looks like your kindly grandmother and plays the good cop with her kind and sharp-witted insights.

"Bringg…" Answer the phone. It's DOT.

"Rod, what's your deadline for the Application Programming Support Waiver?" Departmental CIOs had clamored for this statewide waiver based on professional services. It encompasses discrete tasks, hours logged, and personnel assigned by IT consulting firms to projects.

PB's Enrico Savelli after tedious review had said, "Go ahead with it, Rod," and the CIOs were ecstatic. We offered a trustworthy smokescreen.

But it's a tricky one and maintain a tight leash—to the CIOs chagrin—for it could become abused, over expended, and relied upon instead of bid out at some point. They aren't keen on my follow-ups.

"Dennis, for you, same as everyone else. Remember to show milestones and estimated hours by task." Hang up. Hear a knock.

"Rod, how long do I have to put the Statewide Maintenance RFP inventory into final shape?"

Ugh, more questions. When will they stop!

"Carl, how much do we have?" Review his progress. It's substantial, which means we're on target. He's smart, methodical, a good worker. Carl had transferred in within a month of Cyndi and Lynda transferring out. He's from the Governor's office and is a whiz at MS-Access, a Godsend for listing our twelve-thousand pieces of statewide computer equipment by manufacturer's model. And Tony matches his prowess.

Need both for each of the five categories: IBM, Telex, Hitachi, Honeywell Bull, and third parties. This is a massive and complex RFP. Must estimate the MTTR meantime to repair and MTBF meantime between failure data based on scarce anecdotal evidence.

"Tired." Rest hands on the keyboard, stare at the screen of tight Mandatory Requirements. Depression settles like a cold dank blanket, upsetting natural rhythms, dampening confident spirit. *Was that the right wording? Or should I ask the techies first?*

As days progress with interruptions from door knocks or phone rings, unsure what's right. Tony, who's also manipulating MS-Access to list agency compliance details for the IT Waiver, pokes his head in.

"Rod, want to have lunch?"

"Ah, sure, I could use a break. You ready?"

"Yes."

We head across the street into the Towne House. Mary and Hank keep up a running patter of "I'm better than you," followed by, "Oh no you're not, what about that party of ten I had." They ignore new patrons' looks. Us regulars are used to it. Mary seats us at a worn booth for two.

"Tony, what do you think Labor will say when we tell them to re-justify their vendor request?"

"I think they'll balk, but they have to put it in their own words like everyone else, and not use the vendor's write-ups."

"Hmmm, right. Maybe call Rob Malone and tell him that. If you run into trouble, I'll call Cecil." We've both seen agencies copy vendor's blurbs verbatim, a no-no. The whole trick to successful continuation procurements year after year is being able to rephrase tired overused justifications in new and compelling ways.

Anthony Gibbons, a gentleman, is thoughtful, not rash, both street and business smart, uses impeccable posture, rises when approached, and is always in a pressed suit, white shirt, and tie. *I like it when we go to lunch and just chat.*

Tony slides over a small blue paperback, rectangular, about thirty pages. He explains it's his first book of poetry and personal thoughts, almost spiritual philosophy, *A New Me in the New Millennium.* The author name is Shawn Dove.

"My pseudonym." Proffering it is a sign of trust, a friendship gesture, is a significant issue.

"Tony, thank you. This is special. I appreciate the confidence and applaud your bravery."

He smiles. We chat, then finish up and leave twenty percent for Mary.

Back at my desk, physical catastrophes play out like the shower scene in *Psycho,* each stab plunging deeper into stronger fears. *What if I mess up and get fired? What if we're driving somewhere and someone smashes into us head-on? What if Janet has a heart attack? What if the house burns down? What if, what if, what if....*

By two o'clock can't enjoy a sixth smoke. Hot breaths shoot forth, turn to clouds of cool mist, and dissipate in the cutting wind as contemplate life's fragility.

Next few days…a palpable downturn.

"Damn meds. Make me feel like a tree stump." Dump lunch pills into the garbage can instead of taking them later when miss targeted times. Smoking distracts and deepens dark disposition.

Down mood improves. Normal thoughts return, then worsen. Wild thoughts intrude, settle down, spike upward. *Losing control.*

Temperaments, attitudes, actions sporadic. *How can I work?*

Irrepressible jumpiness turns to criticism. Staff skirts my approach.

Once home, we argue, even curse—something not done—and never in front of Jesse and Kate. Both of us stop before getting rabid, especially if raising voices in angry outbursts. Then, stony silence from Jan, with only perfunctory dialogue until I cough up an apology.

But sharp words cut like machetes, and their slashes do not go dismissed.

Sunday morning arrives overcast and shrouded.

Last night's snow blankets the lawns and roofs and is three inches thick, but roads and sidewalks just wet. We sit in our living room, Jan on the couch, in her woolen pajamas, me in my thick white terrycloth robe and cobalt slippers on the love seat across from her. Kids read or play in their rooms. Janet scans her requisite Sunday *New York Times.* The local *Times* funnies hold little interest for me.

"It's toasty," Jan says.

Too warm. What the hell is Doonesbury trying to say?

Aware Janet's speaking, but can't focus.

"You don't know what you're talking about!" Stomach and chest bubble and roast. *Can't control this!* Throw funnies in the air, rise and cross room, rip open front door, push against storm door, step outside.

"Thunk!" Stomp down front steps and path, the driveway, out to the sidewalk. *Which way? Gottagetouttahere. How can she sit there? Can't she see the troubles ahead?*

She appears in the doorway.

"Rod ... Rod! Where are you going?"

Stop at the sidewalk.

"None of your business!" Storm, storm up the street. Thirty-five-degree air surrounds thrumming on-fire body.

"Gotta wipe this sweat!" Smear dripping hands on the robe, clench sides, plod down the street, turn the corner, continue raging around the block, onto Route 524.

"Where're the cars?" No traffic encumbers the otherwise busy road. No Catholics enter or leave St. Vincent DePaul's Church down the block. Spot a space under a big bush with green and brown leaves, a cubbyhole next to the wet sidewalk. *Gotta sit.*

Plop down in the March snow. Robe flops open. *Who does she think she is? She's on top of me like a waterfall, and I don't breathe underwater for Chrissake!*

Cross legs. "What the fuck do you want from Me?"

Fume as a few vehicles pass. *I don't care what you're lookin' at.*

A black and white Crown Vic sidles up to the curb, no flashers.

Oh, Hamilton Police. Who called them? Can't be here for Me...

Oh.... Shut your mouth. Don't say a word.

Settle hands on knees.

Two officers climb out and one asks, "Hey, how are you?" Both appear friendly. The younger one approaches with caution, blue-clad arm out-stretched, offers his left hand. His right, *near his holster.*

"Why don't we go for a ride. We'll have you feeling better in no time."

Don't look into his eyes. Don't say a thing, can't hold it against Me.

Rise to full five-foot eight-inch height with honor. Ramble to the car, duck into the tight back seat.

"Thud."

Not ill, not. I'm fine.

They climb into the black interior. An officer turns, faces me through the wire screen, opens his mouth and moves his tongue.

Can't hear him.

Quiet! Let Me think.
A hot maelstrom churns inside
as emotions burn

173

4.2 MORE DAYS WITHOUT DATES

Stop. "We're here." The EMT opens both doors and jumps down.

Spied white spotty cloud chunks in shadow in an indigo sky through the rear glass as we passed thousands of feet below them. Eye the EMT set aside his pocket-sized manual, which he's thumbed through and studied as we drove.

Two men in lab coats tug my gurney out the rear of the red-lettered ambulance. There's a large two-story orange brick building before us, with a concrete path to its double doors. One lab coat undoes wrists, waist, and leg straps. Able to turn, stand up. Catch the low-key **HAMPTON HOUSE** sign off to the right. Acres of rolling grassy knolls dotted with mature pines and long-stringy weeping willows greet us. *Will this be another zoo with outlandish zombies?*

Staff guides arm and body inside to a well-kept office area.

Once admitted, escorted to a dull, wallpapered examination room.

"Have a seat." A doctor enters and injects right arm with Haldol, followed by Thorazine. At least that's what he says. Senses dull, mind calms, and body feels numb, like gums and lips shot full of Novocain at the dentist's office. Shown to a green-painted room with two single beds, a nightstand, two chairs, and a bathroom with a green-tiled shower stall.

Collapse. Sleep.

Begin the accustomed routine. Stagger into line four times daily at the dispensary, behind either stiff-legged or erratic males and females with droopy looks, each in jeans. Mumble name, nurse eyeballs wristband, offers a white paper cup the size of a shot glass with two white horse pills and one blue capsule in it. Hands over a bigger Dixie cup with water from a yellow plastic pitcher.

She watches as swallow in front of her. *Don't want problems. Do as told. Need a smoke!*

Shuffle and scrape the main floor on vinyl tiles. *Why can't I focus?*

Random, shooting, curious thoughts curl, expand, and twist perceptions of this fearful and familiar locked-down environment with aides, group TV/activity room, and modern cafeteria. Any spirit and energy once possessed peels away like once tenacious fall leaves billowing from their wind-torn, unprotected branches.

As mental cumulus clouds lift after a week of mindless days, told to attend mandatory group therapy sessions at ten o'clock each morning. Meet fellow inmates in a large, gray-walled room with slim windows.

Their pasty-gray, frowning faces look like morose clowns with reverse smiles under a big top as eighteen of us seat ourselves on black plastic chairs with chrome legs. Schizoids, bipolars, and psychotics are semi-

174

alert, the rest dower. A few adolescent females lounge with legs curled under sweat-panted bodies.

The ringmaster, Doctor Armbruster, sits on one side in the circle. Six-foot tall, trimmed black hair, straight nose, he resembles a young Rock Hudson. Try to stay cool and join the depressing discussion, preoccupied. *What am I doing here?*

Can't look into their woebegone eyes. Can't listen, not listening, only hear disjointed phrases.

Rock Hudson speaks and asks questions in soft tones. Inmates respond with tales of troubles, self-recriminations. *What's this nonsense? Get to the point for Chrissake! Gotta get outta here.*

Stand up. Rock commands, "Rodney please sit down." *Humph!*

Cindy repeats her tale of misery from the day before.

"She has no idea! We're all stuck here. Forget the outside."

Rock Hudson stares with grim lips. We're only supposed to speak after raising our hands.

A teenager with circles under his eyes and a lime green streak in his hair says, "I need to get home."

Shout, "We all do, num nuts!" *Don't care about their feelings. What about mine? Is Rock Hudson glaring at me?*

A kid named Jimmy gripes he has no money. Spit out, "That's hogwash. Work for it." Ruffled Doc tries to keep cool and continues.

"We're going to be patient and listen with respect…"

"What're you gonna do if I don't?"

In a loud, deep voice Rock Hudson says, "Rodney, you need to leave **now**. Come back to group tomorrow."

Rise, stride out, slam metal and glass door.

"You have to act better in group," whispers an orderly in the hall. Survey him, still pissed. *Gotta have cigarettes, Gottagetaway. What do I hafta do? Be the Prince on his white stallion saving the day?*

Inch up to a girl with long stringy brown hair who wears bellbottoms, and a mottled pale green blouse,

"When you goin' home?"

"Well, my doctor told me one week if I reach the third privilege level."

"Privilege level? What's that?"

"They probably told you. Maybe it slipped your mind?" *She's kind. Slipped My Mind?*

"Good behavior and taking your meds daily earn points. At level two, they let you stroll the grounds outside. At level three you go home."

Ah, that's it. Maybe I can fool 'em. I can just act nice, they'll let me smoke, then leave. Or I can escape. Follow her out.

Later, plead to whoever will listen, "I'll be better, I promise."

Three days later, grateful, approved to smoke outside after meals. *Oh yeah!*

Strict fifteen-minute break times mean surveilling the clock like a cat watches a lost mouse so as not to miss the smokers' call. There's always a queue of itchy, pathetic nicotine addicts lined up at the sliding door.

It's a hemmed-in, grassy area surrounded by the single-story brick building, wings on two-sides, and a six-foot-tall gray wooden fence without ledges in between. A sliding door from the main lounge is the only egress and regress. We're packed in, SRO, cramped into the boxlike pen like cattle in a slaughterhouse. *Why no barbwire on the fence? Could I climb over it? Bet I could.*

A lone sapling stands in the middle of the tight square, branches jut high enough to shelter under from the cold drizzle. Stoop under, hold trunk, as icy-water drips and pierces exposed skin like pointed daggers. Wait for the orderly to flick of his lighter. *C'mon, get to it.*

Push the back of the person in front as we crowd in, wait turn, toke on the flame and inhale. It's warm, a thick spring mist that smells like crushed pine needles to starved lungs that haven't breathed nature's wonders since winter set in. Once in the pen, only time for two.

On visits at night, Janet brings coveted Salems, clean underwear, and bags up dirty wash. Everyone here lives in jeans and cotton tops.

"How're the kids?"

"They're at my mother's."

Share snippets about others here. *Oh, I'm so much better than them.*

"Rod, please don't curse." She studies and listens, interjects little.

"How're things at the office?"

"Anne's taking care of things. She says to just get better. And I've spoken with Joann, who's handling your days off, and that's fine too."

"Uh, thanks." Joann, Chuck's executive secretary, is capable, reserved, and discreet.

"Listen to the doctors, they know what's best, okay? And take your medicines. You're here to rest."

Hear her words, but the impulse to escape is formidable. Weigh options. *The opportunity will be clear.*

"Ah, yes, I will."

Like a chained prisoner on a Georgia road gang, shuffle around the hallways. Avoid any eyes looking at me. Respond in grunts. Stay in bed for hours with its rubber pad, green sheets, and green pillowcase. The mattress sags.

Lead weights and chains lighten from neck, shoulders, arms, and feet.

Wake at dawn. No one else up. Plop at the oak table in the common lounge area, fill spaces on Mandela designed graph paper with colored pencils. Get up, sprawl on a couch, stare at the dull walls and the few placid pictures of bucolic farms. Follow the big overhead clock overhead, "Tick, tock, tick, tock..." until its long black hands move as if in pain, and slow, until showing exactly seven.

176

Ask orderly behind chest-high counter, "When's the coffee gonna be ready?" It's always lukewarm. Tired of planning elaborate escapes, they're lukewarm too.

At nine join arts and crafts sessions in the west wing with a handful of others. Paint a coarse white clay pot with a green glaze that turns black as soon as the brush touches it.

They say, "It'll be fired in our kilns." *I'd like to fire you.*

Each day ask, "Can I get my pot? Is it done?" A week of waiting and inquiring, later shown shelf with other clay creations. At first, don't recognize its bright emerald-color with slight yellowish highlights. The planter looks like bamboo on the outside, eight inches in diameter, six inches high. *Love it. I made that!*

But not able to fondle it, admire it. *Damn, why can't I have it?*

Earn privileges, share meals with Janet in the airy, light-filled, modern gleaming cafeteria, its blonde pine tabletops, open steel-beamed ceiling, remind me of IKEA's at Plymouth Meeting Mall.

"How are the kids?"

"They're fine Rod, I told them you're away for work."

"How're you?"

"I just want you to get well."

A veneer of civility blankets our verbal exchanges. Look forward to visits like a condemned inmate on death row. *One day, freedom!*

The second privilege level gained when allowed outside the brick prison onto the mounded grassy grounds. Enjoy an unsupervised stroll. Circumambulate the compound. Find a spot under tall pine with high branches. Lay body on the cool grass, as dormant mind stares heavenward.

"Ah, human again." *Oh, the Sun, to feel earth through My fingers, to bask under this pine and inhale its heady scent. All Mine. To soar in the wind, the glorious free-blowing wind, the breath of God moving the branches as its lists. Hafta get better. Hafta show I'm improving.*

Return after an hour to the tight security. A downer, a snake pit of sullen-looking faces, no enthusiasm, no inner lights. *I want outta here.*

Two more weeks pass in tall slithering weeds of gradual recovery, then discharged.

Janet arrives, drive on county two-lane roads in near silence. Arrive home, rush in, place the planter in the bathroom. It's a treasure, shiny with glaze, a perfect-sized pot for the shelf it's on.

Settle in bed for R&R. Janet caters like a nurse in a hospital ward of recovering heart attack victims. Over the next week, she encourages some yard work, and we attend a Nineteen-day Feast. No friends or family ask for details, and true to form, move past it as if talking about it would resurrect the episode full blast.

When had left Hampton House and they handed over the green planter, exclaimed, "O frabjous day!"

Resolve to swim through that mucky pea soup of depressed feelings, keep emotions steady, and not swing downriver again over roaring rapids into a cauldron of stirred up desires for Kingship of the world. When seeing that ceramic pot and its philodendron, peace reigns. Feel pride at the shelf-worthy container and healthy plant.

No images of its once quarantined source intrude. No sense bemoaning the return of mania this time. Only hope is that higher doses of Carbamazepine, instead of Tegretol, and extra milligrams of daily Geodon do their jobs and balance off-kilter brain chemistry.

It's a tightwire act, and I'm not the Great Wallenda or even part of the talented family. Too little medication and will spin away to the north side of China. Too many racing and foreign-sounding thoughts and will slide to the barren South Pole and sullen isolated depression.

Pills should produce stability.

They better.

Janet can only take so much.

Baselines hard to find
Returns to rehab common
for iffy patients

Drenched in brain chems,
normal balance tenuous
Normalcy?
For whom?

Return to Administration and submerge mind and talent into perfecting the FY95 IT Waiver and other procurements by working overtime until caught up. Delegate commands in sharp words and decisive pronouncements day after day to cut through red tape objections.

Receive a pink interoffice envelope from HR. *That's curious.*

The half-slip reads as usual, but with an addition.

4-28-94   Permanent Appointment $56,261

Excellent. Passed the probation period.

Prior education of forty-four college credits, Certified Public Manager certification and other training, and expert experience has paid off. If the economy keeps chugging, Supervising Contract Administrator will stick. *Oh, and if Chuck keeps chugging and sticking too.*

This title is a perfect match. Although a soupy morass with its over two thousand job titles, thank God Civil Service has this one on its books.

Once home burst into the kitchen, "Jan, come see what I got."

"I hope it's something good."

"My salary's back to where it was. It took two years but look."

Pass her the slip.

"The money's great. A permanent appointment to what?" Explain.

"That's good news, Rod. You'll have to thank Chuck."

"Oh, first thing tomorrow."

Saturday morning vacuum Kate's room while she's at a sleepover at her friend Marci's with other girls. Notice Whiskers, curled under her bed, sleeps, but she hates the vacuum and skedaddles when it's nearby.

Turn it off. Inch closer. Poke. Again. She doesn't stir.

"Jan? Better come here."

She enters. Tell her the news.

"Aww. Well, we've had her sixteen years. That's a shame. It will devastate Kate. She loved Whiskers. I'll miss her too."

"So will I, especially when she was next to me in bed."

We all loved our mild-mannered, cuddly calico house cat.

Wrap her in a paper grocery bag and find a spot between two maples and bury her still curled up.

Kate sobs.

Rehab works
Good news re job, but loved pet dies
Which is next,
good or not?

4.3 FOSTERING DIVINE EDUCATION

"Thanks!" "We love you!" "And the food!" We share claps of praise for Ardeshir and Pouran Dean in their expansive sunken living room before Bahá'í Sunday School ends for summer break. Our mixture of forty-five parents, children, and adults are indeed grateful for their hospitality.

Also, on behalf of the Assembly, it's announced the school will be named after Bill and Ruth Foster, an older biracial couple we met in 1973 who lived in Princeton University housing. Bill worked as an engineer there and we all loved him.

Ruth, Caucasian, who doesn't mince words and stays homebound by severe eczema, raised their three children and supported Bill's endeavors. A down-to-earth black man from Chicago, he had pioneered to Liberia in the early 1950s and established the first Bahá'í community. He instilled in our young and energetic Hamilton troop a love for memorizing Bahá'í texts, instead of spouting imprecise truths. Having met and worked for the Guardian, Shoghi Effendi, he revered his weighty epistles and book *God Passes By* and promoted it and others in early nighttime classes around the state. His older experience doubly beneficial since there are no Bahá'í clergy who run affairs or pontificate Bahá'í truths.

Bahá'u'lláh's principle of the independent investigation of truth means each individual dictates their own path of search and discovery.

In the 1970s and 1980s had accompanied Bill to his classes like those at Al and Dorothy Weiss's in Plainfield thirty miles up north, Betty Ann and Paul Turko's, an interracial couple, in Lakewood down south, and even the Hurdlow's in Willingboro, besides ours in Hamilton. During the six-month oil embargo of 1973 and 1974, Bill had carried five-gallon cans of gasoline in the rear of his used Buick station wagon to ensure he wouldn't run out of gas. In winter, the windows were partly rolled down.

One time I asked Bill about white people's prejudice towards him.

He wiped his forehead with an ever-ready handkerchief and drawled, "It's like this.

"When I'm in a store buying something at the counter, and the clerk throws a nasty look or comment my way, I don't know if they're a good person havin' a bad day or a racist. So, I give 'em the benefit of the doubt, ignore it, complete my purchase, and walk away. It hurts less to think they didn't mean what they said."

Exhorted to eradicate racism, classism, sexism, and religious prejudice, I'd seen bad examples from some people I had met and in the news. As a Catholic white kid growing up in a mixed city of ethnic groups, both poor and middle-class, had to fit in to survive rough neighborhoods, which meant we couldn't avoid each other but better not taking sides. Besides, confrontation didn't work—a knife fight with an older Spanish youth over a game of pool proved that.

Lucky for me, it was a draw.

There was tension between blacks and whites. Most boys carried penknives, and we knew it. A stiletto was serious. We practiced by playing games of mumblety-peg in the dirt.

In Trenton in the fifties and early sixties, it was wise to skirt kids who were different, yet there was an easy camaraderie on school playgrounds and basketball courts, or at the Boy's Club and CYO centers. But at Catholic mass every weekday morning and Sunday, and in parish schools, only local Spanish families and whites attended.

No one socialized outside the color of their skin.

The N-word or C-word invoked chest-pounding or worse, so did not hurl epitaphs to strangers unless among friends. The F word and its variations was used so often it held little meaning. Along with the middle finger, it never raised eyebrows. Unless you added "mother."

One thing—never heard Mom curse once.

Studying their inspirational and morality charged writings when first encountering Bahá'ís when nineteen and searching, knew that holding on to prejudice was antithetical to being one. Soon had to suppress the automatic response to stream curse words in mixed company. That meant not invoking Christ's first or last name either, so common no one considered it vulgar. Colloquial versions were as customary as hats and scarves on women's and girl's heads at Sunday mass.

Had thought then, "Let words roll off and don't get defensive." Yet thin skin abounded. No one turned the other cheek in confrontations.

Once married though, became frustrated with Janet's even minor corrections. She became just as frustrated with my impatience and inexcusable habit of blurting thoughts aloud, or mild curses.

"Rod, will you let me finish?" She hated it when her father could never wait for anything or anyone when he was in a hurry, and he was always in a hurry. It was too easy to jump to wrong-headed conclusions. What I thought was obvious wasn't always so, and Janet proved it many times.

To keep my mouth shut and withhold black or white judgment was an elusive virtue in a world of gray when both sides believed they, and only they, were in the right.

Prejudice—a knife
that stabs two hearts with hatred
Love alone heals wounds

How does she stand it?
Faults outnumber virtues
Love alone overlooks them

4.4 EUROPEAN INTERLUDE

"Here are the top twenty of this year's class," beams the principal.

We're proud and glowing as Jesse sits onstage with the Steinert seniors on Awards Night in the auditorium. He also receives acknowledgments from the National Honor Society and Peer Leadership.

Then all see and hear, "The Bahá'í Unity Award for sharing a positive and encouraging attitude, and a one-hundred-dollar check, go to Jesse Richards." During other handouts, Scott Mcnear has announced it, beaming, from the podium. We clap too, with broad smiles. The Assembly has given awards to seniors at the high schools for years for their go-lucky spirits and school-life contributions.

Jess handles the kudos with aplomb, and neither preens nor brags.

A week later Jan's mom exclaims, "Oh Janet, how grand he looks in cap and gown!" Mom and Dad next to us in the football field stands concur. Hundreds of other relatives and friends clap, whoop, and name-call their sons and daughters. As the mob of graduates tosses their green or white caps, we smirk and snap photos.

Jesse had earned excellent SAT scores. He's well-prepped for college, wanting to go, and we've always expected he will, Kate too. The plan is to use savings, parts of our salaries, and EE savings bonds taken out of my payroll check to ensure both have no roadblocks.

"Great grades, Kate!" are also in order as she moves from Reynold's Middle School to Steinert High. She's a sweetheart and her network of cool-headed friends admire and like her.

We had agreed early on that we would help them but not do it for them. We're pleased when Jesse, rehired for the summer at McDonald's on the Drive-Thru crew, is upbeat and greets visitors with extra spunk.

"Do you believe it!?"

"We're going," says Uncle Buddy and Aunt Hilda. So do Uncle Tony and Aunt Frances. Kids are also welcome. Soon more make plans to come.

To the family's delight, stepbrother Ralph Junior, thirty-one, had announced his engagement and a June wedding date in Sweden. He and his attractive Swedish fiancé Yvonne had invited family to attend, and everyone is abuzz with excitement for a memorable trip to Europe.

Ralph, fourteen years younger than me, had met Yvonne while both worked at a Swedish bank on Park Avenue in Manhattan. They'll be married outside Sweden's cultural, media, political, and economic center. *Stockholm!*

Ask and Jan says, "You can go. But stay with your family and remember to take your pills." *Yea!*

Kiss her with a firm "Thanks, Hon!" and unbridled anticipation. She's resigned to stay home with Jesse and Kate and not attempt the eight-hour flight and everything entailed. Within a few weeks, twenty of us will go.

On the day of departure, our entourage meets at Mom's to board a livery van to Newark International Airport. We hobnob as we carry luggage out to the coach vehicle and find seats.

Uncle Buddy, in his gregarious manner, asks, "Rodney, are you excited to be going?"

"Pretty thrilled! I'm happy for Ralph. I thought Chrissy would be the one, but Yvonne must be special."

"That's how it is, isn't it? Somehow the one is the one." Think of Aunt Hilda and their three kids, Charlotte, Mark, and Jimmy, and how well they mesh. The visits to their house in rural Blawenburg on holidays and growing up were playful, happy times, away from Trenton's constricted city streets and among the open arms of the pastoral Sourland Mountains.

When first married, Jan and my three-room apartment in the Borough of Hopewell just four miles from Blawenburg was our garden palace, complete with an outdoor twelve-foot-long grape arbor over a picnic bench. On warm summer nights we hosted casual Bahá'í introductory chats called firesides for those interested.

The twenty-four of us in the van jabber and pulsate with unbridled excitement, not only as our first trip as a group but for Ralph and Yvonne's one-of-a-kind wedding.

From Newark, we fly nonstop and touchdown with enthusiastic cheers at Arlanda International Airport that welcome us to June's late daylight and a stimulating new vista. Losing seven-plus hours slows down no one.

"Made it! Look how gorgeous it is!"

Ralph has arranged a transport bus, and our goal is the village of Saltsjöbaden on the beautiful and wind-blown waters of the Baltic Sea coast. We travel twenty-five kilometers southeast to the quaint resort town and chatter and observe the green and wheatgrass rolling countryside. The sheer summer clime, refreshing air, clear skies, dense greenery, smiling people, and small dwellings with painted doors in vibrant colors, seem more than warm and inviting.

Contemplate the joys of spiritual and physical matrimony. Happy for the soon-to-be bride and groom and their upcoming adventure. Remember the sun-filled noon outdoors on the Jersey side of Washington Crossing State Park where Jan and I married ourselves according to Bahá'í and civil laws.

At first sight of her had said, "Wow, hon, stunning."

Dazzled by her puffy-sleeved white dress with sprinkled purple violets, she had sewn herself, trembled with expectation. Her flowing red hair glistened in the same sunlight streaming through the tall trees, alluring. Electricity crackled between us, waiting to say our vows.

In sandals, thin white loose slacks, white billowing low-cut shirt, and a new beard, rubbed palms together waiting for the next moments.

Forty friends and family, some gatecrashers, watched.

We had chosen Greene Grove as our spot in the woods, and readings, with care. First, Barb read "Love possesses not, nor would it be possessed; For love is sufficient unto love," from Kahlil Gibran's *The Prophet.*[25] Mister Baker, in a suit and tie to add an official air for conservative relatives, then read a Marriage Prayer by 'Abdu'l-Bahá. "Wherefore, wed Thou in the heaven of Thy mercy these two birds of the nest of Thy love...."

It quoted the *Qur'án* also, "He hath let loose the two seas, that they may meet each other; between them is a barrier which they overpass not...."[26]

Heard that and thought, together, one, apart, two, on the sea of life, our children will be pearls between us. A few more readings and we sealed our union with our own words, then spoken vows to each other, said separately.

184

"We will all, verily, abide by the Will of God[27]."

Our unity sealed and cemented itself with one tender kiss.

The moment of silence broke with claps and kudos. During the cake-cutting ritual and afterward we socialized in a gay atmosphere as Bob took photos, his first professional job as a wedding photographer.

Except Dad wasn't there. His father Charles had passed the night before. A weird coincidence, not lost on us. It was like Tricia Nixon's elaborate televised wedding ceremony taking place in the White House Rose Garden under rainy skies, as we made the rounds to tables and friends.

We scooted to Beach Haven on the Jersey shore in Jan's parent's VW bug, my 1963 VW faded red van broken down with a kaput alternator the night before. On our way there, we visited the six-story-tall Lucy the Elephant built in 1881 and toured inside it. At our beachfront motel a complimentary bottle of cheap champagne in a prominent red plastic bucket awash in ice sat next to our low bed as we opened the door.

We both laughed. "Won't be needing that."

We soon proceeded to our giggling nuptial enjoyments.

Ice was the farthest thing from our minds and bodies.

She, older, takes a chance on me
Love hides futures
of what love becomes

In our tiny dorm rooms across the lane from the huge Swedish A-frame lounge and conference center attached to the brick resort chalet, we Americans unpack. We regather for dinner, and some remain late and kibitz while old-timers depart early to bed for the next day's festivities.

On-time, we ride in a van and arrive the next morning in suits and dresses at the four-hundred-year-old brick and stone church and disembark.

"Here they are!" With fifty friends and family on both sides, watch the distinguished couple drive up to the weathered stone and brick house of worship in an open-topped, sienna-colored, 1925 Rolls-Royce Phantom with wide, white-walled tires and its elegant, elongated frontend chauffeured by Yvonne's brother, Ronnie.

The traditional Swedish-Christian ceremony on high wooden platforms inside its dim interior doesn't dawdle like long Catholic weddings. Fetching blonde-haired Yvonne in white, and handsome black-haired Ralph in a gray tuxedo, face the minister in his plain black cassock as he addresses them before the high age-less altar. Simple and dignified, they exchange vows then encircle necks with a quick, passionate kiss.

"Congratulations! Stay this happy!" and other advice, along with tossed rice, waves, and big grins, swamp them as the exit. They drive off with huge grins, waving to us well-wishers.

Our bubbly talkative group boards the same reserved coach and travels to the reception at the historic 1893 Grand Hotel in Saltsjöbaden.

185

The large luxury hotel stretches and looms over a picturesque marina packed with the stark white masts of sailboats, a few forty feet long. Their swaying masts contrast with the hotel's solid three-story white walls and black-topped turrets. After sampling casual hors d'oeuvres on the grass at the marina's edge, a server escorts us to the long dining room. We sit and face each other at a twenty-four-foot-long oak table in a constant babble as we dig into a sumptuous native dinner-feast.

Congratulatory wine and champagne toasts follow, one in Swedish by our host, Mister Bergstrom, Yvonne's father. His words are kind to us as he begins, "Dear friends from America...." All return the heartfelt toast as I drink water to not compromise Bahá'í law.

The next day at noon our group gathers at the train station for a trip to Stockholm's Slussen station 18.5 kilometers away. The ancient city's packed tiny shoppes along narrow cobblestone streets hold stimulating and attractive handmade jewelry and small collectibles gobbled up as mementos. We stroll its sundry stone-carved bridges over the surrounding endless waterways of bays and blue-green rivers and note the close two-story buildings with peaked roofs. It's old charm features add to our startling pleasures of history-laden Europe.

We return by train to the conference center, with dining, kitchen, and large A-frame lounge prepped for our comfort, as we tell embarrassing family stories and laugh at each other's past escapades over lamb dinner.

Uncle Buddy says, "One evening Pat called me, frantic. 'Rodney's gone; we can't find him.

"I hopped into my car and drove up and down Princeton's streets. I found four-year-old Rodney walking six blocks away on Nassau Street in front of Saint Paul's Catholic Church. But in 1954 there were no undue alarms for one's safety, except for Pat's."

That would be a pattern of behavior until age nineteen.

Before six the next morning, reconnoiter our housing unit and find a cabinet with some keys hanging on hooks. Take a set and start up a white van parked outside. Go searching for coffee.

After twenty minutes on the highway, stumble upon a small convenience store twelve miles outside our tiny resort village. "Great."

Stop and buy coffee for a few dollars. Regain the highway and see only a few vehicles ramble atop the two-lane yellowish asphalt roads. Admire the raw natural beauty of the rural area with mild sloping hills and green or wheat-grass stalks atop flush low, rolling fields as head back. *Love this. The peaceful nature of nature, hiding in Man.*

Pull the van into the same spot. Place the keys back in the cabinet. Enter the room and lie on the bed. *What a glorious place. Should I stay?*

At breakfast, adults chat and sip coffee and tea, share stories, and laugh. Younger cousins, nieces, and nephews listen or absorb themselves in Game Boys while we remark on the stunning benefits of Sweden.

No one accosts me about the missing van and overhear no discussion of its absent status. In between traditional Swedish meals we carouse, play, chat, and laugh at Uncle Buddy's and other's jokes. That night we visit Yvonne's parents' home first, then her brother and sisters. They are lovely and happy to meet us and quiz us about America. At Ronnie's, he pops in a video of his yellow early model Camaro in a clandestine midnight drag race on a Swedish highway and we watch enraptured along with the secret cheering crowds shining their flashlights while he grins.

Wake at dawn. *Our last day. Gotta do something.*

Enamored by the breathtaking ambiance of this olde monarchy and democracy combined. *Gotta explore, I only have a little time left here.*

Try to ride out again, but the key cabinet is empty. *Shucks.*

Once outdoors, it's easy to sense that nature here is a vibrant character in a novel of dramatic beauty. Sweden's rich history, vast natural charm, and a tableau of ancient loveliness overwhelm my detached façade.

Skin… tingles. *These grounds are exquisite.*

It's not the slight chill in the air or the breeze from the winds that prick.

Pace the shoreline, climb on top ten-foot-high boulders thrusting up at the choppy edge of the murky, choppy Baltic Sea. Stand, stare out across to the far shore. *At one with God and Mother Earth.*

"Should I cross to that island rock in the middle?" No boat in sight, so let it pass. Sit on my rough-hewn boulder. It offers solid curves to caress, crevices to trace with fingertips, and mounds of moss to cup with roaming palms. It has weight and gravitas. Its ancient strength migrates up arms, shoulders, neck, and head.

"Who am I? Can anyone say?" Look down, "Who am I to ask?"

Four hours later, as we gather to depart, we each convey our unfettered praises for Yvonne's family and their kindnesses. Their old-world charm and country's history have merged with the new and changing one ahead for Ralph and Yvonne, holding much promise.

And offspring to love, if lucky.

A marriage of souls
made in heaven on earth,
matched by twin hearts
in love

"So, Jess, excited?"

"This should be great!"

In fall 1995, we move Jesse and his key belongings into his shared dorm two-person room at Drew University.

"Jess, be careful with your laptop, now." We had chosen a Toshiba to satisfy his unbounded curiosity and meet the school requirement.

A small liberal arts college in the town of Madison up north, the town population is fifteen thousand. The school offers personal attention through assigned advisors. He is excited and ready to excel.

We greet his sociable, stocky roommate who helps us lug items from Jan's dark blue Pontiac TransSport to their first-floor room. Thanks to a healthy one-third scholarship, and Jesse's attraction, the choice was easier.

Stroll the campus after he's all settled.

"Busy around here today!" The hubbub and diverse friendly students, well-maintained buildings, campus store, sheltering maples and oaks, and even roaming bands of black squirrels, speak well of its well-regarded President, Tom Kean. Everything about the school is admirable, mirroring Kean's personable, well-educated, and politically astute qualities.

Tell Jess and Jan, "I shook hands with him once in 1984 when he was Governor. Nice guy. We had booming years under him."

We leave excited for his prospects.

Back home, at Steinert, Key Club members vote in Kate as Secretary, and after classes, she scores the first goal of the season in field hockey, earning high praise from teammates and claps of glee from parent fans. Work hours don't allow me to watch her play, but Jan's there often after her classes and bus duties end at Mercerville School.

Kate continues to gather friends around her pleasant, outgoing personality.

Jesse chooses Art as his Major, not a surprise. Soon the Department head takes him up on his offer to reformulate and redo its web pages. He designs the opening page as a palette, each glob of paint color a link to other pages.

Brother marries well
Son starts college, daughter shines
Is this perfect yet?

Roll through a red **S T O P** sign leaving our development for the office one morning and earn a ticket from a no-nonsense Hamilton cop. Hadn't seen his patrol car hiding across the road on PSE&G's right of way.

Proceed into Trenton, cautious, embarrassed at stupidity.

Ahead, on the shoulder of Route 129, see a forest green Mustang with its distinctive red taillights flashing. Pull behind, exit car, and see its flat rear tire. Approach the woman in the driver's seat.

"Need help?"

"Do I! My tire's flat and I don't know what to do."

"Do you have a spare?"

"I guess so."

"Unlock the trunk and I'll change it for you."

"Oh, would you? Thanks!"

Ask her to wait outside the vehicle, lift the lid, manhandle the spare loose, up, and out, and move through the motions by rote. It takes fifteen minutes with added leverage from my four-pronged steel-hardened lug wrench.

Afterward say, "You're all set. Have a good day," and head back to my white Saturn as she offers, "Thank you."

Thankful too, it's not raining or snowing. Or at night. It's hell changing flats then. Not the first time have stopped to assist on the roadways. Have changed plenty of our own.

Stranded travelers
are friends who need helping hands
It could've been me

5.0 LAST EPISODE?

5.1 "FOOLED YOU!"

"Darn. I'll miss him.""

We'd received the letter. Doctor Argueta, confidante, and pill prescriber for sixteen years, leaves Greenspring and starts his own private practice on Nami Drive in Hamilton, our predominantly white community of eighty thousand. Will miss him as a third conscience and wish him good fortune.

Greenspring consigns my case to a Doctor Wolf. Janet and I agree to try him. Make a late afternoon appointment, as do for all my doctor visits.

Our first meeting is in their new office on Bellevue Avenue in Trenton, across the street from Mercer Hospital. The thirtyish male doctor with well-groomed short black hair and manicured fingernails sits behind a blonde desk in his white shirt and dark tie. A little stiff. He doesn't stand or offer his hand in greeting like Doctor Argueta always did.

"Hi Mr. Richards, I'm Doctor Wolf. Tell me about yourself." He sits back in his rolling, high-backed chair and folds his hands.

Describe only highlights of my bipolar episodes. *Keep this short.*

Words rush. *Wait, be normal, he can't read thoughts, only My face. Stay deadpan. Stay cool. Slow down. Tell him only what he wants.*

Repeat, "Things are fine." *Stop twitching. How come he doesn't ask to see My tongue or hold out My hands like Doctor A did? Concentrate. Don't volunteer a thing. Don't slip and ask him a hundred questions about his qualifications and background.*

He turns a page over and scans the underlying sheet. "Have you had any racing thoughts?"

Don't know you from Adam. Stop fidgeting! Stay focused, Rod.

"No, none." Janet's not here; it's easy to lie.

"Do you need any medication refills?"

"No, I'm good."

The anxious session ends. At the receptionist's window, schedule an appointment for early March. When home, hug Kate. Janet presses for details.

"What was he like?"

Hide snickers. "He's okay. We talked for fifteen minutes. He's not as good as Doctor A, but I see him next month." Stride to the sanctuary of our bedroom. Turn on TV before dinner so won't have to answer more questions. Smile at such cleverness.

We say we're "Fine"
we say it all the time
but out of our freakin' minds

191

5.2 FLEE

[Friday]

Damn clock.

Stare at the Cablevision box. White digits turn over minutes... 2:11 it screams 2:12... 2:13... 2:14... *Close your eyes.*

Squeeze them together for the fifteenth time, but they pop open. *Sleep, for God's sake.*

In a fit, snooze.

Wide awake, 6:25, Janet's turned away. Her audible snores rise, wane, and emulate lumberjack's buzz saws in a forested library. Woke her once to challenge them and heard about it the next morning.

"Did you have to wake me? It's bad enough with your snores."

"Sorry, if it happens again, I'll sleep on the couch."

"That would be thoughtful. You know I need my sleep." Mrs. Hyde without it. Bolloxes her attitude the entire day. When my snores wake her, she pushes to stop them with a mild effect. In arcane dream states, too often wake to find my legs kicking her or fists throwing punches at shadowy figures in the foreground...

"Whoop . . . Whoop . . . ." She reaches her left arm out, pushes the center button down. It's seven. Rising, she dons her robe over pajamas, slides tiny feet into slippers, enters the bathroom.

Listen, eyes closed, as she washes up and brushes her teeth.

She pads to the kitchen to make hot tea, and picture her sitting on the kitchen stool reading *The Times* page by page, as she extracts and records the names and photos of people she recognizes or past and present students. Faintly hear the TV weather report.

Get up. Pee then brush and turn on the shower. Thrust fingers into the spray and adjust the temperature until hot, but not steaming. Step in, shut the glass door. Relish the forceful dousing.

"Ahh, love this Waterpik showerhead." *Blessed in all ways.*

"Today's what? February second? Must get Jan a birthday card."

Hate to decide what to wear in the mornings, a colossal waste of time. Since the eighties, lay out clothes the night before. This morning, a gray sharkskin suit, Regular 42, a sleek fit, hangs on our closet door with a white long-sleeve shirt and black belt. Black casual rubber-soled shoes rest on the floor and red power tie hangs from the doorknob—standard office attire. Dress in four minutes, spritz on Polo for Men by Ralph Lauren, always a birthday wish with other stalwarts like puzzles and black socks.

My thoughtful wife enters, "It's in the thirties out Rod, so wear your warm coat."

By then she's in the bathroom, takes a shower, then dresses. Door ajar, she applies makeup for school.

Step to the half-open door, "Bye hon, I'm leavin'. See you later, have a good day."

"You too. Drive carefully." An oft-stated phrase because she's never had an accident or traffic ticket and means not to. I've had plenty.

Pull out black London Fog overcoat from the living room closet, a factory-outlet bargain, and put it on against the chill. Pocket wallet and thirty-three-dollars in cash, then strap black Casio on right wrist before leaving in my Civic.

An uneventful ride in medium traffic. Sing along to classic rock tunes on WMMR. Cruise west/north on the blessed three-lane highway Interstate 195.

"Thank you, Feds, and NJDOT." Merge onto Route 129 and reach the heart of Trenton, a total six-mile commute. Enter the thousand-car State garage on Bank Street with my keycard, back into a spot, lock up, light up, and turn onto Willow Street, alert. Appreciate the free parking. *Employees should have free parking. That's only fair.*

As cross at the light a yellow Mustang brushes by making its turn. "Bastard! Watch where you're going!" *Damn yellow squeezer.*

Walk the next short block. Insert card key and enter rear doors of 50 West office building. *Always quiet before eight. Nice not having to walk far on nasty days.*

Take an elevator to our shared lobby with Pensions. Use card key, no one around. *In a hurry.*

Rush to office, feel a slight flush. *Shut the door, Rod.*

Agitated, high-strung. *What will the zoo be like today?*

"Wait. I'd better leave the door open, or staff will think I have someone in here with me." Open it. *Keep up appearances.*

Pace through the morning office background noises, skip through papers and notes, avoid the break room conversations. *What to do?*

Let lie project folders. Pat shoulders and neck, hard as rocks. Stop... clear webbed thoughts.

Nine, ten, eleven, twelve, until one o'clock passes. Then speed up with urgent demand.

Listen...

Hear it, clear and firm as if presented by an actor on stage with an overhead mic, in a "honeyed-tongue."[28] Inhale its arresting fragrance.

HAIFA

Ahhh. "The Bahá'í World Center" *The Universal House of Justice.*

193

The Holy Land, ancient and current historical and political significance. *Time to meet them. Will they be ready for Me?* If not, will barge in on their deliberations.

They've got to be expecting Me. I've gotta go!

Bolt from 50 West to the garage, race home skirting traffic using dirty tricks along the way. Janet's at school, so are Jesse and Kate.

Run to the den, find hidden container in the desk drawer. Race to Yardville Bank around the corner. Sign in, give key, teller removes our safe deposit box, shown to room alone, retrieve passport, return box.

"Three hundred please," from our joint account. Teller peels out twenties. *Gotta return key. She can't suspect.*

Speed the eight blocks back. *Don't have much time!*

"Shit." Left bifocals at work next to the PC. Without 'em, can't read. Grab old aviator pair from a top drawer of bedroom dresser. Return key to its hidden red box. Overcoat at work too. *Don't need a London Fog where I'm going.*

Hop into Jan's dad's old red Civic, a hand-me-down, with four-wheels for wings and VTEC engine for a jet turbine. *Where to?*

"Only forty miles, hurry!"

Drive 85, 90, on the Turnpike and jet in and out of the clearest lanes, or scoot behind and tail the slowpokes until room, so can burst into the next lane. Exit 8, 8A, two lanes widen to three. Speed past 9, 10, 11, 12.

"Ahh, 13A."

Leave toll booth onto the concrete highway, look for parking signs.

Newark International Airport
Long Term Parking

Enter. Grab ticket. Zip into first available spot.

Thrust jet in open slot
aimed toward soul's secret goal
five thousand miles east

5.3 SEARCH FOR PASSAGE

"Where's the damn shuttle?" Pace under the PASSENGER PICKUP sign.

A white mini-school bus arrives, step aboard, jounce up and down with the few other riders. Hop off at international flights Terminal B. Once inside, browse, select a Mounds bar and flashy spy novel.

"Four eighty-nine, please."

"Okay." Hand her a five.

"Thanks, I'll eat this now and save this for the plane." *Explain or she'll think I'm weird.*

Junior clerk pays no damn attention.

Find **Check-in**. Trot to El Al's front desk. *Must buy a ticket to Haifa for the next flight. Israeli airline is safest, but slow down.*

Saunter up to the clerk in a blue uniform at the empty counter.

"Can you please tell me the next flight to Haifa? I'd like a ticket."

"Tomorrow, we're closed for Shabbat. Tel Aviv is the earliest."

Vague idea. *Shabbat... holy day?*

"Do you have any luggage?" *She can see I don't.*

"No."

A well-dressed man joins her, asks, "Can you please wait, sir?"

Thirty minutes on edge in a plastic cushioned chair. Squirm. *What's going on? He asked me to wait. I'll still catch a flight, got to.*

Shakier, check silent Casio display and its increasing numbers. Jumpy. Newsflashes flit by on a TV screen nearby. The Internet has one-hundred-thousand websites, Clinton battles a Republican House of Representatives, the Macarena is crazy popular at weddings.

When will it board?

A smiling middle-aged woman in a navy skirt, white blouse, crossed navy tie, and a swarthy man in a suit and dark blue tie motion to me. Woman asks, still smiling, "Passport and driver's license please." Hand them over. Man walks away with them.

"Why are you going to Israel?"

"Visiting the Bahá'í Shrines on Mount Carmel."

"How long are you staying?"

"Three days." Had heard many Bahá'ís visited Haifa and received three-day passes.

"What luggage do you have with you?"

"None." *Again, they have to ask?*

"Do you know anyone in Israel?"

"No."

"Okay, please take a seat, sir, we'll call you."

Sit in the same spot. *Hey, you're holdin' Me up. I need to go!*

Neither the passengers rushing back and forth, nor the over-used and predictable plot of the spy novel distract from worry.

My new... worry. Need El Al for a direct flight, right? Try a different airline? Oh can't, they have passport.

The reservation clerk speaks, "Mr. Richards?" *About time.*

Walk to the same counter stall. She hands back passport, license.

"I'm sorry sir, we can't accept you."

"What's wrong? Why not?"

"I'm sorry, we just can't," the man reiterates.

"Thanks for nuthin." *Sonofabitch.*

"Humph." Leave as clerks watch.

They seem jittery.

Stomp away. *What? Why? Dammit! Wasted an hour. Bastards.*

Scratch beard as look for another flight.

El Al more than tough
but can't fathom rejection
Why don't they like Me?

5.4 BRITS OFFER AID

How to get there?

Thread way through the teeming masses. Parents push strollers or chase errant toddlers. Others tug luggage on wheels, while youths tote backpacks or carry bulging gym sacks. Individuals, couples, and cliques stand in check-in lines, most animated, expectant.

Stock-still, examine the big board entries. Regard BA direct flight to London's Heathrow boarding at midnight. *Hmmm.*

Find Check-in, jump into line. *Be patient.*

"Can I get a window seat please?" Hand over passport. Book passage via VISA.

"Thank you, sir, for choosing British Airways." *No questions, great.*

Find an assembly-line café. *Sandwiches look awful, old, stale looking, discolored edges. Leftovers from lunch.*

Buy a large coffee and croissant. Cream and sugar at side counter. *Umm, coffee. Tasty for an airport.*

Sprawl on a chrome-topped café table, tipping back coffee after coffee. People and kids and bags of matched and unmatched colors, shapes, hard or soft backpacks, carry-ons, purses, shopping bags—endless. Mouths open in questions, stares, or blank faces as they search for flight arrivals, departures, or cancelations.

Carry my hollow metal chair over to chat up two girls. Discover they're best friends from Harrisburg returning to a fine arts school in Geneva, and they went sightseeing in Manhattan.

"How d'you like Times Square?"

"So cool but mobbed! And the cabs, cars, trucks, police, unbelievable. But everybody was so so nice. Just like Europe."

"Headed that way. I'm meeting with our world council. I was summoned." They leave.

Join and engage a dark-suited businessman, his suit matches his wearisome mood as he confides he's on the way to Boston after three days of tiresome confabs for a venture startup. He ventures off.

Check Casio. Hours to go yet. *Must move.*

Wander until find and pass through the checkpoint. Walk the terminal length to the Gate and waiting area. Look out and the 747 nose looks immense through the floor-to-ceiling windows, with a body hundreds of feet long with a longer wingspan. *A jumbo plane. That should be neat.*

So, what am I going to say? "Dear members of the Universal House of Justice, I stand before you with an important announcement...."

"I'm very pleased to be at our history-making meeting...."

"He said I must meet with you...."

Impossible to concentrate. Futuristic civilizations interpose themselves as steel and glass gleaming mirages with fluid but stable political structures. *Hmm. Start with full employment, and better transportation. Inner-city monorails?*

Flew cross country at fifteen to live with Dad in California and flirted with a tall blonde stewardess, she with me. Then back again at seventeen. Last year to Sweden. *No fear of planes. Can handle Myself, have since a kid.*

Insha'allah. Can do this.

Obstacles are bullshit. Meant to be surmounted, crawled under, or skirted. Mission clear. *Chosen.*

File onboard with two-hundred others for the hours-long flight. With time changes, London's arrival time should be around seven a.m.

Jet off. A surge of swift G-forces shove body down and back into the seat as the miracle behemoth rises. No urge to grip armrests. *In God's Hands.* Glance out. Amazing cityscape and vehicle head and taillights beam across a long and winding roadway of ribbons. *Relax, you're fine. So high. Love it.*

Peer out the oblong window, as float above the twinkling eastern seaboard. "Heh, heh, heh."

Quickly gain altitude. Settle in. Blackness obscure's view. Try reading spy novel; ludicrous. *Should I be on alert?*

Pull out flight magazine and read page by page, article by article, while adjacent passenger naps. Pull flap open, put it back in its pouch. Meditate as stare into the oblivion over the Atlantic.

Open inflight magazine a second time. Skim pages, find crossword. *Good. Always carry a pen.* Exercise Catholic school vocabulary skills for twenty minutes. Adore word puzzles, jigsaws, hand puzzles, jumbles, and cryptograms. Finish except for seven letters out of one hundred.

Start anew, thumb its pages one by one, peruse ads. Island paradise vacations, gold Rolex watches, and Tiffany diamonds pop off the page. *They want to pop their sticky fingers into my wallet. Trinkets and baubles for the weak-minded. But no harm can come from them—if priorities straight.*

Hmmm. *Should I sleep?*

Lay head back, close eyelids....

Secret wish put in motion
Fly headstrong to destination
Bor-ing

5.5 RENAISSANCE MAN

Intermittent technicolor dreams surface and dive like Day-Glo flying fish along the Atlantic coast in storm-tossed cresting foaming waters. Gaze outside for the fiftieth time, reinvigorated, as under first light we skim above the Emerald Isle, ancestral home to Mom's original Cavanaugh clan. *Will have to visit someday and greet my cousins.*

Move eager limbs. Want to shake hands, pat backs. Stand up, glide up both aisles, search for a smile, offer nods and right hand or left. No one's a stranger, only a potential friend.

"Hello, nice to meet you. Enjoying the flight?"

Overhead signs flash. Return to seat. Approach Heathrow. *Ah, he's here. Expects Me to visit.*

His gravesite's on the city's outskirts. *How could I not pay respects? The scion of the House of Bahá'u'lláh, the Pearl of Great Price.*

Shoghi Effendi, appointed by 'Abdu'l-Bahá, his grandfather, as sole Interpreter and Head of the Faith in 1921.[29] Recall the story well from Bill.

Shoghi Effendi, not yet twenty-five, stunned and overcome by his grandfather's death and the mantle of authority he bequeathed, retreats to the mountains of Switzerland to gather strength for the herculean tasks ahead. He drops out of Oxford to assume his crushing duties guiding the infant faith—and ends up tied to it for thirty-six years.

His words, his national and global plans—vibrant, educational, encouraging—inspiring action, service, and sacrifice in his readers and listeners. In all ways, he aided and exhorted the Faith's small cadre of devoted followers to attempt the spiritual conquest of the planet.

His unforeseen death in London in 1957 sent aftershocks throughout the Bahá'í world. His physical heart gave out in his sleep, *like Dad's*. But his astute mind, confident spirit, resolute heart, foresight, and insight, with us forever in his copious letters, book, and translations.

While memories of Dad live in one 6 x 8 x 8-inch box in my basement. How long has it been? Seventeen years since I felt your lifeless body. What have I done that you would be proud of?

What would you be proud of, Shoghi Effendi?

[Saturday]

Casio reads 7:15.

Disembark, convert twenty dollars to British pounds and coins at an ATM. Observe hopeful passengers or tired ones as they traverse the airport concourse. *Now what?*

Many headed left. Spy wall sign.

199

I can go anywhere. Should I follow the moving throngs, posted arrows? What town is his grave in? Is it the Great Northern Cemetery?

Skirt outdoors under the second-story roofline, stand next to a wide pillar and light up. Enjoy each pull of my cheeks on the Salem. *Better call information.*

At the Tube entrance, enter an open phone booth, dial 1-0-0 per label to call information. "Number for Bahá'í National Center, please?"

Write it on left palm. Hang up.

Insert coins. Dial. Connects. A bright-sounding woman answers.

"Good morning, Bahá'í National Center. May I assist you?" *Must be on best behavior or they'll send me away.*

"Hi, ah, I'm a Bahá'í visiting London and wondered how to get to Shoghi Effendi's gravesite."

"And your name, sir?" *Are they looking for Me?*

"Rodney Richards."

"Yes, Mr. Richards, thank you for calling. Will you be staying in London long?"

"No, just to visit the Guardian's grave."

"I see, and where are you, if I may ask?" *Why's she asking? Who is she? Why does she want to know?*

"I'm at Heathrow and there's a Tube connection here."

"Good. Take the Blue Line to Arnos Grove on the other side of London, near the end of the line. Find the New Southgate Cemetery, just a short walk from the station on Brunswick Park Road." *Oh, she's giving directions, not turning me in!*

"Ahh, it's not Great Northern Cemetery anymore?"

"Oh no sir, they changed that name when the suburb of New Southgate established itself." *Glad I called. I AM going to find it.*

"Okay, thanks a lot."

"Is there anything else I can help you with, Rodney?"

"Ah, no, unnecessary. Thanks."

"You also, Rodney!" hangs up. *Is she reporting my name to her superiors? No, meant to be here. Guided here.*

Buy a round trip pass at a kiosk, wait on Blue platform five-minutes, as one smooth silver-white car with a red top pulls up, stops. Londoners herd on, quiet, unremarkable. Considerate of personal space. *They don't squeeze like Manhattanites.*

Take a window seat for two. *The Way... clear. Always... clear. If you read the signs.*

Traverse city limits and local stops. The sleek train exits the tunnel. Ride through flat green countryside, low hedges, fieldstone drywalls. Nine kilometers of silence on this Piccadilly Line. No one sits next to me.

White plastic seats with mustard-colored thin vinyl cushions seem as familiar as Manhattan subway cars, only cleaner and less worn. Black, yellow, or red graffiti symbols don't mar any surfaces. Close eyes, hear whooshing, muted conversations, crisp announcer's voice cries out station stop after station stop. Nod off.

Look up, out. Low green fields of wheat, brush, and bushes. A few spread-out thatched-roof cottages pepper the sides of the wide stream we've followed until we enter a tunnel. *This is in London too. Jan's mum born here.*

"Arnos Grove." *She was right. And why wouldn't she be?*

Casio reads 9:10. Emerge from the underground exit onto a wide street with a few quaint brick shopfronts. Tight two-story brownstones line the opposite side. A circumscribed newsstand straddles the station wall, packed with sundries, snacks, and small flower bouquets in water-filled dark-green plastic pots. Kelly-green tarpaulin sides and a top tied to chain-link fencing define the space. A young, sinewy man unpacks boxes.

Pick a bunch of red carnations in clear plastic.

"I'll take these, please."

Pay the hectic young man two pounds, receive change.

"Can you tell me the way to the Southgate Cemetery?"

He points up the block to his right without looking in My eyes. "That way, chap," as if he's done it before.

Thought that'd be the way, and I'm right.

Confirmation from the Holy Spirit.

"Thanks!"

Guided.

Plane, call, train, store man
confirm sacred new goal
"He who longs," waits…
…and waits…

5.6 DELAYED BY BEAUTY

Thought we only had these in Jersey?
See the street sign **Betstyle Circus**. *Does Circus mean circle?*
Saunter on brick sidewalks, neat but lumpy, wooden planter boxes on white-trimmed windows hold shrinking peonies. This area of North London clean, not littered like so many American streets and highways. Stride past well-kept two-story row homes with no front yards near busy lanes, and approach the broad, round traffic circle.

No traffic lights, only crosswalks. Reach it and wander through oncoming cars.

"Beep, beep, beeep!" Ignore blasts. Raise an arm.

"Pedestrians have the right of way!"

Continue onto the next blocks and find a long, winding two-foot-high fieldstone boundary. *Cemetery wall, I'll bet.*

Main entrance looms on the right. An iron Gothic gate arches over the narrow asphalt entrance drive. *Knew I'd find it. Not a problem.*

Have seen photos of his gravesite, dignified, with a single nine-foot white marble column supporting a Corinthian capital and white marble globe, a golden eagle perched atop it, wings spread, its head and beak held high. Mature trees flourish in the background. *Where might it be?*

A sprawling place, no end in sight. No visiting mourners to ask, too early. Squint atop the aged gravestones and monuments, up the winding minor road. Notice stone and wood cottage on the right with a slate roof.

ENTER

Turn right, approach. *Anyone inside?*
Knock hard twice on the weather-beaten thick oak door.
A stout Englishman with his broad toothy smile swings it inward. "Welcome chap! Join us."

Grasp his calloused, aged hand and enter. The gray interior comprises a 15 x 15-foot room with a minuscule kitchen to the side. A small **TOILET** sign hangs above a door in the back. *Gotta go soon.*

Adjust eyes to dim light, two fellows behind a square table and four chairs stand to one side chatting.

Is that...? Recognize Mark Granfar, a young Persian Bahá'í from Long Branch.

"Salaam, Rodney!" He stops chatting, steps over, offers an embrace.

Exchange "Alláh-u-Abhá" in unison, just as most Bahá'ís do when hailing each other.

Rodney, last time I saw you was at the Jersey City District Convention, remember?"

"I do. Who could forget Nick Genovese, eighty-years-old, with his Sicilian accent, saying the *Tablet of Ahmed* from memory. I couldn't."

Wild, running into a friend three-thousand miles from home.

Compare notes on events, people. *Hafta play along.*

But then he shoves a thick-bound coffee-table book before my chest and turns pages, pointing out gorgeous color photographs of the Bahá'í Shrines in Haifa. *That's where I'm going after this, Mark.*

"I have a few copies of this exceptional new book about the Shrines. You can see for yourself they're beautiful photographs, some never shared. It only costs seventy-five dollars and part of the proceeds support the World Center." Hands over the hardbound open book, thumbs through its wide pages. Two inches thick, it weighs pounds. *I'm not interested in this.*

"Wow Mark, awesome book. It's beautiful. But I'm traveling light, not even staying here. On my way to visit those very Shrines. Sorry, I just can't lug around that book right now, but it sure is fabulous."

Ya gotta be kidding. You're holding Me up.

Hand it back. Mark is crestfallen by his downcast eyes and head.

Mumble, "Uh, can I buy it from you some other time?" *A shame: he's just trying to make his quota.*

Morning's fading. Haven't phoned.

"Well, gotta go." Give a last hug, march for the toilet, and do business. Wash up. Straighten up, soak hand then whisk it through hair. Had mentioned Janet and the kids to Mark, *guilty of desertion.*

Reenter rustic room. Interrupt caretaker who's speaking to a friend.

"Is there a phone I might use? I'll pay for the call."

"Of course. Just leave some pence in the can."

He leads me to a large box on the tiny kitchen wall. Follow typed instructions above the gray rotary phone.

Stay calm, focus.

D e e p breaths...

Is there any Remover of difficulties....

Must fulfill mission goal
Not buy pretty pictures
of where I'm going

203

5.7 A FRIEND'S ADVICE

Hear the buzz tone, pause, buzz tone, pause, buzz…

"Hello?" The baritone voice is groggy.

"Ah, Bob, it… it's, Rodney." *He will understand.*

"Oh my God, where have you been? Janet's worried sick, everyone is. You woke me up, but, ah, that's fine. Where are you?"

"At Shoghi Effendi's grave."

"In London? What the heck are you doing there? When you didn't come home from work yesterday, Janet phoned Anne and they had no idea where you had gone. She's beside herself." *Don't get into this, Bob.*

"But I have to do this."

"I don't believe it. I just don't believe it…. Are you coming back?" *Do I tell him?*

"I have to, ah… still on My way to Haifa."

"Bob?"

"Haifa?! Why? What do you mean? You can't be serious. What do you plan to do there? What's wrong? Rod, look, you need to come home as soon as you can."

"Can't right now. Must finish this."

"Finish what? What are you up to?"

"Can't tell you. Something I have to do."

"Why can't you tell me? What do I tell Janet?"

"I'll be there in a few days."

"Are you serious?"

"Yes, I'm okay. Tell her not to worry, can take care of Myself. Listen, hafta go."

"Tell me you'll be careful, and call Janet, will you?"

"I'll try."

"You promise?"

"Yeah, I will."

"What else can I tell her? She needs to know."

"Just the truth. I'm safe and will be back soon."

Silence.

"Oh, ah, okay, but… stay in touch."

"Okeydokey will do. Bye Bob."

"Bye Rod, and please… be careful." *Imagined worse. Can't talk to Janet, it'll upset her. Maybe later.*

Leave three pounds in the jar by the phone. *She's amazing. My consort and private houri in paradise. Loves unconditionally.*

Has her own will, is independent, strong, smart, can manage anything. Her response to any stimuli is immediate action. But incapable of not

204

worrying—about me—or scurrying over kids, finances, health, school, house—even on mundane days.

Ever since our honeymoon days in Hopewell, we had a pact. Always share our whereabouts.

But hafta finish this.

Duty done, in a way
Duty now to pay respects
to true brother

5.8 GRAVE OF TEARS

"Can you please direct me to Shoghi Effendi's gravesite?"

"You'll find it not far up the main drive, on your left. Do you know what it looks like?"

"Yes, I've seen photos."

"May peace be with you," the stout Englishman offers.

"And you too, thanks."

Turn and wave. "Bye gang, have a good go at life."

Mark says, "Khoda Fez, Rodney."

Shut the large oak door, head out. *Ah, the Guardian. Unique.*

Turn right, walk along the drive. Spy the distinctive marble column on the left. "Almost there."

The meticulous plot, outlined by a low marble gray wall and bordered by grass, sports rows of flowers with drooping white bells, and lines of short, square-trimmed bushes, with a crushed red-tile footpath up the middle to access the sacred spot.

"Crunch...crunch...." Gaze fully on the column, globe, and eagle atop it, in its central spot on a tiered white marble base. *White, the symbol of purity of spirit.*

Glance right and left. Deserted except for monuments and headstones—each a remembrance of a living soul in a physical body. *Alone with corpses again. Once alive with spirit and personality.*

Alert as noisy pigeons coo roo t'oh and doves coo in the serene and safe park-like space. Brisk morning air streams outward with each increasing breath. Chest heaves. Sense heart hammer, knees buckle.

Place red carnations on base. *Wish I knew what flowers you liked.*

Stand erect with respect. His uncountable achievements, a statesman, husband, mentor, leader. *Designated the Sign of God on earth.*

Eyes water, a torrent of tears rolls. Gasp like a fish swallowing air.

Collapse onto cold marble platform, cradle head on arms. "I'm sorry Shoghi Effendi, I'm sorry. We should have done more."

I should've done more.

How he longed for his great-grandfather's and grandfather's teachings to take hold in people's hearts. How he longed for us to be courageous. How his sacrifices, his systematic plans, his meticulous gardens displayed in those Mount Carmel photos of Mark's, how they inspired and guided us. *What if he had lived longer?*

So few LSAs and NSAs established when he passed. He, the one desperately needed to shepherd this Faith through obscurity, snatched away. *Only ten years older than Dad.*

"Oh Shoghi!"

Weak arms push down against the cold stage. Rise, legs unstable.

"I'm sorry, so sorry." He, unable to choose a successor from his bloodline, nor from the dearth of faithful or loyal relatives. *And I am here for a better future, the one you saw.*

Wipe eyes with fingers, dry wetness on pants. Tremble in frustration, impotent to change the world with one power-laden word.

Stop it. Better to continue instead his vision of unity and love. They're possible. They exist like this tall white column exists.

Step backward.

Clear eyes, leave the sacred site, turn right. Stride past the cottage, maintain a straight-ahead gait. Pass under the iron arch. Reach the street and turn left and follow the low wall toward the circle.

March firmly along brick and cobblestone paths, step across the road watchfully, find station easily, wait mere minutes. Board the train back, slump into a seat. Ponder quotations from his brilliant *Dispensation* letter penned in 1934, when we needed clarity on what we believe—and what we shouldn't believe.

The Tube speeds on its channeled course to the airport. *How soon can we stop the madness?*

Uncountable signs from God's innumerable Messengers and Their lieutenants of what we could become are everywhere. *But we say "Bah."*

Too enamored of our own creations, our physical comforts and material wants. Too many neglectful of their souls and the well-being of their fellow human beings. Yet attention to spiritual principles would solve hunger, poverty, prejudice, injustice.

Love, kindness, generosity, cooperation, justice, sacrifice, compromise—heavenly virtues that bring about the greatest good. Not man-made political structures, economic plans, or legal systems that favor the wealthy and well-connected over common folk.

Thanks to God for pure hearts everywhere that do what's moral and right. Minds and bodies that strive for peace and order, who combat evil and chaos. Souls who build up and don't destroy. Souls who love and care for all instead of hate and harm.

Beloved of All Hearts
left us so suddenly
Just like his grandfather

5.9 THE SOULS OF ROMA

Eyeball terminal **DEPARTURES** screens at Heathrow as passersby scurry like blind squirrels searching for winter nuts. *Flights to Haifa?*

None showing. *Shit.*

Walk toward familiar El Al counter. *Will they turn me away again?*

Clerk pinpoints me, we lock eyes; she glances down… looks up. *Mind playing tricks?*

Blow past, hide behind milling travelers. Slip away. *Did she recognize Me? Can't be.*

Colors, tones, shapes, bags, clothes, shoes, sneakers, stand in stark relief. Focus fixes on nothing and everything for split-seconds.

Return to big screen. A British Airways flight to Rome leaves sooner than others. *That'll get me close.*

Approach ticket counter with credit card. *Or has Janet canceled it?*

"Next flight to Rome, please."

Show passport, slide card over. *Will it work?*

"Please sign here."

Scrawl signature. Slip reads "£242." *How long will it take?*

No questions, but no thank you from the clerk either. *Crap! Would've paid anything to fly direct. But can't risk capture.*

"Next please." *Yes! Will be there soon.*

Light up Salem outside. Fifteen minutes later, unpack another.

Find airport McDonald's. Munch through two small cheeseburgers, fries, then gulp Coke. *Ugh.*

At Mac's exit see an alert bobby in his indigo uniform with hands on his wide black belt with black holster and handgun. *Huh, didn't think they carried guns.* A big, mottled chestnut and black German shepherd lies by his side. The large dog rests, friendly, slack-jawed, its thick pink tongue hanging down, panting. *Hot in here?*

Bend down to pet his head. A growl—not from the shepherd.

"Please don't sir." Look up, the bobby is stoic. Straighten. Shove off, don't glance back.

Skedaddle to the outside. Inhale the life-giving nicotine in deep tokes. *A smoke after eating is satisfying, always satisfying.*

Inside, store windows, shop counters, and shelves blare signs and prices for duty-free goods. None pique interest.

At the Gate. Queue up and board. Plop down, kick up as thrust builds, takeoff flawless, whisk eight-hundred-ninety miles east.

Wouldn't it be nice without crime? What if nuclear fuels were smaller, lighter? What if there were cinder block-sized fusion reactors? What if there was no stereotyping, no false judgments, no hasty impressions? No poverty? Or no dictators, criminals, or demigods? What if Russia was a multi-party democracy? Or even America? What if U.N. Peacekeepers had charge of borders? What if we spent Defense Budgets on replacing crumbling infrastructures or building new ones? Or universal education? What if the U.N. Security Council didn't have to worry about vetoes?

Weariness lifts bending probabilities and possibilities into an ordered life, free and equal.

Whines grow louder as approach our destination. The twin-engine jet sets down at Fiumicino Airport. No luggage, wait on my toes for the chaos in the crowded aisle to subside. Trundle out with the flowing mass. *Patient Rod. Must get to Haifa.*

Envy the pilgrimage of Roman Catholics—Vatican City, the Basilica. *May as well visit. Can't erase those years growing up, despite Father B's encounters. Took advantage of his twenty-dollar bills as much as he did of me. If nothing else, you didn't tarnish God, Jesus, and the Bible despite your two-faced example.*

Inside the airport, approach green ATM screen wide-eyed and exchange pound notes for Lira. Find the announcement board. Alitalia flight leaves at 1645. Time enough to scout.

"Over there."

Around twenty miles.

Follow green signs, reach arched terminal with a train track, but empty. Purchase round-trip ticket at the kiosk and wait under a wide steel-canopied enclosure. The single track starts and ends right here.

Sit and wiggle on a hard green metal bench, gaps as wide as its flat metal bars. No one to chat with, stand, pace for twenty minutes. Sit.

"Thank goodness." Blessedly, the train pulls in. The last car has worn black iron rungs leading onto the short black iron platform and a green door. Firmly grab handles and hop up. Take a window seat on the right, fourth seat in, next to a clean big window. *Good.*

Face up front. A lurch, then rolling. *Better.*

Peer through the glass at Italy's enchanting landscape. *Land of my great grandparents, named Ricci, not Richards.*

Hand conductor ticket. No questions, no odd glances, no *"Grazie."*

Rome. The Eternal City, City of Seven Hills, City of God. *On the way to meet your representatives. I can do this, easy.*

Only six bodies share our car. Average except for a charcoal gray Armani suit man, darker than my ash-colored one, no tie, purple shirt, open white collar. A peasant woman in a white worn apron and orange headscarf sits two seats over.

The Italian countryside is flat with stuccoed residences on both sides and hills beyond as we speed by at sixty miles per hour. Unique pine trees intersperse the scenery and are odd because they're two-stories, straight up, then green, thick, with sprouting finger-like branches spread-out in a V-shaped top. Sporadic sentinels.

Eerie looking. Surreal. Not swaying. *No wind? But the Great Wind of God is blowing. It's a maelstrom.*

Homes low, tannish bronze color. Look like stucco and stone. Pause at another local stop as the train fills.

A young twenty-something male sits down facing me, not saying "Ciao." A handsome youth, with shoulder-length thick black hair, olive skin, a black leather jacket, black pants, and a purple shirt. He immediately peers out the window.

Smile. Big. "Ciao, and good afternoon. How are you?" He turns his head with a blank look.

"Me, Americano, part Italiano."

He smiles, returns light banter. Pick out his halting English when he asks about America and baseball.

"Phillies?"

"*Nada*"

"Yankees?"

"*Si,* yes!" We share impressions, me in clear English, he in accented Italian English.

"I watched Mickey Mantle and Roger Maris play at Yankee Stadium." This man never heard of them.

A loudspeaker barks the stops, in Italian, then English.

"Your country, here, beautiful." Gab about the U.S. Not politics, though.

Ask him, "St. Peter's Basilica—Vatican?"

"*Metropolitana di Roma.* Posters."

Does that mean Metro? Could be the subway, like in D.C. Rode it twice to Crystal City and IBM classes. Love that modern Metro, that history-making city. *Hell, I was born there.*

"Follow *segnos.* Ah, signs," he says.

We continue to chat.

"Roma, five minutes." Quiet now, we grin.

Stop with a slight jerk.

"*Arrivederci* my friend."

"*Addio paisan.*" *Easy-peasy.*

Exit to drab, large Roma Termini Station, with three-story-high chrome portico and glass-curved roof intermingled with stainless steel struts.

It's drizzling. Find a hawker, pay three Lira for a compact black umbrella instead of two Lira for one with black polka dots on a purple background.

Step outside, look across the plaza. Hear the traffic with its short, blaring, high-pitched beeps. Rome appears low, ancient, without tall buildings. Trees rise sporadically, not the kind seen from the train.

Find no clear subway entrance. *Must be below, inside.*

Return. Lose minutes wandering brown grungy catacombs, scanning confusing posters and arrows, until decipher *Piazza San Pietro* pointing to St. Peter's platform.

Leary of pickpockets. Carry wallet in front left pants pocket ever since Tina Balletto had said at a visit, "Don't keep it in your back pocket. Your spine will be unbalanced if you sit on it."

Enter first faded bluish-gray car that stops. Sit and watch until stop. Amble out with the crowd. Notice nine-inch square signs, interspersed on walls every block, which lead the way. Navigate narrow cobblestone streets and stop at a small glass-framed shop, La Sulameria, that looks like a Deli. It has eight tables. Order, pay, munch provolone and prosciutto panini. Gulp Perrier.

Ugh. Good bubbles, but tasteless. Pepsi or coffee better.

Should have ordered coffee. *Is Roman coffee any good?*

Leave. Rest tired spine against storefront under their short red awning. Cup hands, strike a match, inhale. *What do I look like?*

Search faces for smiles to return or engage in conversation. They look down. Not one viable candidate.

Head left. Track light blue arrows until stumble upon the distinctive clearing, famous Saint Peter's Square. *Magnifico.*

The vast piazza, as big as a stadium, is a floor of worn gray slabs and cobblestones trod by millions of believers and tourists.

Behold its round immense space, an impressive semi-circle of colonnades on both sides with tall thick, four-deep, gray-streaked Doric pilasters that rest on their worn plinths, while towering above, marble-carved saints look center. The Egyptian obelisk of red granite rises eighty-two feet into the overcast air like an index finger raised to Heaven. In contrast, the book-sized bronze rust-colored Stations of the Cross, hardly discernible, simple bas reliefs, depict imitations of the trials suffered by the Son of Man on the Via Dolorosa. Approach them.

Stroll beneath one to the next, pause and scrutinize each, visualize their scenes on Jerusalem's ancient streets. Sympathize with Christ's physical and emotional sufferings, yet His spirit must have ached. Each scene etches into my psyche after having watched annual church processionals with six-foot-tall chrome cross lead the way during Lenten services.

The Basilica, a massive façade from the front, can't fathom its depth. The eleven faithful Apostles carved in white weather-aged marble crown its yawning entrance. On the left side, semi-golden gates into the Vatican are closed. *Should I ring the bell? Is this why I'm here? To inform the Pope of this new Day?*

211

Pause. Two Swiss Guards in their blue, red, and orange uniforms stand at attention holding their tall spikes, eyes fixed like stone.

Pass by and stride across the wide major steps.

Enter the atrium, then the nave. It opens to a far expanse in the form of a Greek cross, with grottos off to the sides. Ornate marble throughout, white and gray, arched walls, like giant Redwoods in girth, sometimes flat columns with curved channels, shiny and impressive in height, in a pattern that supports ceiling and dome, which soars one-hundred thirty-six feet.

Marble inlaid floors glisten.

Nine formative-years in Catholic churches, daily Latin masses in their vaulted-ceilinged expanses, their painted biblical scenes looking down at us sinners. Their picture-laden stained-glass windows. Now all float underneath dreamscapes of saints.

Trappings, dogma, ceremonies, stories, and sermons. Mysterious practices, Latin words, guilt-driven morals, arcane demands, and constant restrictions, distant, yet visceral.

"Mea culpas, mea culpas, mea culpas do not forgive Me for Who I Am. Only You can do that."

This awe-inspiring and grandiose spectacle; immense. Ten times, more, the size of St. Mary's Cathedral on Warren Street, the largest church in the Trenton diocese; a lunchtime resting place when felt lost. *Now here, in need of fortifications.*

Tread lightly afoot. Avoid eye contact with faithful tourists. One high walnut post-framed baldachin sits in the middle with a gold cross atop it, Saint Peter's tomb below. Dozens of Bishops of Rome sepulchers lie closed under the marble floor. *Some of you, men with faults and fleshy whims. United in imperfection as we all are—and death.*

It's quiet. Disconcerting. Life-sized stone figures are empty shells, cold statues with gray-white bearded faces, and flowing robes. Spirits have departed. However, living spirits of awe and inspiration fill the hearts of visitors from around the globe. Looking from above the towering dome, from heaven itself, the Eternal One must see each one's worth.

Spotlights shine as approach the heartbroken and inconsolable Virgin Mother, ensconced in a grotto behind a plexiglass bulletproof panel. She cradles her cold dead Son with tender arms and a beatific but forlorn stare from white-stoned eyes. It is the Pieta, carved and signed by Michelangelo himself. *The picture I had chosen on Dad's Memorial card a lifeless copy.*

No wonder I've been sent here, reminded of a greater death, death nonetheless, but only of the body. Not the death of a spirit that changed history, but of a soul that embraces all souls.

Clasp both hands, pinkish in the high overhead lights, look down, then at the nestled Christ's marble carved body draped across Mary's torso and knees. Add colors, heat. Sky-blue robe for her, a bare cloth sheet cover for His loins. Rosy cheeks on her, drained; gray for Him. Sighs from her, no breaths from Him. The blush of resignation from her, the blood of supreme sacrifice sapped from the body and face of Him.

"Hail Mary, full of grace, the Lord is with thee; blessed art thou amongst women and blessed is the fruit of thy womb, Jesus. Holy Mary, mother of God, pray for us sinners, now and at the hour of our death. Amen."[29]

Stand two few feet away, tears trickle. First, for His disappointment in the Jewish leaders and mobs who reviled Him, then Judas' betrayal and Peter's denial. Tears also group and slide for the Manifestations' sufferings at the hands of those who bear Their Names but fail to serve Them with constancy and faithfulness.

We're so blessed. Jesus the Christ's resurrected spirit has returned as promised, despite humanity's infidelities. *God's Plan.*

Step backward with heavy feet, soul free, as if a rain cloud obscuring the sun's heat and flames has blown past. Peer towards heaven, the glorious high arches and the dome four-hundred-fifty-feet above our puny human frames and admire God's handiwork expressed through men's hands.

How do I get to the dome? Search for a stairwell or doorway leading up.

Distracted by inspiring frescoes and statues. *Once, they were devoted living souls. So few saints and fewer saintesses acknowledged. So few champions at the beginning of momentous movements.*

Picture a future teeming with millions of champions, none puny, none afraid, devoted to unifying humanity.

Pivot, head to the square. Stop on the outside stairs. Stare at the large centuries-old plaza, note stormy sky, thunderclouds looming, wind streaming. Walk. Blunder upon the Postal Vaticane on the right side and its smudgy bronze doorway. Enter, select and buy a postcard, postage.

Print the memorized address.

Hi everyone, Mom. Did you ever visit Rome? The Basilica? The Vatican? I'm seeing it with your eyes. Love to you and all. Be home soon
Rodney

Raise flap and drop card into a worn bronze chute. Exit. Meander through the near-empty Square.

Refocus gaze upwards upon rusted Station XIV, when the Son of Man's body, placed in Joseph's tomb with love-filled hands, caused hearts and hopes to break. Sadness tugs at Bible stories of man's inhumanity to man that tortured and murdered Him, and man's humanity toward the Son of Man that buried Him.

That tomb a symbol, sealed, unsealed, the ever-pervasive Holy Spirit that can raise a dead soul to physical and eternal life. Too many dead souls in living bodies, but Thank You, forever alive in Your words and example. It's not too late.

213

Proceed and tread narrow sidewalks, note the close-knit domiciles and storefronts. Like a mouse who eats crumbs left on a trail, find the Metro Station and enter the gray-blue car. Sit and glance at packed passengers, dressed mostly in jeans and tops, some light jackets, note that blues dominate. *Blue for down moods.*

Peer at the rough hands of working men and women, and their black or brown tough-skinned shoes. They are silent. *What're their stories?*

Empathize with their blank faces. Connect with them through throbbing Italian blood but no joys, no exuberances, peek from any faces. *They're so close to grand centuries of history though! We could be a new race of women and men, as fingers of one hand, sharing similarities instead of fighting over differences. Kick this old century to the dustbin of outworn shibboleths. Imagine. The Third Millennium a chance to renounce what has separated us.*

Humanity's glorious future. *According to scriptures, guaranteed.*

Mumble the promised assurance made by the Son of Man, desired despite competing definitions of kingdom; "...Thy kingdom come, Thy will be done, on earth as it is in heaven."[31]

How much more pain before we attain it? Must we allow tyrants and aristocrats to destroy social order and freedom? What about Justice? What will it take to motivate hearts toward service and unity?

Ride the subway car to the train station, subdued and quiet as it is loud, even though want to shout, "Wake up!" like Jehovah's Witnesses imbued with the real meaning embedded in New Testament scripture.

Climb into the red and black train car for the return. Sit in the direction we're headed and survey the peaceful and serene beige terrain out the large window. Meditate. Nod off. Safe. Secure.

Reach airport, disembark.

Eat dinner and drink cola from the cafeteria. In and out for a smoke, two. Slump on a hard-gray chair with little padding. Loll left, right, stare ahead, lids flutter. Watch the clock. Another nicotine rush breaks the tedium. "Thank you, God, for fresh air and a clean restroom."

Buy a ticket. Move to the Gate. Next stop, Tel Aviv.

Then, with haste, Haifa.

Men's temples to God
hewn to honor Holy bodies
When can They rest?

Where have believers fled?
If champions awake,
triumph is assured

214

5.10 THE PROMISED LAND

"Where do you think you're going?"

"Umm, Tel Aviv, aren't you?"

"Yup, just pullin' your leg young fella'."

Traipse onto the Alitalia green, white, and red jet getting set to leave. Like the joker behind me, its passengers file through the narrow aisle into cramped seats. Weary, burden-laden, and not just by carry-ons, we settle. A crowded, noisy cabin with active toddlers, crying babies, and parents shushing to no avail. Read, think, plan, ignore children's whines. Meditate, snooze, awake to cries. The Brooklynite behind me talks nonstop.

Fourteen-hundred miles to go.

As we approach Tel Aviv-Yafo, our flight attendant hands out declaration forms adults must complete. Pull out a blue ballpoint pen from jacket pocket and fill out card in bold block print. The man next to me sees this, holds up his, turns. Had heard his thick accent earlier.

Smile, tell him, "For VISA. For Customs."

"No… unerstand Ennglis."

"Let me do it for you." Proffer left hand. He hands it over with a broad grin. Use his passport information and complete it, checking all "No's." Return both and we shake hands vigorously.

A rush, then crush, as the air-braking Airbus pushes us down tight and into the backrest. Arms loose on armrests, smile at others, hangars, planes, and the runway rushing nearer. Land intact in a powerful hard "Whoomph" of the tires and long loud "Whoosh" of air.

My christening to this ancient land.

We rise from our seats.

The man once next to me gushes, "T'hank you," along the length of the plane's exit tunnel. Ignore him and only nod. *Don't want attention.*

Through customs checkpoints without a hitch, tramp down the wide concrete ramp at Ben Gurion International Airport with the mob of passengers onto the great circular concourse. *Only two things to do. Locate an ATM and get directions.*

Find and fiddle with a machine, receive shekels. *Good, credit card still works.*

Ask passerby, "How can I get to Haifa?" He raises his arm and points left to glass and chrome double-doors.

Once outside, on the right, rests a single set of elevated train tracks, but they're empty. Light up. Weak purple streaks from the setting sun stream through the falling dark blue patch of birdless sky under the exit's canopy.

"Ahhh, holy air." Inhale the cool breeze and smoke. Bow to this history-laden place, where Giants of the Lord of Hosts taught, suffered, and ascended. Thousands stood on their shoulders. The Tanakh, the Torah, Old and New Testaments, the secret accounts of Thomas, stories of their sufferings and tribulations, miracles and joys, and spiritual triumphs. Thousands of stories retold to hundreds of millions.

The access road on the left shows a line of vans masquerading as taxis. A smiling, skinny, dark-haired youth approaches in jeans, loose white shirt, and scuffed white low-cut sneakers without laces.

"Where to, sir? Haifa maybe? Sharoot leaves in ten minutes. Parked here, just six dollas American." *Can he tell I'm American? How? Should I ask? No. But he looks expectant.*

"Haifa." *Mount Carmel shields you.*

Tee the cigarette. Pay him in cash and jump into the rear seat of the white van marked by wide black scratches and multiple dents as two-female passengers already dwell in the middle. Fifteen-minutes pass with four-added until we're full, while our driver stacks their luggage high in the rear tight space. He shoots onto Highway 2 and swerves through traffic.

Converse loudly and discover two women are also Bahá'ís heading to the Shrines. We share hometowns, and when we discovered the faith, where, from whom, and the signs of the times. Longer in the faith than they, keen as hear the magic in their stories.

Drive one-hundred-kilometers north on the asphalt four-lane highway with its concrete divider. *As good as any highway in the States.* The young driver weaves in and through traffic like the pro he is, honking at slower drivers that block him. *Okay, where can I stay?*

"Anyone know a cheap hotel?"

Driver chirps, "Tower Hotel on Herzl Street be good." *A tower sounds appealing.*

"Great, please drop me there."

We enter the bustling streets of Haifa. Spin to the first stop, my hotel. Share warm goodbyes, kisses on cheeks to one Persian woman, handshakes to the two pilgrims heading to the fancy Dan Panorama. It looms over the city from the mountain crest a kilometer away.

The eighteen-story white concrete building we've reached, staggered discrete levels tall and impressive, look curved on one side and see why it's named "Tower." A market faces opposite.

Register inside with trusted credit card and passport, and the clerk assigns a room on the seventh floor. Take one of two elevators up. Enter the room and on the right is a bathroom half the size of the room with a porcelain sink, commode, and tub/shower. One low twin bed, thin gray wool blanket hiding it, matches the wall tones.

"Sure, could use a few colors in here." One end table, lamp, and clock. 5:40.

Casio shows 5:45. *Heh, heh, always ahead.*

Waist-high wooden dresser with four-sticky-drawers stands in the middle of the main wall with a small TV on top.

The carpeted area, confined and stuffy, leaves just enough floor space to navigate around the bed. Push apart curtains but the window won't slide, and no screen on the other side.

What do I say to the House members?

Should eat.

Must appear dignified.

Pocket the door key, leave the circumscribed room. Ride the elevator to the lobby, walk past the front desk into the restaurant, and pull out a chair at an empty table for four surrounded by a dozen deserted ones. Order kabobs and rice and have no trouble being understood. Grilled ground meat patties appear, short and rectangular, semi-tasteless without a coating of pepper, not what Persian dinners are like which are longer, on skewers, and browned. These, mild but good compared to preferred over-spiced food.

Thirsty. Tolerate a semi-cold Coke.

Charge it to the room, go back, take deep drags on cigarette down to its nub, into my hot, burning throat. Two left. No cigarette machine in the lobby. "Wish you had a balcony."

Strip, take a shower. Steamy water cascades down shoulders, back, and legs, turn, revel in the refreshing pulses on head, face, chest, arms, and stomach. Soap up, rinse off.

"Ahh."

Turn knobs right, step out, dry with the thin white bath towel, dress, don suit, return downstairs.

"Must find wheels."

In this thousand-year-old city
will address world's
true government Seat

5.11 JUMP

Stride through the lobby and sidle up to the counterman.

"I'd like to rent a car for a few days, please."

"If you can wait in the lounge, Mister Richards, someone will be here in a few minutes." *Good. He trusts Me, My credit.* He raises the phone.

Sit, no distracting TV, twiddle thumbs, notice bluish thumbnails, turn pages of the Hebrew newspaper on the table. *I need to do this.*

Two well-dressed men in white suits and black skinny ties appear within twenty minutes, exchange a few words with the clerk, then advance toward me. Stand, they smile, we shake once, one brandishes papers in his other hand. They sit on adjacent tan couches with a plain three-foot square wooden coffee table between us and spread blue-lined papers like a checkered tablecloth.

Show passport, New Jersey Driver's License, as they explain. Rapidly scan the two-page English contract. *Not worth it to change this boilerplate.*

Scrawl initials RR in two places and sign on the red X line.

"What's the date?"

"February third." Date it. Hand over credit card. The taller man takes a carbon copy slip, places it and card in his portable plastic machine, slides a bar across, slides back, and hands over the top sheet. *A white late-model sedan. So easy. They haven't asked what I need it for, where I'm going, or why. Boy, drivin' round here'll be fun.*

Retreat to room. Strip down to jockeys. A clear plastic-covered cup sits on the bathroom counter.

Grab coins, a gray bucket. Open door.

"Oops!" Nudge shoe into the door jamb with big toe. Notice hairy legs as walk the empty gray-green hall. Select a Coke from the machine, then accost the black ice-maker next to it. Some "plop, plop, plopping," onto the tiled floor. Pick them up, toss them in.

"Anyone else on the floor?" No response.

Return. Kick shoe inside. Waste half an hour punching TV remote numbers. Fill cup with ice, soda. Lay down. Sip.

Jump up full frontal toward the double window. Unsteady, sway, intone "OMMM." Push curtains wider, peer out again. Scrutinize squat, tall, square, or rectangular shapes blanketing sight like a quilt with their lit windows for eyes and seams. Streetlamps glow below. Lights twinkle on the tanker-sized ships in the harbor as they wait to unload.

"Why not push through this like Princeton House?" *Eternal peace lies just beyond. A new spirit for this shell-casing. Will meet Dad and Stephen. We'll hug and swap stories. Why not here?*

Body twitches, leaps, smashes through the paper window…

tumble through the air, down one story, two, three, four...
fall free in stop-motion, like thumbing through a flipbook...
float, serene, swing, limbs weightless...
forty-six years sail by...
every dawn on every calendar, every sun at noon, every glow-red sunset...
every shadowed moon shape at night....
every hour on every clock unfurls and unwinds, past the wasted minutes

Orange cover and bold title of novel catch eye.

Floating stops, room comes into focus.

Fall into bed, open book. Can't concentrate on words. Fuzzy.

TV shows are blurry, abominable—most in Hebrew. Being Catholic and American, know Latin roots, a few Arabic and Persian words, some pickup lines in French, curses in Spanish, exclamations in Yiddish. My Italian consists of the names for pasta. *Wish I was a polyglot. In the future, we'll all be. At least for our native tongue and an auxiliary language. Enough with these barriers. A New Day comes, with a New Sun of Reality.*

Strike match for last Salem and draw smoke. Memories as an unrestricted youth weave through inner vision, driving my '65 Chevy SuperSport, with 327 horses under the long hood, four-on-the-floor, mag wheels, encased in a golden shell, unrestrained, then the motorcycles. Open to risky encounters, pursued erratic escapades begun in eighth grade. Ignored most school instructors, adults, rules.

Recall French class and assigned name, Phillipe. Mom chose Philip for confirmation name. "He was one of Christ's Apostles," she had said.

A miracle-healer and preacher.

Take a deep draw of smoke, watch it spew into the air, study the white filter, and pale blue ringlets on the white cigarette paper as they flare and turn to ash. *History. I've seen it so many times before, we all have. Do we ever learn?*

Shut eyes from the curling smoke, draw in the last drag.

Hold.

Snuff out the butt in worn glass ashtray, blackened by tar stains.

Philip.

They crucified him upside down in Greece.

Saints are loyal
to their Master's Voices
Time to complete core mission

5.12 NOCTURNAL JOURNEY

[Sunday]

Two o'clock.

"Damn. Did a professional valet park this?" The white Audi is tight up against vehicles on both sides and must squeeze body between them to open the driver's door and wiggle inside. Fourteen other full slots surround us. A white square support column is eight inches from the left bumper.

"Glad this is facing out." Pull up, turn, inch back and forth, steer the wheel in opposite directions, inch forward, reverse, again, until inching clear of the next vehicle and pillar. It takes longer than it does to interpret the directional signs on Israeli roads once out on the street in the rain.

"Perfect out here. That's why God invented wipers." *Left my glasses.*

"Seein' fine." Near-and-far-sightedness merges. Super sharp, super alert. Rain dissipates as drive and mists settle in. Scarce traffic.

Follow signs to Tel Aviv-Yafo, one states 90 km, as thick patchy fog blankets the roads. Drive on the southern route at 160 kph but on short stretches between sloped curves speed up, and the speedometer glows green at 170. Highway eerily deserted, then a handful of cars pass in the opposite direction, a concrete divider between us. The freeway, beautifully paved asphalt with glowing white lane lines, rolls gently between steep hills on each side.

Lose sight of the surrounding highway in a near-constant fog cover that shrouds windshields, windows, sides, and roof.

"Don't crash into embankments."

Tires crunch gravel.

"Damn, rode off to the side again!" *Is this where I'll die?*

Arrive in Tel Aviv, the great white-gray fog dispelled. Traverse empty city streets except for lines of parked cars. Stop in the lane on a high hill with a large open panorama.

Kill engine. Exit the Audi, examine the inhabited area for movement or lights, but only a few streetlamps glow. A dog barks in the distance, intermittent. Nothing else stirs. Coal black building silhouettes of low and middle heights push against the lighter night sky dimness. Far removed but discern minute details like windows and doorways. No windows emit yellowish glows.

Can't hold it.

Pull zipper down, part legs behind the open car door, pee in the middle of the street. *Relief.*

Zip, take a few steps, scan the mildly hampered horizon. One massive building far to the left looks important, three or four stories above others, impressive length, and buttressed by thin, square columns around its girth, with curved arches atop connecting to the building roofline. It stands out amidst its shorter neighbors. *A prison? Concert hall?*

Clouds pass across the yellow-gray moon as shadows dovetail runaway thoughts. No soul, no animal, no bird, no wind, no creature stirs.

Bring right wrist up. Casio arms on three and twelve.

Unbounded energy subdued by stillness, shadows, but eyes sharp. *Where to next? What to do?*

Size-up city.

LEAVE

Mission almost complete.

Start Audi, spin it round. Speed back toward Haifa on same roads. Turn off headlights midway when no other cars appear. Flick them On. Off. On. Drive under the hazy glow of the yellow moon, road clear.

Moving vehicles are as scarce as lightning bugs in winter. This night journey, riding this powerful four-wheeled horse, is as quick as an antelope racing across the savanna to the shelter of its copse.

The return—always different from the setting out.

Find hotel and garage entrance. With precision, back Audi into the same tight space. Leave keys in the ignition.

Reach room, strip in bathroom. Turn on hot water faucet full left turn. Steaming water gushes, clouds rise. Grab hangers from the closet, drape suit jacket, pants, shirt, separately. Hang them over shower rail. "Maybe I can steam the wrinkles out?"

Rinse black socks and gray jockeys in scalding water; stings mean nothing. Red hands drape them next to the towel. "Must look good today."

Steam-has filled the space, the mirror clouded. Write **H A I F A** with right thumb.

Have no sundries. Wipe teeth with forefinger and cold running water.

Lay down.

"Almost done, or am I just beginning? That was great, *Just the Beginning.* Showed it multiple times. Just like I did for Alan Lakein's film, *How to Get Control of Your Time and Your Life* at work for every BDP employee. One of Chris's brainchildren. What was his question? Oh, yeah, 'What's the best use of my time right now?' Heh, heh, well, I have a priority."

Sit up on the minuscule bed, curtains still thrown wide on the sides of the large-framed window. Stand, peer out harder, contemplate Haifa's glowing city lamplights as the megalopolis it is. Remember Louis Armstrong's tune, "What a Wonderful World."

"Maybe."

Pace the gray-walled cell, switch off the TV. Close eyes.

A vision takes center stage...

Lounge on the comfortable black leather rear seat...

A presence hovers on the other side of the wide bench...

Turn. No one there. But not alone...

Can't see the driver's face in the rearview mirror, but he's not wearing a cap...

Swing sideways left, then right... tinted windows obscure view... push head forward, gaze outward... we're traveling on one side of a deserted four-lane highway at high speed...

North or South, East or West?

Limo's lights are the only illumination... striped, crisp white lines flash past the vehicle...

Vaguely sense entourage of blinking lights, other large murky vehicles behind us, but hear no sirens...

"Whoop, whoop" of tires along the smooth surface is the only sound...

Where can we be going?

The inmates of heaven and hell are breaking out...

Traffic's diverted...

We're headed to The Seat, and they've cleared a path.

Summoned, on way to meet them, to share the truth, to share reality...

WE'VE STOPPED TIME

I know. You've chosen Me. I won't fail. Bet Mister Lakein never considered that priority.

> *Weighty task ahead*
> *Midnight chariot assures*
> *we'll consult on time*

5.13 GARDEN CITY

Hear Hebrew phrases calling from the room's TV as they clamor for attention. Anyone's attention. Ignore them.

Casio hands on 4 and 10.

Turn off the steaming faucet. *Nowhere to go. Restaurant shut.*

"Why not a dang coffee pot in the room? Write it off or do somethin' for your guests! And I need a cigarette."

Nap, turn, rise, TV on, lie down, rise, off, repeat. Close eyes.

Bedside table clock glares 7:13. "Gotta get outta here."

In the bathroom don jockeys, socks—damp but tolerable. Don suit. Exit hotel. Muse on the brisk morn, the lofty goal ahead, hungry to meet the nine men. Stop a mother with her toddler son in a stroller, wave, laugh, they return the spiritual communion, young hearts to another, knowing smile to knowing smile.

Troll downtown through beige and honey-skinned citizens, and what shows of mine is olive too except for a pale fleshy face, brown hair, and white-tinged beard. *They come across like Me but aren't all in suits like Me. Are We that different? Different destinations, different purposes, assume we'll succeed. The same. But The Fates, ah, The Fates.*

"What do you want humanity?" Security, jobs, mates, health, family, education, friends—*what else?* Love, respect, consideration. Justice. Fair justice, principled justice, not blind to feelings or circumstances. No imprisonments for stealing bread to feed one's family like peasant Jean Valjean in *Les Misérables.*

Peer into mismatched shops that line the trafficked street. Center-city swarms with face-scanning walkers of all ages as they sidestep one another to pass on the sidewalks. *Manhattan without skyscrapers.*

Distinctive red Marlboro sign ahead. *Aha.*

Approach the hole-in-the-wall store, but inside it's jammed with demanding bodies and voices. A half-open glass window two feet away beckons. Reach right arm through.

"Marlboro!" Hand over bills to a grasping palm. Box of red and white exchanged. Don't wait for change, stop at the corner, light up.

"Ah." At a coffee shop, buy one medium black.

"Oh, better."

Continue to follow single-minded city-dwellers so intent on their destinations. *Like Me.*

Cross street on the green signal with the crowd. Turn left. Up the block, enter the short beshadowed concrete-walled and ceilinged tunnel supporting the rail-line. Toss coins into a black instrument case in front of a gray scruffy man playing a reedy tune. *Oboe maybe?*

It's echoing haunts in the narrow passageway, and its clear timbre summons the recesses of mandated desire. Turn round, inch nearer, stop, shut eyelids, relax bones, listen. Ascend with him to his lyrical paradise on his ardent notes, succumb to his penetrating spell. Dig into a pocket, drop two bills into the yawning black case, back away.

Keep moving. Big day today.

Find a cheap bookseller and drugstore with sundries. Racks of used paperbacks dominate the space. Snatch an orange toothbrush, travel toothpaste, short black comb for rear pants pocket. Grab a nut bar. Pay pleasant enough clerk. Receive change.

What'd I give her?

Continue trolling. Eyes search street as chew. Spy yellow sign, bold black letters.

DISCOUNT CLOTHING

It's on the opposite side of the street. Its appearance, like the Red, White, and Blue Discount Store in center-city Trenton, popular for us hippies in the late sixties, is mildly inviting.

Cross the road and enter the basement store that blares Israeli music from corner loudspeakers. Select straight black jeans, a plaid red and black flannel shirt with black buttons and try them on. Jeans fit and match black casual shoes; shirt sleeves stop above the knuckles. Change back into suit.

They bag up purchases and collect cash. Return to walking this foreign and welcoming city, civilized and cosmopolitan within ancient vibes, winding narrow paths between and behind dwellings, and steep streets.

"How interesting, colorful." The mix of words in both Hebrew and English on store signs seems familiar but some street signs harbor unpronounceable names. Stroll, wave.

"Hello," to eyes pointed my way, like Mom always does. *She always smiles at strangers and offers kind words. The least I can do.*

Return to the Tower, hit button number seven in the elevator, rush into the room. Brush teeth, comb hair, leave bag, hop on elevator back down.

Ask the desk clerk, "Directions to the Shrine of the Báb and Bahá'í Gardens, please?"

"Gladly. We are blocks from the Shrine, so here's a bus schedule." He traces the Uptown line.

Wait outside on the corner under a sign. Ride one and exit at the Shrine. A low visitor center lies next to it. Enter the stucco brick building on the right, saunter to the low wooden counter after the gray-haired gentleman finishes his turn.

A smiling middle-aged woman looks up.

Blurt out, "My name's Rod. I'm visiting from the States."

"Are you a Bahá'í?

"Yes."

224

"When did you arrive?"

"Yesterday."

"Can I see your Bahá'í Identification please?" *Why?*

But remove it from wallet and hand it over. *Why My ID? Can't I just be a visitor?*

She takes it with a smile of thanks then moves five steps to the rear office. She's searching for something, then goes to a computer screen. *Is she checking up on Me? Have Bob or Janet told them I'm here and that they should send Me back?*

She types. Returns with ID and a tan card, handing me both. Card reads **Bahá'í World Center** in the top left corner, near the rounded edges of a nine-pointed star in the middle. Assume the same words in Hebrew on the right corner. Big bold text: **VISITOR** stamped in the center. Below it:

Mr. Rodney Richards 4 February 1996

Can't she tell I'm a mister with a name like Rodney?

Typed on its reverse side is **Visitor Identity Card** even bolder. No indication I'm a Bahá'í. *Ah, the three-day pass.*

"Oh, thanks." Glad I'm not caught. *They're not El Al.*

"Enjoy your visit, Rodney, and please have some tea in the next room before heading to the Shrine, if you'd like."

Two samovar-type metal dispensers sit atop a long table layered in a lacy white cloth with white cups and saucers. Pour and the rose tea looks strong but tastes weak. Observe others as they sit on carved wooden benches, cushioned, lining two opposite walls. Some obvious couples, one mixed racially, talking in hushed tones. Two mothers appease their young with sugar cubes while husbands chat with men next to them.

Prop up the doorway to a smaller room, gulp the lukewarm tea from the bone-China cup. Place it on the thick wooden table. Exit.

Turn right and trod the white pebbled path to the Shrine next door. Feel the spirits of thousands of pilgrims' souls hovering about the holy site. Its core first-floor walls, composed of interlocked layered white cinder blocks, denote purity. Pink pillars connect arches interspersed around its main shell, supporting the second level. Underneath it, circumambulate the sacred spot on its crushed reddish stones. *Symbols of the drops of blood from the Báb, his holy person riddled with bullets.*

Circle three times. *Oh, My poor Báb! Another martyr for the Lord of Heaven and Earth and whatever lieth in between.*

Cross the unadorned sacred threshold and enter His stark room, head down. *The Prophet-Herald, the Gate. A manifestation of God in Your own right.* Holy. Innate knowledge at an early age. Revered by followers, with a magnetic personality and energizing powers. *You and your followers set ablaze Persian society.* Only thirty years young when you were executed by a firing troop of seven-hundred and fifty muskets.

Taupe Persian carpets cover the floor and the raised platform of His resting spot with its low black iron fence, simple, sacrosanct. Placed in careful positions, a dozen gilt, bronze, and pewter lanterns of assorted sizes and shapes, all lit, reminiscent of His era. They sit atop one of the holiest points on earth. Kneel on haunches next to the rear wall in the pure, white-painted room, facing the flat raised sacred tomb.

Dear God, let Me be worthy of Thy mercy.

No expectations. No wishes to wish for. No sins to ask forgiveness for. No hopes to hope for. No one to pray to but God and His Holy Messengers. This spot, like Jerusalem and Medina for so many. This spot and Akka with its tomb of Bahá'u'lláh's remains, the most current repositories of Holy Spirits on the planet. *Twin Manifestations, Twin trumpet blasts.*

They detract not one whit from God's past Holy Ones. Each and all brought spiritual renewal and grace to the planet.

Arms shake, heart tingles, body throbs. *I'm here!*

A young man enters. Push off the carpet. *Your turn to be alone.*

Walk backward through exit portal, not turning away from the holy site.

Next door, enter 'Abdu'l-Bahá's empty mausoleum room painted pure white as well with light Persian carpets on the floor, plain like that of the Blessed Báb's, but plainer still. On the left wall facing hangs a facsimile of His Tablet of Visitation in a glass frame. Read aloud it's printed script, "He is the All-Glorious! O God, my God! Lowly and tearful, I raise my suppliant hands to Thee and cover my face in the dust of that Threshold of Thine ...."[32]

Recall cherished days with others in Rochester memorizing this prayer of servitude.

The gleaming parabolic dome far above this holy verse, covered in golden-glazed tiles mid-way on this Holy Mountain, can be seen from anywhere across the wide Bay of Haifa, as shown in Mark's book. A lighthouse like none in the world.

Spotless. Freed from sin. *Oh lord, release Me.*

Exit with head bowed. Cross between two pillars, *Nothing out of place, a place for everything, even spirits.*

Plain red terracotta pieces or white stones cover paths through Eden-like gardens with cypress and juniper trees, manicured bushes, and plant-lined paths in brilliant pink, purple, and red Bougainvillea. Martyr's blood that blooms heaviest when scorched by torrid suns of trials and tests.

Beloved icons, the Báb, Bahá'u'lláh, and 'Abdu'l-Bahá, still live through Their wise words and tireless examples. The Holy Ones don't die, in every age, no matter Their Names, Their spirits live on. Visualize a new race of men and women through Their eyes—peaceful, happy, and just, overlaying oceans, valleys, and mountains. In that world, inner beauty matches outer beauty, and humanity acts as true stewards of each other and earth's resources. Physical angels abound. *Just like now, but do we recognize them?*

Pass by the Visitors Center, continue onto Hatzionut Avenue in a collective haze. Clutch the Hand of Certitude as We walk toward the Seat of the Universal House of Justice.

Will they appreciate My message? My company? What name should it be? UniCorp? UnityCorp?

Rehearse finer elements of the Corporation. Envision notes from 1979 scribbled at our kitchen table.

Directors, seven

Departments, five

Products, varied, endless

Success assured

"And now too, new goals to spread the cause, to cast wide nets not single fishing lines into the teeming ocean of humanity. To reach everyone through our examples, deeds, and words, so every person finds God's Promise and Fulfillment."

"God is with them, it's their choice to respond. Always been that way, will forever be so. We choose our own paths."

Souls seek diverse ways,
but search within and out
for peace, hope, and love

God's eternal Voice
calls all souls to Him,
"Love Me, that I may love thee."[33]

5.14 A STEEP APPROACH

Hasten along Mount Carmel's western slope.
Shuddering waves of confidence confirm resolute will.
Next to the sidewalk locate a single waist-high filigreed black iron gate.

ENTER

The Seat looms one-thousand feet above the Mediterranean's calm royal blue, flat as glass, peppered with tankers at anchor. Wide heavenly vistas shine from above and the sides to encompass the bustling city. Cream pillared buildings jut out ahead, as this Babylon's hanging gardens surround it in an arc of multi-hued foliage. Eager eyes imagine paradise. *Here. They are here.*
Unhitch the gate's clasp, pass through unchallenged. Latch it closed. Don't see a breathing person, only sense One Soul. The panorama instills reverence that could only surface from viewing the magnificent. *The Faith has attained planet-wide status in only one-hundred and fifty-two years. Surely humanity can get its act together. I can help.*
Sudden conflicting thoughts and images of violent wars ripping humanity asunder flood inner eye. *Go away!*
Walk up the mountainside into plush irrigated gardens along lengths of white-colored pebble paths and low rows of bluish-green hedges and man-sized cypress. Sets of encircled marbled column tombs, taller than my body, cap-stoned, lie on the path. Simple dignified graves of Bahá'u'lláh's saintly wife, youngest son, and eldest daughter, together with one for 'Abdu'l-Bahá's blessed wife—the Holy Family. *Shoghi Effendi had these monuments built and landscaped as permanent tributes.*
Stop, drop head, mouth the Prayer for the Departed. *They are praying too, for the living to take up the call.*
The meaning of human reality is not gleaming silver towers that pierce horizons with their prominence, but what it enshrines in these simple tombs. Shining examples of sacrifice, love, suffering, and family unity. *Like all family's experience.*
Reverence penetrates anew.
Turn, search, find the middle path. Tread straight-up the mountain steeps with no carved steps. To the right, view the full-scale replica of the Parthenon built under Shoghi Effendi's direction. The symbol of ancient Greece, the birthplace of democracy, Bahá'í archival items stored within, precious relics and mementos of faith. *A history of heroism.*

Straight ahead. Straight to the center of humanity's guidance. Ordained by Bahá'u'lláh Himself, their decisions inspired, the International and Universal House of Justice, who do "whatsoever He willeth."[34]
They'll know what I have to do. I'll spread the Message and The Corporation. I have to do both before the world goes to hell.

Trudge, grind, dig shoe toes in, climb the fifty-degree angled mountainside to The Council Chamber of the World. The building's mass predominates. Sixty thick white Italian marble columns, each wider than two persons and over three wide stories high, gird its exterior and gleam with their broad fluted Corinthian caps. Trudge further on loose white stones and pebbles, climb harder, breathe quicker, up the incline like nothing ever trekked.

See the broad carved steps that lead to the base of the arcade's columns. They beckon to the bronze doors beyond. *Ninety feet. Almost there.*

Pause next to a single nine-foot-tall sapling, standing strong in the center of the thin stony path. Outstretch right arm, grasp tight its trunk under its short green branches and leaves, which fills fist and spirit with firm assurance but provides bare shade.

Wipe sweat from forehead and face with palms.

Clammy under confining clothes as breathe morning air to cool.

Gasp, then puff, then a deep inhale for lungs to recompose. Fire lights belly and belies the rays of heat from the sharp-eyed sun in the clear azure sky. Lift hand, shield eyes from its penetrating rays, as gaze up at the striking edifice, its white low dome crown and green roof visible from the horizon on the mountain's heart. *Janet and I helped build this. I urged believers to donate toward its construction.*

Solid earth and stone support now trembling legs.

Dare I knock? Will they welcome or spurn Me? Do they know who I am? Will they accept My ideas?

Make out the windowed glass between the columns. Visualize the ten-foot-high, wide, closed chestnut-colored doors below it. The only public entrance. *They will open them for Me. Just take these last steps, climb the stairs, and knock. Didn't Christ say, "Knock?"*

"I have much to say. Each passing day exhausts the allotted time. Civilization totters, teeters on collapse from its ponderous weight of veils and distractions, unaware it can save itself, unaware of what God has sent."

Push forward. Lean… forward. Climb. Right… left… right… left.

"Crunch,… crunch… crunch… crunch…."

Pass a sea of lush green grasses on either side.

Regain footholds on the steeper path.

Right… crunch. Left… crunch. Right… crunch. Left… crunch.

"Crunch… crunch. Crunch… crunch. Crunch… crunch."

Hear intonation… low… deep.

229

5.15 A NEW COMMAND

Hear intonation again, louder…

TREE… BEYOND WHICH… THERE IS NO PASSING [35]

"Oh…."
The symbol of The One. The Alpha and the Omega, the end and the beginning. He has breathed the Word of God into the dying gasping lungs of humanity. The ageless Life Bringer, the Manifestation, returned yet new. *The Divine Lote-Tree, eternal…*
No such dimension as Time.

…you may not pass…

"No. Can't … We can't go on … can't. . ."
Look back. The sapling stands alone twenty feet behind, forlorn. It's a marker, a sentinel, guarding the single route.
Welling up, surging out… *Not worthy. I'm not Him. Bahá'u'lláh is the Prophet for this age, not me.*
Falter, tears form, cry, cry for humanity's waywardness. *Can't do it.*
Retreat, re-grip the sapling hard, feel its smooth bark, strength, then lower right arm, hand. Pivot, shake. Peer down at footholds, concentrate. Step back, withdraw, down, one step, two, three, four….
Pause. Carmel speaks…

Persevere…

Falter, descend, its precarious perch. Further, meander atop pebbled paths. No person in sight, no one asks, "What are you doing here?"
Hear larks, spy sunbirds of yellow and blue, red and brown. Life endures.
Pass by the holy family vaults. Reach the thick iron gate, feel its solidness, unlatch its bar, walk through, close it, reverent.
Reach Hatzionut Avenue, see vehicles speed by as if nothing has changed, but the world has changed, I have changed.
Wander downhill the long blocks, half a mile to center city.
Clear mind, no intrusive thoughts, clear heart.
He will inspire Me.
Air fresh, spring-like. Thoughts enter, faster.

TELL THE MASSES

"Yes. Must intensify efforts."

HAVE FAITH

"As ye have faith, so shall your powers and blessings be."[36]

On God's Holy mountain
found soul's desire
and imbibed humble pie

5.16 EXILED

Back at the Tower, enter room, doff restrictive clothes. Splash face, arms. Water chills burning desire.

Look in mirror. Cry, heave, sob for what was not to be.

Dry, pull on new jeans and shirt. Brush teeth, comb hair. *Must leave. Time to return. Not appropriate to stay.*

Take a last look.

Reach lobby counter and speak with manager. He picks up the phone. Wait.

A white-suited man arrives and checks the mileage on the Audi, then we settle up for the rented car.

Check out and the efficient manager phones for a sharoot.

Zip toward the airport, mum, don't offer smiles or eyes. Lost, peer out the Toyota van's window. *Where else to go?*

Watch hundreds of blurs within blurs. *Humanity still has a chance. It can turn around.*

Arrive at Ben Gurion's entrance, close-mouthed. It's semi-busy, like fevered thoughts of a glorious future civilization.

Where are the revolutionist clerks?

Plop onto another gray hard padded plastic seat, place brown paper bag with suit clothes in it on next one.

I may need them again.

Now what?

There is tomorrow, isn't there?

> *Head home Kato,*
> *as fast as Green Hornet flies*
> *Not yet time to proclaim*

5.17 ISRAELIS RELENT

Direct sunlight exposes vestiges of soulful failure through large gleaming windows behind me as I smoke. Don't dissolve into self-pity or disappointment as preen. *I still have power to alter destiny's trajectory. Hell yes I do.*

Inside, find **MEN** door. Step through and do business. Splash water on hands and stinking face. Swish some mouthfuls and spit out. *Did I grab the brush and toothpaste?*

Check bag. "Crap." Wipe teeth and smoky tongue with index finger as scan mirror. In it watch finger rub cancer cells away. Grab paper towels. *Should I buy another toothbrush?*

"Why be fearful?" *No, everything will go My way.*

Exit left and march to El Al counter revolutionist.

"Excuse Me please, is there a direct flight to Europe?" She strikes keys on her computer.

"Flight 315 leaves for London at ten-oh-five. *From there, can go anywhere.*

Do you have luggage?"

"No, I'll carry my bag." *She sees what I carry. Will that be a problem?*

"Do you have anything to declare?"

"No. I'll take the flight if you have a seat. Window, please." Convey passport, VISA card.

"Thank you, Mister Richards." *Don't fidget.*

Receive ticket, ID, and card.

"Thank you."

"And thank you for flying EL Al Airlines."

Take a gray seat in a row of lobby seats. *No rush now. Home soon. Made it to the Holy Mountain with no plan and just a credit card.*

He must have other plans for Me.

Spent. Rest. But uncomfortable. Can't sit. Go. Open **MEN** door again, deserted. Empty paper bag, check suit pockets, stick pen in back pocket. Dump suit jacket, pants, shirt, and bag into upright trash can. Peek around, step outside, further outside, further.

Walk in a hurry to transport roadway circling the airport. *Ah, a smoke.*

Hungry. A modern glass and steel restaurant is across the drive. Inside, bypass the hostess and empty tables, and slither up to an attractive woman with long, light brown hair.

Smile wide, "Hi there, name's Rod, from the U.S. Looks like we're both stuck here. Would you mind some company?"

Scan's face, clothes. Smiles, waves to sit, "Okay...."

Pull out the chrome-plated chair facing her.

"I'm Brigitte, from Stuttgart."

The server in black slacks and white shirt zips over and hovers.

"How about a turkey sandwich with lettuce, tomato, onion, no pickle, on a hard roll, mayo, with coffee and cream. Oh, ah, please, and we need sugar on the table as well. Brigitte?"

"More espresso, please." Skinny server stops, stares, turns on his heels.

"Are you coming or going?"

"Returning home."

"Me too, New Jersey, close to New York City."

"I've never been."

Show the sights with hands, the subways below the bustling above, the crisscrossed streets and skyscrapers full of human diversity, the ten thousand yellow taxis zooming like mad bumper cars, the dozens of outstanding museums, like the Met and MoMA.

"There's an enormous park there too, right? I've seen pictures of statues, people picnicking, lakes, a castle, and a circus too?"

"Central Park's over eight-hundred acres, maintained to a tee for all its visitors, with variegated plants, boulder-rich to climb on and benches to sit on, with ponds, hidden paths, fountains, and gardens amidst skyscrapers and hotels on all sides. It's a treasure amidst the sprawl. New Yorkers and world travelers love it."

"Ah, nice. A great green park, where office buildings tower like the Alps, I imagine. That would remind me of Switzerland. Love the visual." She gushes and relates the green wooded beauty of cottages, chalets, and white-capped mountains near her home.

"Much slower hustle and bustle."

"And what language do you speak there?"

"Mostly Swiss German, but French too."

"Your English is quite good," elicits a smile. *Try to bring a smile, Rodney, share a compliment. Too bad she can't compliment me on my German.*

She sounds the expert. Europeans blessed, multilingual.

"What do you call someone who speaks three languages? Trilingual. What do you call someone who speaks two? Bilingual. What do you call someone who only speaks one language? American."

"Ha-ha, true I think." Between bites and sips, chat for fifteen minutes. Steal short stares at her firm Barbie prettiness and fair, ruddy-complected skin. An intimate tension rises. Touch hands.

Coffee tastes robust, thick, hot. Like my loins.

Five more minutes. She rises. Pushes her chair in.

"It was pleasant to talk to you—Rod. I have to check my flight, have a good return trip."

Stand, offer right hand. Shake twice.

"Alvederzane." At least I know that one.

She turns toward the Terminal. Peruse her hourglass shape in her tight yellow blouse and tighter white jeans.

Would she like a companion on her trip?
Glance left out the floor-to-ceiling windows. *Nothing else to do here.*
Rush to cashier. Watch Brigitte promenade out through the restaurant's double glass doors.
Sunrays spotlight her swaying hips.

Twenty-five years
of wedded comradeship
perish like melted ice

5.18 LIMBO

Rush into Terminal. "Brigitte?"

Her memorable shape has disappeared, our encounter blurs….

Move on Rod.

Take a seat but should board soon. A female El Al clerk approaches, "Please follow me, Mister Richards."

She leads to wooden doors marked **Private—Do Not Enter.** Once through, curious small 6 x 7-foot three-walled rooms pique interest. Numbers are nailed above doorframes. Drapes cover openings. See through slits they're not offices, no desks.

She leads to number **3**. Opens the curtain.

"Please take a seat." She draws the green covering behind her and there's a hospital cart lengthwise against the wall. *What's going on?*

"Someone will be here soon."

Minutes later, as wonder what this facility is, the privacy curtain whips aside and a man wearing thick-rimmed glasses enters with a short woman carrying a clipboard. She closes curtain. Both wear spotless starched lab coats. Man moves close, flashes a penlight into one eye, then the other. Question's pop, pop, pop like gunshots on an Army shooting range.

Retort "Yes," "No," "Doesn't matter," "Yesterday," "Feel okay," "New Jersey," "Soon."

Mousy woman jots notes on her pad.

Man says, "Please wait." They leave, whip curtain closed.

Hear inaudible whispers of "manica" twice.

Is this necessary? What about my flight? Blast them and this place.

Huge white crystal rockets, hundreds, shoot from far-flung silos that dot the landscapes of countries with no names, every name. *Done here. Need to go. What's the holdup? Who are these people?*

Long minutes pass. Curtain parts. *About fuckin' time.*

No words. A woman motions. Leads back to the passenger area and its rundown, rigid plastic seats, gray, only gray. *Where are the colors? Is the world only gray?*

Plop down. Not afraid. *Important. Must stay calm.*

After twenty minutes adrift, a petite, attractive woman in uniform approaches and bends down close to right ear. "Be patient." *Am I dreaming?*

"They're arranging transport."

Patient, oh so patient, as patient as a gasping man waiting for Last Rites. Yet itching. *I'll leave by car, train, horse, or mule if I have to.*

Head to the sundries counter, buy two postcards and postage. Address one to Mom, the other to the Harrises. One card a field with rolling hills, with cut rolls of man-high yellow wheat, green forests in the background. It could be a scene in Sweden. *France?*

Mail them in a slotted box.

A counterwoman approaches, motions to follow. We approach the **Olympic Airways** kiosk, and she says a few words to the clerk in Greek. She rises, knocks on the door behind the counter, opens it into a 9 x 9-foot-wide disheveled office. Scattered desk, stacks of files, gray metal bookshelves overflow behind it with colorful binders, papers, and scraps sticking out. Gray file cabinets line the wall with more binders on top, with two thin chairs in front.

"This is Mr. Richards, who requires transportation."

*"*But I have a ticket."

No response. The gray-suited swarthy man, no tie, with a bulky frame and potbelly, stands from behind his sloppy packet and paper-strewn desk.

"I'm Manager here for Olympic Airways."

"Hello. But why am I here? I have an El Al ticket to Heathrow."

The woman leaves and shuts the door.

He offers a cigar and a chair. *Should I take it? Put him at ease?*

"No thanks, don't smoke." Sit down in a metal chair, shaking legs tipsy on the parquet floor. *Am I out of here? Do they know Who I Am?*

He lights up. Wisps of blue clouds and a rare smell fill the space. He speaks like Spiro from Towne House Restaurant only with a high-pitched voice in more accented tones.

Cigar man smiles. *Smile Rod.*

"We will help you." *About time. Crazy El Al, who can figure them out?*

Meet for thirty minutes, he tells jokes, laugh. He chatters, listen. He asks questions, respond. He fills out a multi-part form with passport information, then swipes credit card. He hands them back and stamps a one-way ticket.

ATHENS Flight 265 Time: **1905.**

"No other flights allowed," he says. *Don't care, at least I'm outta here.*

Stare out the window as our jet rushes through black airstreams.

On my left, two well-dressed brown-haired women converse across the aisle, as if they've known each other for years. On my right, a Texan tourist, pony-tailed, gray-blonde hair, who sings and plays guitar for a living. Speaks and looks like Glenn Campbell might. Ply him with questions about the music industry and Texas, not sharing my Greyhound bus trip through the flat panhandle in '67. Dislike the middle seat.

Never again unless forced to.

But invigorated. *Invigorating!*

Arrive at Athens airport, ringed by barren mounds and short scruffy dusty mountains. Disembark into the large one-room terminal twenty yards long, empty of furniture except for a few rows of low seats.

All grays.

Approach a female in an airline uniform studying a document at her desk. She doesn't look up, then waves to take a chair. No explanations for the rebuff. *Another gosh darn clerk who is no help.*

Wait, twist in seat, say memorized prayers. Approach her again. "Can I go outside for a cigarette?"

The woman in a navy skirt and matching but lighter blouse answers, "Don't leave the building." *Huh? Not even for a smoke? You kidding? Where can I grab one?*

Hunt and find a side exit. Pass through floppy, translucent plastic door strips to a loading dock. Light up and sneak my Marlboro since no one in sight. No hassles.

Return. No one took notice. Sit until safe.

Rise, ask her, "Can I get a plane to the U.S. or London?"

"Wait for papers." *What papers? I have a passport.*

Wait. *Did the Israeli man at Newark Airport phone here? Did the woman at Ben Gurion call?*

Every two hours check-in with whatever clerk appears. The same. No progress. Not a word, no explaining. *Hate that the most.*

Pull on knuckles, no pops. Never tried to crack them before. Rub eyes, palms clammy. Wander dull-white circumscribed expanse of the terminal. Find **MEN** room in the filthy cold white and light blue basement, wash up. Return, waiting area is one large room, few doors. *Where are signs, restaurants, shops, coffee?*

Nothing but a black-handed clock on one end, the long hand minutes past ten. A flight board on the sidewall but few flights out listed. None headed to Newark Liberty. Fifteen people wait. No one converses. Observe, always observing, note plain dress, careful movements, ages, book readers, non-readers.

There is one sign, up high, a logo with an outlined sun, two birds on the wing, black bold text **AEGEAN**. *A Gean? Is that the airline?*

Find peaceful unreserved hideaway in a deserted L-shaped section of the large room, crouch on top of a thick white plastic table, in the smaller wing of the one-story building, the entire space empty of adornments or windows. Nothing else, no one there. Stretch side to side, meditate, muse out loud, stretch, perform ten jumping jacks.

Still no magazine stands, no coffee, no food, not even a drinking fountain. Swirling ideas and flinging thoughts carom and bounce until they pass in a desert of baked-on sweat and boredom. Energy levels fluctuate, doze off then snap alert; wired, awake. Spy guards in blue uniforms holding their Uzis on shoulder straps in both hands at the ready, posted by a single, gray-tunneled gate to the plane entrance.

Is Greece totalitarian?

Watch as a group of passengers depart into a grayish canopied tube-like corridor. Blow past them and the guards' guns, the only exit to planes.

Can I sneak in with them?

Look for an opening.
No.
Visit the woman at Olympia booth again. Looks up, shakes head, "No."
Gnash teeth through the night hours. *Damn. What is it with these people?
Why not run? What will they do, shoot Me?*
Curl body onto three padded chairs, bring hands under head as in prayer.
Feel beard hairs high on cheekbone.

*Questioned, approved,
shunted away;
no paths of escape
for manica*

5.19 ESCAPE

[Monday]

The black-rimmed clock with its paper-white round face the diameter of a basketball shows the short black arm at five, long at three. Inside the terminal harsh light glares from the same overhead fluorescents, same shadows in empty corners and under a few legs and seats. Stumble to **MEN** in the basement, crap, wash up.

Sneak through the floppy strips and smoke. *When will I get outta here?*

Sit on appropriated thick white plastic table, cross legs, fume at the boredom. Stomach growls. Doze.

Two hours later watch dawn's glow flush the sky pink from my smoking platform.

The basketball clock declares nine when hidden doors at the side rear end of this dead space open like a cave door to "Abracadabra!" to a much bigger and longer terminal, full of shops and product displays with clerks selling touristy goods, foods, and drinks. Full sun streams through its upper curved skylight windows.

"The First Day and creation starts. Let there be light." Walk up to a coffee counter, peruse its pastries. *Oh, thank you, God. Double that for baklava.*

Its soft pasty flakes and mushy body melt with a sweet oily taste on parched, hungry tongue. Feel saliva where none before. Gulp the coffee. Return to reservationist counter again, to the morning's mournful shift woman. Tell the full story this time; receive a blank stare, no words of encouragement.

Leave for a secret smoke. Return to Twilight Zone penitentiary, then sit cross-legged atop my reserved table. *Expand World-Center into World-Megalopolis. Copy Manhattan's street-laced infrastructure, L.A.'s freeways, and Silicon Valley's connected business hubs.*

Move dozens of sites. Institute a system of uniform weights and measures. Use English to translate all languages. Institute universal health care, international job banks, and skills training schools in all disciplines. Rebuild crumbling water pipes, resurface roads, reclaim cities' brownfields and slums, bury all electrical cables underground. *All planned out. In Control.*

At twelve lip-sync the Noonday Prayer.

Watch small hand pass one, two, three, on the clock. *What did El Al flunkies say? Inaudible creeps.*

With a silent touch, a new clerk rouses half-stupor with, "Follow me."

Expectant, she opens a rear door. Hadn't noticed the entrance to a long thinner terminal section and another counter. This time indigo-blue uniformed men pore over forms behind a draped table set below a 4 x 8-foot **AEGEAN** sign. *Where are Uzis? On the shelf below?*

They ask questions, check documents. Lean on the table.

Don't blow up.

Answer by rote.

"Can I please sit by a window?" Contain smoky ire, bursting to berate their plodding. *Why did you hold Me up?*

Receive tacit approval. *About fucking time!*

Pay for flight to London, *No problem, been there.*

Escorted to idling lime-green shuttle bus. Step up, scurry to a seat, twenty passengers file in, four stand holding onto bars. *All wearing jeans, every goddamned person in the world wears jeans. When we were hippies, they mocked and sneered.*

Sit, feign disinterest, notice furtive glances. Tram runs in a wide circle to a rundown terminal some distance away. Pushed to the left squish the comely woman's jeaned thigh who sits next to me with mine, as we make an even wider arc across the tarmac.

The new terminal is much smaller with a ring of tan hard orange plastic seats in a large circle. *Wow! Colors! Forty passengers in all?* Brothers, sisters, fathers, mothers of all ilk's and ages, children in the majority of seats.

Enter **GIFT SHOP**. *Need a memento.* Search the busy cramped shelves, select a 4 x 4-inch small boxed white and red chessboard, with sixteen white and sixteen rust-colored pegs molded into chess characters an inch high. Add a coffeecake. Pay with the few dollars left.

Stroll in front of seated passengers in the terminal holding area and survey potential chess masters. Ask an older gentleman, "Hi? While we wait, care to play chess?"

"I don't mind."

He opens with pawn to king four. Safest when it's an untried opponent. Always liked games. Bob, on a two-year chess kick, had invited me often to play back in the eighties. Otherwise, it was backgammon.

Short matches transpire while we wait. Chat a little. Win three. During the fourth, about to move black bishop to attack my third opponent's knight.

The flight's announced! We rise, some lifting, pulling luggage, we bunch up and file out, walk across the tarmac to the plane, and board. Grab assigned window seat. Close eyes. *Athens, birthplace of democracy, good riddance.*

Watch brown scorched hills dotted by scrub bushes surrounding this desolate place fade out of sight. *You tried your scorching fires on Me and failed.*

On the plane doze or otherwise converse with seatmate. Ask the middle-aged guy, "Have the time?" The black Casio, set to alarm at noon, gone the way of toothpaste, brush, and comb.

"Six-thirty."

"Thanks." *Good a time as any. Plenty of time. In God's capable hands.* And the pilots. *Trust in God but tie your camel—be smart about it. Headed back! Done with cowardice and fear. Time to speak out.*

The Mission—postponed—for another day, another opportunity. *When it arrives, will the body of humankind be thriving or only left with pockets of survivors?*

Since the symbolic time of Adam, only He knows. *But we each have a say. That depends on how we treat each other, how our leaders treat us, and how nations treat nations.*

But if we destroy the nuclear warheads before the idiots destroy us, then we have a chance. Besides, there are plenty of other ways to die.

> *Long waits dampen spirits*
> *yet upbeat dreams*
> *for humanity still live*

5.20 EXPOSED

Since Orville Wright first raised a thin muslin wing at Kitty Hawk in 1903, trust pilots and aircraft to perform without flaws and they have again. The flight of escape from the limbo of Athens and a pounding touchdown welcomes a spate of thankfulness despite interminable waiting.

"Hey, I'm crawlin' here."

Itch and squirm as let fellow riders disembark first into Terminal 4. Heathrow's busy in its hollow long narrow walls of glass. Amble up to a counter with a short, pretty black-haired accommodations clerk, perky and shapely.

"Hi, Miss Gorgeous, where can I stay in London?"

"May I ask how long you'll be lodging?"

"Just as long as it takes to know you better. But ah, only one night, fly out again soon." Flirt with no shame or inhibition. She completes two phone calls during our flippant exchanges.

"I've booked a room for you at the Radisson Edwardian and hailed a carriage. Here's a twenty-five quid voucher—because you're interesting."

"As you say, that's lovely, no? So, what time do you clock out?"

"You'll be gone before that, chap." Lovely but won't share her number.

Twenty minutes outside Heathrow, the hotel's stories of light brick and tan stucco seem pleasant enough, like Rome's. Check-in with loyal credit card. No one else in the luxury lobby. Bellhop in red and white striped cap escorts me to a tasteful room, as small as Haifa's single, bed raised high off the floor.

Turn on TV. Nothing makes sense except local whodunits. Flip channels. Keep flipping. Watch then flip. Pace alongside the high bed, battle nervous jitters. *Too hot in here.*

Strip clothes off, throw them, glasses, atop mattress. Bedside clock reads 11:25. *Hafta move.*

Step out into the royal-red carpeted hallway. Impelled, stroll through deserted hotel corridors. Turn the handle of a random unmarked door on the right, painted white with cove molding trim to match others. Saunter into an all-white ballroom except for long beige curtains half-opened along the far wall of glass.

A cocktail party of fifteen well-heeled good-looking adults' mills in cliques and tête-à-têtes about thirty feet away, engaged, drinking white wine in an alcove staged just for them. *Or is it champagne?*

The men wear suits or tuxes, a few sport white hair. Animated women in ankle-length black skinny dresses, some in see-through bright pastels of in short skirts, mingle among them. They're rapt in conversations, joking, laughing, in gay moods. The large rectangular room we're in holds twenty tables covered by off-white linen tablecloths, no glasses, no silverware, nor cloth napkins. Formal white chairs surround them.

All empty except for me standing in the middle. *Where am I? They haven't noticed Me.*

Some turn. *Can they tell I'm American?*

"Bloody hell, what's that bloke doing?" a grumbling voice says.

"Tsk, tsk." Buzzing chatter subsides. Hear whispered derisions of flaccid penis, light laughter, but no one calls out or approaches. Wind back through the tables, turn, stroll out a different unmarked door. *Ha, these folks not impressed. So, what? No rush. I'm the master of time.*

Out in the hallway, "Shit. Where's My key? Where's My room?"

Pad down a corridor that looks identical to others in white wallpaper with thin red stripes. Scoot behind a clerk's cubbyhole in one corner. A red house phone lies on the countertop. Pick it up, punch 0.

"Front desk. May I help you?"

"I locked myself out, lost my key." Supply name, describe surroundings, nearest door number, thirty-two.

"Someone will be right up sir."

Bellboy in candy-striped uniform and matching cap arrives. Without a word or dirty glance backward, he leads to the room, passing no guests. He unlocks the door and hands over a key, neither of us embarrassed.

Dress, no socks or shoes, lay on the bed, watch an abominable snow-interrupted TV. Switch channel after five minutes of insanity. No decent programs or movies on "telly." *Ab-so-lute-ly terrible. Producers need to do something. The U.S. is much better.*

Get up, pace. Engage in a lengthy conversation about it, converse with 'Abdu'l-Bahá for a time, listen to His uplifting, chanting voice. Understand....

[Tuesday]

Lay down. Leave BBC on. Too scary calling Janet but had mailed postcards. *At least I did that. What will she do?*

Thoughts race, cannot stop... *Justgowiththeflow.*

Skip through consequences of an upsetting return. Close eyes.

Before dawn, phone front desk. "Can you please call a cab for Heathrow?"

"We have a service sir, I'll ring them. About fifteen minutes. Is that acceptable?"

"Excellent."

"Thank you, sir, he'll wait for you." Put on socks, shoes. Pocket the chessboard, wallet. Take the polished wood-paneled elevator to the lobby, pay hotel clerk, ignore cost. *Don't care. Necessary.*

Out front, a friendly, well-muscled, well-dressed cabbie with black chauffer's cap, black suit, and black tie over white starched shirt opens the rear door to the midsize late-model car, it too black. Soon he speeds toward Heathrow on a divided highway through pouring, black, blowing, hard English rain in full blustery swing. Caught in the blinding white sprays from cars and lorries ahead and to the sides, it obscures the road ahead.

Wipers scrape windshield at double speed. Vehicles of all shapes and sizes hurtle toward us on the other side of the concrete barrier in their double lanes and splash waves of water over the divider onto the hood and windshield. Move to the left side of the backseat to avoid them.

The driver is half-Irish and talkative. We bond over Mom's Cavanaugh family name. Spell it.

"It's with a 'K' in Ireland," he confides.

Arrive. Pull up close to terminal entrance. Only a five-pound note in right pants pocket next to cigarette pack and he doesn't accept credit cards. *Shit!*

"Let's go inside to an ATM, I'll pay extra."

Both of us run heads down and skirt under pelting raindrops. *Smart cabbie coming with Me.* Ditched a cabbie back in Ewing that way once. Told him "Stop here. I'll be right back with the fare." But it wasn't my parent's house—that was down the block. Walked around to the rear like going to our back door and ran like a hellcat.

Pass into the main entrance and under shelter. Inside we search for an ATM and British pounds. Use one, glad to hand over a five-pound bill as a tip. *Friendly guy.*

"Thank you so much. Sorry for the trouble, Sean." He nods and leaves. Watch him rush through the easing rain to his car. *What was his name?*

At eight o'clock buy a ticket on DELTA. Only three brief hours to wait. Visit the same McDonald's, large black coffee, which can't stomach, but too sleepy to protest. *Need it strong.* Munch two Egg McMuffins. Smoke outside under a different canopy. Wait. *Soon, home soon. Patience.*

Lounge until called at the appointed Gate. Only a few passengers line up. Board.

When aloft and in coach seat, play games with a Nintendo-like controller on a small video screen built into the backside of the seat ahead. But controls lock and can't get any movement on the screen.

"What's wrong with this picture?"

Move empty seat to empty seat, trying five, ten, twenty controllers. They lock within minutes of attempted frenzied manipulations. Firmer ministrations and mumbled prayers fail. "What the heck is wrong with these things? Hell, piss, and shit you'd think one would work."

We must be above thirty-thousand feet. Get up, stroll the airborne monster ship unhampered. Few lights on, thin blue blankets cover a minimal number of sleeping passengers, their heads on pillows.

But a large bulky white door with big red letters and red and yellow stripes in the far rear of the wide plane on the port side attracts roaming interest.

"Oomph, oomph, oomph," push its two-foot-long white molded plastic door handle down. "C'mon Rod, you can do this. We've got to fly." The urge grows stronger.

Cute young blonde flight attendant happens by, rushes over.

"May I help you to your seat sir?" She's distracting in her solicitous manner.

Stand up straighter.

"Ah, sure." Leads to a rear seat, no one else in the row, in front, behind, or across.

"Please remain here sir, I'll return in a few moments." Minutes later she sits across the aisle, maintains constant vigil, and offers pitter-patter speech.

Go to the head—she waits outside the door. Inside, throw house and car keys down the tiny trash bin.

"Clink" sounds echo through dirty hand towels. *Someone might steal and use them. Should I throw wallet and wedding ring away too? Throw 'em away. You don't want them to know who You are, do You? Better not, Jersey DMV awful, too many hassles.*

Tug wallet out. Passport out. Twist gold band off. Place them on the brushed aluminum sink. Stare down. Stare ahead. *Is this the end of the line? Will they take Me away? What do I need ID for, I know Who I Am.*

Light knocks, "Sir, is everything all right?"

Unlatch the door, fold it open. Return to coach seat, her trailing. The bright smiling girl says nothing. Her straight white TV model's teeth are framed against her beautiful piercing hazel eyes and offset her attentive personality. *Hazel, like mine.*

A glow surrounds her svelte and youthful body.

Another guardian angel....

At 30,000 feet,
attempt to fly home
on superhuman arms

246

5.21 LIBERTY

While conversing with such a sociable guardian, she produces a small pad and pen.

"Can I get your name and address, please?" Comply. She writes it.

"Do you have any luggage? Can I call a spouse or friend when we arrive to pick you up?" *Who will meet Us at the airport?*

It's Liberty International Airport, better known as EWR. We just call it Newark.

"No luggage, travelin' light. Call Bob." Give 609 number.

Later ask for pretzels and coffee from the wheeled cart.

"Cream and sugar, please." Enjoy the crunchy taste and caffeine rush, and angel's description of her short airline career. Minutes and hours pass with sporadic chit-chat as ruminate on America's deficient, divisive, and competitive political system.

"Yeah, gerrymandering is the worst. An impartial panel should demarcate voting districts, nationwide. But even then, the popular vote doesn't even matter. The Electoral College with its arcane state-by-state rules and handfuls of electors elect the President, not the people. Popular vote be damned. Many voters know it's a slap in the face."

She says little as more time passes. Continue to rail.

She's polite.

Cabin overhead lights flash, **FASTEN SEAT BELTS**. The captain makes the all-important announcement. *Yes!*

Soon the push of the landing approach invigorates blood. The smooth, powerful touchdown on the runway signifies familiar turf. Taxi to our Gate. *Home. Screw you El Al, screw you AEGEAN.*

Young angel and another blonde angel her age in the same blue uniform lead the way off the plane. They waltz like ballroom dancers through their shortened customs and entry line, up to a uniformed man in a booth encased in plexiglass. My beautiful escorts show their badges, pass through. Booth man looks at me. Walk up.

"Sir, can I please have your ID and passport?"

Pause.

Hand them over. Inspector's eyes scan them, peers into my face, touches keys, stares, hands them back.

"Thank you, sir, you may proceed."

Drop them in front left front pocket. Fondle ring. Take it out, slip it on left hand finger. The two considerate golden-haired goddesses lead us through ARRIVALS to a circular drive, in front of the DELTA logo.

Bob and Barb are parked at the curb. Bob steps out.

Angels ask, "Mister Harris?"

"Yes, that's me." They turn back and start into the terminal with sweet waves and "Goodbye."

"Thanks, girls!" They pass through the glass doorway.

He strides to the sidewalk and waits, arms at sides.

"Bob, you SOB! I shudda figured you'd be here." Wrap his wide girth, look up into his warm familiar embrace, feel his forehead kiss. Like we do, raise on tiptoes, and return one on his cheek. Bob also pinches asses in jest and friendship; not now.

"Rodney, I can't tell you how good it is to see you. You've had quite the adventure."

"Yeah, it was cool. Glad I went, but gotta have a smoke. Gotta!"

Bob grimaces but stands aside at the curb. Light up as he waits, pacing. Smoke until done. Tee the butt. Barb, still in their car, is on her cell phone.

Bob's saying something.

"Rod, do you know what day it is?"

"No, not particularly."

"It's Tuesday, February sixth. You've disappeared for five days."

"Oh. I wudda never guessed that long."

Bob swings open the rear door.

Climb in, sit, squeeze Barb's shoulder, lost in thinking ahead. Not thinking. *Bob drove to Mercer in 1979, didn't he? Important, We must appear normal.*

Bob speeds down the Turnpike and familiar roads to Trenton. Ruminate, gab, pontificate in back seat.

On Brunswick Avenue see **Helene Fuld Hospital Emergency** sign on the right, hospital on the left. Pull into the loop. Exit the car and enter the Resident Psychiatric Unit.

Meet Janet, who's solicitous. Strong furrowed brow. No raised voice, no screaming, no snide remarks, no questions. Soft tones.

"Rod, are you all, right?"

Lay down on a stretcher in a bare green room. *Will they give a sedative cocktail?*

Janet comforts, "You have to sleep, Rod."

Head collapses onto a hard-minuscule air pillow, body flops, turns, flops. Try to lay still for her, close eyes partway, as she coddles head in her arm. Sit up.

"Jan?" Talk, semi-rational, not about the excursion. Then a new white smocked gentleman with a stethoscope enters, a professional-looking Indian doctor. He smiles, his kind-heart obvious.

"Missus Richards, I'd like to speak with your husband alone, if I may. Please follow me, Rodney." Janet assists as climb down then leaves and takes a chair in the hall.

He leads to his half-walled, half-glass-enclosed office. Sit in a hospital green plush chair with Scandinavian wooden legs and shape. Cross right leg. Answer questions without elaboration. *Keep it short.*

"I only need sleep, Doctor. I'll return to normal in no time. Just need a few more pills." Rational. Clear. Level-headed. *Show him you're fine.*

"The racing thoughts stopped. Not planning to save the world or anyone else. I recognize what I did was off key, and it won't happen again."

One phrase reverberates, *Please... release me... let me go.* Engelbert Humperdinck's song played at Dad's apartment on his record player so often in 1966. *Must avoid the insane asylum. Don't want to shuffle and wander through morbid halls again.*

Janet's there on our return to the green room. Climb up and lie on the high bed-cart.

"I'm fine. Believe me, it's over."

She leaves when the doctor calls, "Missus Richards?"

They begin an intimate verbal exchange I can see through his office glass.

What are they saying?

Fools only fool themselves
Disappearance means
trust has fled too
Damn it.

5.22 CARRIED AWAY, AGAIN

Toss, turn, kick at the thin green sheet. Injected once, twice. Try to sleep on the skinny padded cart with its tiny hard pillow while Janet soothes and coos.

"Rod, you need to pay attention." Two burly orderlies loom next to her. "You have to come with us."

Blurry, dazed, in a rocky swaying ambulance ride. Don't care if shackled, umpteenth time.

"Where... are you taking me?"

"Carrier Clinic in Belle Mead, about thirty-five minutes away." *Aw hell. Gotta go, no choice now. Gotta play along.*

Sleep. A day, a night. Two. No waking dreams. No visions, no voices.

Again, with shuffling and bowed head. Again, with interviews, check-ins to the nurse's station, little white Dixie cups, meals in line holding rectangular lime-green or rust plastic trays. Again, a semi-parochial, paranoid, hemmed in place. *Gotta escape, find My Mind. Losing it.*

We eat in a small dining area of wooden picnic tables covered by a thick red plastic cover on top, white cotton felt on the bottom, with a white vase in the middle holding a single red plastic rose. It's like summer days spent at Robin Dee Day Camp as a boy but without horses to ride or games of Mumblety Peg to win or lose.

Chew and keep head down as sit on two opposite benches, three of us on each, silent, chomping, some using their forks to push food clumps around on their plates. Meals are salads, meatloaf, and mashed potatoes except for breakfast with scrambled eggs, limp bacon, and cold white toast.

The patient lounge has two short wooden bookcases, three shelves each, a handful of worn outdated books with torn jacket covers, three boxed games. A large screen black-framed color TV sits on a cabinet, tan couch with faux leather facing it. Splay out, watch one stupid show then two, but ennui unrelieved, growing more frustrated.

Rise. Peer through half-glass doors. *Can't see anyone outside. Is there barbwire on the walls?*

Ask a nurse, "When will my wife be here?"

"Visiting hour starts at seven." The only contact with the world except for flaky new patients consumed with their troubles. When together, listen as Janet shares.

"I just want you to get better Rod." She brings a pack of Salem's. They keep all cigarettes in a tray at the nurse's station, two allowed max, doled out at break times. I give some to other smokers bereft of their own.

Kids can't visit, can't see Daddy this sick.

Awake next morning before anyone else. It's five on the big clock. Still night shift. As soon as an orderly shows up at seven, beg him to put the coffee on. Wait next to the empty station. A nice young man proffers a filled Styrofoam cup, black.

"Ohh, thank you sooo much!"

Milk it for twenty minutes. Only coffee and cigarettes during the day hold interest. No arts and crafts to distract.

Group therapy session starts, with sixteen patients in a circle and a doctor sharing his discourse, or maybe it's supposed to be a discussion. *Or is it drivel, or self-loathing? What are they saying? It's not my problem!*

"Why are you saying that?! I can't solve your issues. Stop it. Stop it!"

Fists punch against the sheet rocked wall.

"Bang, bang… bang, bang…." Two brusque men rush in and manhandle flailing arms and torso.

"Stay off Me. Get your hands off!" Recognize what they carry, something from other hospitals and movies. *Hell no!*

They thrust both arms into the straitjacket, lace and snap as fast as they can with tired practice. *Struggle!*

Drag and push back, drag and push along the corridor. Socks slip on its linoleum. Watch as sunlight streams through windows in slow motion. Then the sunlight's gone.

But bright recessed bulbs blind eyes. Shut lids tight.

"Off, off."

"Oomph!" Throw body at white-tufted padded walls and bounce off.

"OOMPH!" Three hard pushes, harder, pushing, but socks still slippery. Can't wiggle out. Padded door slams.

Collapse in the middle of an empty room on the thick gray mat.

"Please, We're sorry. I'm sorry!" Eyes water and can't wipe them. *No way out!*

Crawl on knees to a gray wall, turn, push back up straight against the pad, stretch out legs. Keep eyes shut from the horrible spotlights. *Where will I sleep? How?*

Spend full twenty-four hours in that… cell. Once out, decry behavior, say to every staff person, "I'll be good."

One morning a pretty teenager, black hair past her shoulders, sits on an Army cot in an 8 x 7-foot room, crying. See her through the half-wall of glass, watch her from outside for a few hidden moments.

She's crying, in silence, cursing herself. A brown army blanket lays disheveled around her quaking body. Her head is on her knees, arms wrapped like a vise around her bent legs, rocking, chest heaving, moaning without pause. Low sobs and curses, curses and sobs. Her agony, apparent.

Twist the door handle, enter on thick white cotton socks, sit behind her, but don't touch. Raise the loose brown blanket and cover her shaking shoulders. *Sad what she's putting herself through.*

Loosely wrap both arms around her upper body; feel her tremors. Lay head on her messy black hair, as irregular streaks of black mascara discolor her pale cheeks. Whisper "It's all right, it'll be all right. You'll be home soon." *What else can I say?*

Lightly clutch her shoulders. *Why is she moaning?*

Still unresponsive. No one interrupts us. Spend minutes in a tenuous embrace. At a loss, extricate sympathetic self from the half-room.

Her lips still twitch, only less.

The Carrier Program has downtime with little to do but have a blood pressure read taken every morning, eat three meals a day plus snacks, take pills four times a day, and go on smoke breaks. Group sessions merge and fade. No windows to look out of except in discussion rooms.

Clear windows would've been a pleasant distraction.

At loose ends, find a bedraggled book of Edgar Allan Poe's stories and poems, my favorite author. Read line by line, underline pregnant passages and words in pen. Annotate interjections on margins. *Thanks Edgar, you take my beating heart elsewhere.*

Regular smoke breaks and flowing coffee are highlights in a sea of glum faces, dull spirits, unfocused eyes, and thin lips, although a few jabberers liven up boredom with their exploits. Spend most time sitting in the Day Room on blue vinyl padded chairs with the TV on, listening to the eighty-five-year-old Italian man curse and fight off staff.

"Stronza! Cavallo! Cazzo! Leccaculo!" We laugh on the sly at their unsuccessful attempts and his unabated eighty-year-old feistiness.

Feel more alert later when attend forums in small conference rooms for ten of us, as facilitators elicit responses on "Meditation," "Coping with Stress," and other topics. Attend an AA meeting in another part of the hospital. Had intoned their wise mantra years earlier. *If only I always had the wisdom to know the difference.*

Mind, body, spirit, confined for four sad, silent, closed-off weeks.

We, sluggishly transforms back into me.

Great meds help normalcy return
and freedom ring
Else locked up longer

5.23 SAFE FROM MYSELF

Janet unlocks the kitchen door and enters ahead of me. Empty my pockets onto the counter. Some foreign bills, three dollars, and odd-looking coins splatter out. Place wallet stuffed with tiny receipts on top.

Jesse's studying at Drew and Kate's in school. Deserted the job, her, the kids. It brought shock and disappointment. Jan, most upset because hadn't called her. Somehow, she doesn't berate or rub it in. But neither on our ride here nor any of our time together has she implied she wants to hear details of my mental disruptions or reasons. Impossible to rationalize my crazy behaviors to her.

On the other side of the counter, she turns.

"Rod, you know I love you, right?"

Nod, *Oh thank you.*

"Of course. I hope you know I love you."

"But I can't go through this again." It's her tone, her resolute voice, only like this when she's adamant.

"Hon, the medications will help."

"They better, because if they don't, we can't live with you. I would want a divorce." *Aw Geez.*

Flustered, but understand. Reasonable. She's not a quibbler. She means it. Alone, removed from her, removed from Jesse and Kate, away from comfort, away from routines, is as sobering as a gut kick and slap across the head. *Only who's the jackass doing the kicking? It's got to be me. I've got to get this sickness under control. Can't let it overtake me again. Too much to lose.*

Within three days Janet phones GreenSpring and lambasts them over how Doctor Wolf had been fooled.

"This wouldn't have happened under Doctor Argueta's care," she almost shouts. She also sends them a letter detailing her vehement frustrations.

We soon praise their wisdom because they authorize eight sessions to meet with Doctor Argueta. First once a week, then every month.

Mental illnesses hibernate
Or attack like
angry hungry bears

Thank goodness Spud found my car at the airport, don't know how he got it out. Return to work and no one delves into reasons for the absence, as if they all know. Assume they do.

Weeks fly by trying to meet the demands of the FY97 IT Waiver and other procurements. All willpower and concentration focus on the reviews, spreadsheet checklist, phone calls, and emails, to the exclusion of personal interference.

As agency requests step through our approval-processing gauntlet, grab the mail from my In-basket. There's that pesky pink envelope from Human Resources with a label on it with my name and unit and nothing else.

"What now?" Tear it open. The half-slip inside reads:

6-13-96 Chief Contract Administration Section $59,332—$80,294

"Whoa, I'll be…. The salary range is much better. I must do something right. Whatever it is, they like it."

Somehow, despite rough or bizarre behaviors, multiple leaves, even hospitalizations, somebody does likes me and my work. Intone a quick prayer of thanks for incredible blessings then email Joann with a note.

"Received the HR notice. Incredibly grateful. Please thank Chuck." Can only surmise that in six years here that all perfect threes on mid-year and annual performance reviews have generated such a promotion.

And maybe since I report to Chuck. As Director of Administration, a deputy state treasurer, and higher than HR's director, it doesn't hurt.

Vow to keep doing the best possible for as long as body, mind, and spirit allow. New business cards are in order. *Will they be my last?*

Janet will be proud.

Although mentally ill
we achieve many great things
if try our darnedest

6.0 EPILOGUE

A monorail or a rollercoaster. That's bipolar and that's life. From the moment we are conceived, every day and night we humans ride them. One moment the ride is calm and smooth, the next we climb up and up and swoosh down topsy-turvy. Across minefield deserts, up perilous mountains, into unexpected valleys, through questionable ravines and down raging rivers. The Conductor knows all the stops and is with us along our circuitous route and doesn't question our decisions or choices, or apathy, along the way. At the last station stop He takes our expired ticket with a knowing wink and a smile.

Our trip here may have ended too soon or lasted longer than we hoped for, but it is over and a new one is starting. The Conductor hands us a new ticket for a world of vast calm seas and friendly oceans. Then, we board a ship of our own making and sail into a realm of insight, spirits, and enlightenment, to learn the knowledge of our own ourselves. We have far to travel to reach our goal, but the One within us is greater than ourselves and knows the way.

I yearn for the Truths I'll learn in the next world as I search for them in this one.

Bouts of bipolar decrease with age. Rather, they're supposed to.

But I've experienced more manic events since 1996 and the trip to Haifa. Janet has stayed with me.

That episode, governed by a messiah complex, is common to many males.

May 2014, I started with hypomania and Voices, almost climbed to full mania, but we caught it in time. Two years later it overcame me. Two Hamilton police officers waited in our dining room as a crisis interventionist said, "Rodney, you can go willingly and be evaluated in the hospital or be committed involuntarily."

I agreed and signed a form. The evaluation at the Princeton Medical Psychiatric Screening Center did not go well. Or, maybe it did.

At age sixty-six I was in a full manic state yet denied it. The evaluation resulted in a month in Carrier Clinic for before returning to normal. What's normal for me and Janet together that is.

But I'm caught in a dilemma. On one hand, I want to share with Janet my emotions and thoughts, so she can understand what it's like. On the other, she does. She understands it's not me when I'm manic but the disease. It's almost impossible for a rational person to communicate signs of illness they see in someone when that someone is gripped in a mental episode of mania or depression. They are incapable of recognizing it in themselves.

Janet can't stand being around me when I'm that way. When I am, it's a race to get me back on schedule, on medication, or into a hospital.

I have never thought of myself as mentally ill, or as a sufferer. Bipolar is a label and doesn't control me. But a big but, I must stay alert and maintain vigilance against symptoms that appear. I must share how I'm feeling and what I'm thinking right away.

It's a balancing act.

I returned to Haifa in May 2015 on Bahá'í pilgrimage and toured the holy sites with other pilgrims. This time, it was a peaceful, fulfilling spiritual experience. We pilgrims had an audience with a few Universal House of Justice members who greeted us personally. As usual, forget what I said to one, Mister Paul Lample, but it wasn't profound.

As a visual learner, speech has never been memorable, my own or others. I have to see it or visualize it. Sixty-five percent of us are that way.

My coffee intake, mostly Dunkin and Wawa with their proliferation of Drive-thrus, averages five medium to large cups before noon. I sent in a tribute to Dunkin and received a $5.00 gift card for the trouble.

Smoking is one of the banes in my character. My May 2017 heart attack came from it, and I needed a coronary stent. My doctor says my lungs are like yellowed blackened Swiss cheese when they should be thick white slices of provolone. I count and curse each one I light.

Janet and I celebrated fifty years of marriage with a trip by train and subway (Covid had lifted), to Manhattan and we visited our son, Jesse, daughter-in-law, and granddaughter. We then walked and stayed at The Standard with a panoramic view of downtown from our room. We dined out at a casual-dress pricey restaurant where they brought fire sparklers to our table as celebration and had decadent desserts. Then we shared memories over coffee and tea of our years together.

We see Kate regularly too and are grateful and fortunate for God's grace and the splendid memories.

All in all, and if not careless, I try to follow a positive path forward, and try not to hurt others. My path has never been straight and narrow, yet as I age, wisdom and love grow, the path gets wider, and I stray less from it.

7.0 INSIGHTS AND TAKEAWAYS
7.1 WE NEED MENTALCARE

I asked Janet once, "What was it like for you during my episodes?"
"Horrible." She looked away, signaling, "Please don't ask."

I couldn't rouse myself to put her on the spot to ask more, no matter how relaxed she appeared. I realized I don't want to remind her of my episodes—too upsetting.

Memories unearth emotions. Emotions revive pain. Pain erodes love. If these experiences you've read have shown anything, it's that while manic, I was incapable, clueless, of understanding the consequences of my actions. Those actions caused pain.

The disease tramples feelings and love between people and for society's norms despite well-meaning intentions even in the best cases.

Whether for me and my family or multi-millions of caregivers, living with someone afflicted with bipolar disease is horrible when it strikes. I have learned and experienced much over forty years diagnosed as bipolar. My psychiatrist told me, "Rodney, you're a five or six for sure." As a five or six having had half-a-dozen full-blown manic episodes ending in monthlong hospitalizations, and periods of hypomania and depression throughout my life, can you imagine what an undiagnosed, untreated bipolar person and their caregivers experience?

If like Medicare and Medicaid we had a program of MentalCare, that is, fully coordinated counseling and support systems for mental illness sufferers and their caregivers at all levels of society, we could solve many more problems. If we coordinated the police and criminal justice systems, the courts and prisons, the healthcare system, and insurance, that would go far. And there's the homeless, even the unemployed, who need income, training, food, shelter, and clothing for stability. Besides healthcare in general.

Geared toward all ages and stages, the overarching goal is to ameliorate the devastating effects of mental illnesses and be model other countries follow.

The Human Rights Council of the United Nations stated in 2017:

- **One in four persons in the world will experience a mental issue in their lifetime.**
- It takes all of us, and our health and prison systems, to deal with that and transition to wellness.
- More caregivers, social services, and psychiatrists are needed.

Janet and I are fortunate. We had solid beginnings of love and trust, solid educations, a caring family, and understanding friends, coworkers, and employers. And good health insurance and doctors. Together they are the legs of a chair. But you can't sit on a one or two-legged chair.

A program of universal, affordable MentalCare would make a sturdy chair. For example, there are 24,000 psychiatrists in the U.S. There are over five million diagnosed bipolar sufferers in America. That's 1 psychiatrist per 208 bipolar patients. Multiply that need for skillful psychiatrists by the list of over two hundred mental disorders on Google and you glimpse the strain on the current system.

Remember, as cited from the U.N. Human Rights Council, **one in four persons in the world will experience a mental issue in their lifetime.**

Over eight billion of us inhabit the planet now. It's estimated by the year 2050 the world population will be between nine and ten billion.

Each of us has innumerable problems and issues to deal with, great or small, every day, besides the devastation of health and life from the Covid-pandemic. These test our spirits, minds, emotions, finances, and bodies. They strain, curtail, or drain our limited resources to deal with them.

These problems will only grow worse unless each of us, every woman, man, youth, and child, has a stable moral, spiritual, physical, and mental core.

Too much of what we are doing now is reacting to mental health problems instead of diagnosing them early and preventing worse mental and societal outcomes.

We have made much progress.

We need more.

We need a coordinated Plan.

We need a Program.

And we need to fund it from our personal and collective wealth.

Note 1: American Journal of Public Health, 2013 May; 103(5): 777–780, *Mental Illness Stigma, Health Seeking, and Public Health Programs.*

7.2 WE ARE NOT ALONE

You may have heard of Edgar Allan Poe, Mel Gibson, Mariah Carey, Ted Turner, Frank Sinatra, Florence Nightingale, Vincent Van Gogh, Ernest Hemingway, Patty Duke, possibly Britney Spears (according to some reports), and Catherine Zeta-Jones. Oh, and the esoteric Russell Brand. There are also untold numbers of philosophers, artists, entertainers, blue or white-collar workers, et al. who are bipolar. Many, although experiencing the worst of their conditions, led or lead functioning, complex lives.

You hear about some of these. But you don't hear about average people going through it until they hit the news, often in tragedies. I was a Hamilton Township Municipal Court mediator for twenty-four years. One man who appeared in a mediation session struck a young woman at a NJ Turnpike Rest Stop and destroyed their property too. He admitted being bipolar and off his meds. He could have faced assault charges. He apologized, it was accepted, and he paid for the damages.

With ongoing trials and studies, new medications have been introduced. Besides versions of lithium carbonate, there's Laytuda, Vraylar, Abilify, Seroquel, Zoloft, and others. Their development, release, and incessant TV commercials testify to the size of the problem.

We have drugs and some clinics, but need more professionals to help, such as:

- Primary care doctors. Generalists who have received some training in mental health during medical school and residency. They often provide basic or initial assessment and medication treatment.
- Psychiatrists. Specialists in the branch of medicine devoted to the diagnosis, prevention, study, and treatment of mental disorders. Together, you develop a management plan for treatment and recovery.
- Psychologists or therapists. They do not prescribe medication but help with talk therapy, called psychotherapy. Talk therapy provides coping skills that can lessen the chances of long illnesses or hospital stays, even suicidal inclinations.
- Nurses. Their advanced training can help in the battle.
- Some social workers who are psychotherapists can also treat bipolar disorder using talk therapy. They do not prescribe medications.
- Audio and video visits on your cellphone, laptop, or PC, Telemedicine, can be as effective as in-person visits. They can also be a transportation-saver and cost-effective alternative.
- Cognitive-Behavioral Therapy (CBT). Besides having a medical doctor and a psychiatrist, one can receive this training as an Outpatient if your insurance covers it. It provides practical methods to control

your thoughts and actions and to counteract signs of depression, hypomania, and mania. Hearing other's stories brings perspective too.

- Support groups. Some groups now meet online. If you don't want to meet people in person at a discussion setting or you don't have access to one, you can subscribe to newsletters or attend Zoom meetings almost anonymously.
- Friends and relatives who care and try to understand.
- Be active. Cultivate a garden, see a movie, volunteer, work full or part-time, spend more time with family, and keep yourself moving and interested in life and people. Don't dwell on your own self. Do what you have a passion for. I became a writer and editor.

As my friend and barber of fifty years, the Mayor of Warren Street, Joe Festa says, "Help is at the end of your elbow."

Of course, belief in God can be a great comfort and source of motivation. Rely on God and be practical. Feed your spirit the truth.

Having said these things, they should all be part of a good MentalCare program.

As in anything concerning your health, consult reliable medical sources for guidance on mental treatment plans and options.

Then please follow them.

7.3 BIPOLAR NEVER LEAVES, BUT…

Taking prescribed medications at the right times is so important I use pill cases when out of the house. I've missed single doses and slipped into mania. I'm still itching and eager to go—impulsive. That can be a sign of hypomania, the stage before mania, so I work hard on patience. The key is to recognize what trigger's one's manic episodes and stop them from progressing. Or I've been morose, isolated, and somewhat depressed.

The best way to avoid extremes is to tell someone you're having abnormal, rash, or depressing thoughts or feelings. The sooner you do, the closer you'll be to stopping the worst from happening.

Some triggers and signs of bipolar are:

- Lack of sleep
- Too much excitement or grand expectations; overly emotional or the reverse, lack of energy and apathetic
- Extreme euphoria or elation
- Stress, especially unexpected or undue
- Racing thoughts
- Grandiose thoughts, like being a leader, king or queen, star, tycoon or savior
- Mood swings—wildly happy or severely sad
- Impulsive behavior like spending sprees or taking off without notice
- Passionate or compulsive activity followed by disinterest, or switching between "must do" projects in quick succession
- All-powerful, invincible thoughts that make you believe you can do anything and will succeed
- Ascribing coincidences to Acts of God or a confirmation that "things went my way" because you willed them to
- Missing or not taking prescriptive medicines in the right doses at the times indicated or messing with doses. Trying to be your own doctor
- Thinking you're right, or know best, and everyone else is wrong or doesn't understand; and the corollary, defending yourself when logic dictates otherwise
- Irritability, like being curt, harsh, or cruel; cursing is a sure sign
- A short temper or uncontrollable outbursts
- Not caring about oneself, everyday things, events, or people and their feelings; avoiding people
- Self-absorbed in your thoughts to the exclusion of anyone or anything; self-isolated or continual guilt; feeling worthless

- Tiredness, listlessness, depression, or bemoaning one's fate, malaise, or catastrophic thinking
- Sexual impulses more than usual or with strangers
- Spontaneous big decisions; costly shopping sprees or big purchases
- Acting with no thought of consequences, like gambling or risk-taking
- Not trusting your doctor(s)

But too often, the manic or depressed person doesn't recognize their illness and says nothing or tries to hide it. That's why when we see such behaviors it's important to ask: Is it *an increase* or *decrease in his or her normal patterns*?

Of course, no one is perfect and will exhibit some of these behaviors. That doesn't mean we or they are bipolar, or manic or chronically depressed.

But looking back I can say I first showed signs at age fourteen and it took a full-blown manic episode fifteen years later to get an accurate diagnosis.

Bipolar is about recognizing changes in behavior. It's a biological and chemical condition with genetic undertones. It's an episodic illness with symptoms that are not a part of a person's regular behavior. It's noticeable and out of the norm for expected human responses. That's when someone needs to intervene, before mania overtakes one's rational senses or before depression causes the loss of the will to live or suicidal thoughts.

If those behaviors described above are systematic and apparent my best advice is this:

Open your mouth, move your tongue, and call or tell someone.

Guardian Angels stand ready to assist you.

8.0 RESOURCES
8.1 MENTAL HEALTH INFORMATION

According to most if not all State laws, any person who is a danger to themselves or others, or considered a threat, can be restrained and/or locked up for their protection or to protect others. That goes for a mentally ill person acting out as well, including spoken thoughts, verbal threats, physical assault, or indications toward suicide. And its legal.

The first line of defense is your local crisis center staff or the police, trained to recognize such behaviors. They are a phone call away. Their raison d'être is to help and protect. Police have wide discretion to determine how a perceived threat should be handled and temporary incarceration or hospitalization may ensue. That doesn't mean police may be cruel or hurtful. Psychological consideration, fair judgment, and proper handling should be expected and received.

MENTAL HEALTH RESOURCES:
- Have your local police number on speed dial. A critical number to have in the face of violence. Otherwise, call 911.
- Have the number(s) handy for your closest Screening or Crisis Center(s). The Nov 2/Nov 9 2020 issue of *Time* reported a new law establishing 988 as a national crisis center phone number and resource. The target for implementation is July 2022.
- SAMHSA at the federal level has a Helpline 800-622-HELP for treatment referrals and information, 24/7, or check their Treatment Center Finder at https://findtreatment.samhsa.gov
  Its anonymous and confidential.
- National Suicide Prevention Hotline 800-273-8255.
- National Institute of Mental Health (NIMH) articles cover mental health, the latest news and updates, and resources. It also has a free email subscription newsletter. Go to **nimh.nih.gov**
- The National Alliance on Mental Illness (NAMI) offers a free newsletter, info, and a welcoming community.
  Helpline: 800-950-NAMI. **www.nami.org**
- Bp Magazine, free info by email, from **bphope.com**
- Henrik at **PositivityBlog.com**, subscribe free for uplifting daily positive outlooks
- *The Road Less Traveled*, copyright 1978 M. Scott Peck, and later editions and publication dates. That book opened my eyes and mind to being dysfunctional or mentally ill.
- Major drug companies like Merck & Co, Bristol Myers-Squibb, etc., all have printed material, websites, and information. Take

what anyone says with a grain of salt. What works in general may work differently on you.

- Major hospitals like Johns Hopkins have websites too.
- WebMD is helpful at **http://www.webmd.com/mental-health/mental-health-helpline**
- Check your government mental health listings, including your County. For example, in New Jersey there's the Division of Mental Health and Addiction Services (DMAHS) at https://www.nj.gov/humanservices/clients/mental/

Finding help in your area, when you need it, may take determination. If you love or care about someone with bipolar disorder, **nail down specific resources now.** Call them and talk. Scope them out. Have them readied in your back pocket.

They may be a Godsend.

8.2 INFORMATION ON THE BAHÁ'Í FAITH

- Contact Information: 1-800-22-UNITE (800-228-6483)
- U.S. Bahá'í website: *https://www.bahai.us*
- Bahá'í World website: *https://www.bahai.org*
- Free online, uptodate access to Bahá'í literature and books: **https://www.bahai.org/library/** You can find all the full contexts of the quotations used herein by entering a few words from the quotation into the Search box.
- *www.bahaiteachings.org* contains personal essays on current topics by a spectrum of writers. I've authored over 220 of them.
- *Bahá'u'lláh and the New Era, An Introduction to the Bahá'í Faith* by J.E. Esslemont, is s thorough and answers most questions. Original copyright 1950 by the National Spiritual Assembly of the Bahá'ís of the United States.

'Abdu'l-Bahá summed up what it means to be a Bahá'í: "...be the embodiment of all human perfections."[37]

Bahá'u'lláh described it this way:
"O well-beloved ones! The tabernacle of unity hath been raised; regard ye not one another as strangers. Ye are the fruits of one tree and the leaves of one branch.

"...love is light, no matter in what abode it dwelleth; and hate is darkness, no matter where it may make its nest.

"Were man to appreciate the greatness of his station and the loftiness of his destiny he would manifest naught save goodly character, pure deeds, and a seemly and praiseworthy conduct. ...

"Women and men have been and will always be equal in the sight of God. ...

"We have enjoined upon all to engage in crafts and trades and have accounted it as an act of worship.

"Trustworthiness is the greatest of doors leading to the tranquility and security of the people of the world.

"Knowledge is the cause of exaltation and advancement. It enableth man to pass beyond the world of dust to the realms above and leadeth him out of darkness into light. It is the redeemer and the bestower of life. It conferreth the living waters of immortality and imparteth heavenly food."[38]

8.3 ABOUT ME

Rodney has been a business and technical writer for thirty years and now writes prose and poetry since retiring in 2009 after a thirty-nine-year career with the State of New Jersey. His story *Episodes A poetic memoir* on living with bipolar disease was self-published in 2012 (out of print). His blog *writewithauthority.blogspot.com* started in 2014.

Rodney's book *Solving the World's Titanic Struggles* was self-published in 2018. It contains one hundred essays of philosophical and spiritual slants published online by BahaiTeachings.org. Volume 2 is due out the second half of 2021.

He has facilitated over 3,000 writing and poetry critique sessions with local writers since 2012 and has assisted fourteen writers edit, polish, and publish their books of memoir, fiction, and nonfiction.

His short story *Bike Slide* was published in the March 2017 issue of the Kelsey Review. Two of his poems appeared online in *The Drunken Llama*. He also owns and operates his own consulting company ABLiA Media LLC which helps writers edit, format, polish, and publish their works. Fourteen books of his clients have been published with more following.

Rodney served on the Rutger's Writing Conference Advisory Board for three years, 2017-2019, and introduced such notables as TV and movie critic David Bianculli, poet Mark Doty, author Mary Bly (pen name Eloisa James), publishing authorpreneurs Arielle Eckstut and David Henry Sterry and others at the annual conferences attended by two hundred.

His philosophy is that every person has a story to share and a unique voice with which to share it.

8.4 CONTACT ME

Contact me by email at **1950ablia@gmail.com** or write c/o:

ABLiA Media LLC
P.O. Box 2536
Trenton NJ 08619

Email is preferred. Please include your full name and email address. You can investigate my manuscript editing, revising, formatting, polishing, and publishing services for writers through my website at *rodneyrichards.info/* when it is finished construction, soon.

Thanks for reading!
I'd be grateful if you'd post a review on Amazon or another venue for your feelings and thoughts on the content or issues brought up in this book. Your show of interest or Likes make a difference. I read all reviews personally so I can appreciate your feedback and respond when practical.
*You can also find me on Facebook at **rodneywriter** or Instagram at **rrichardswriter.***
Thanks for your support!

Rod

PS And write your story! I hope to read it someday and learn from your experiences. It's easier now to self-publish or hybrid-publish for next to zero or little cost. Do it!

9.0 ENDNOTES
9.1 EPIGRAPH SOURCES

'Abdu'l-Bahá, cited by Shoghi Effendi in *The Advent of Divine Justice*

Dr. Wayne W. Dyer, *Inspiration Your Ultimate Calling*, Copyright 2006. Hay House Inc. USA.

Stephen R. Covey, *The Eighth Habit*, From Effectiveness to Greatness, Copyright 2004 by Franklin Covey Co., published by Free Press, a division of Simon and Schuster, U.S.A.

Naked City, 1958-1962 ABC TV show

Rodney Richards, haiku in homage to Edgar Allan Poe

9.2 REFERENCES AND NOTES

1. bp Magazine, bphopeBUZZ, Myth #2, *Bipolar Disorder is a Personal Problem, not a Societal One*, Feb. 7, 2021. Also, according to NIMH statistics, an estimated 2.8% of U.S. adults had bipolar disorder in 2018. An estimated 82.9% of people with bipolar disorder had a serious impairment, the highest percent of serious impairment among mood disorders. An estimated 4.4% of U.S. adults experience bipolar disorder at some time in their lives.
https://www.nimh.nih.gov/health/statistics/bipolar-disorder.shtml

2. Depression and Bipolar Support Alliance (DBSA). NIMH statistics reported on 10-25-19. https://www.dbsalliance.org/education/bipolar-disorder/bipolar-disorder-statistics/

3. "...world is but one country...." Shoghi Effendi, *The Promised Day is Come*, Copyright 1951, 1961 by the National Spiritual Assembly of the Bahá'ís of the U.S., Bahá'í Publishing Trust, Wilmette Illinois.

4. "...nethermost fire...." Bahá'u'lláh, *Gleanings from the Writings of Bahá'u'lláh* CXXV, translated by Shoghi Effendi, Copyright 1939, 1952 by the National Spiritual Assembly of the Bahá'ís of the U.S., Fourth printing 1969, Bahá'í Publishing Trust, 110 Linden Ave, Wilmette, Illinois.

5. The term queer or homo was used among youth I knew in 1964 to connote homosexuality. Now in 2020 the LGBTQ+ community has and is gaining civil rights and some religious tolerance that acknowledges their chosen identities. Both Father B and Monsignor F of my past parish were identified by name and photo in early 2020 in *The Trentonian* when the Catholic Church released such information.

6. Alláh-u-Abhá. Marzieh Gail, *Bahá'í Glossary*, copyright 1955 by the National Spiritual Assembly of the Bahá'ís of the United States of America, Fourth printing 1969, Bahá'í Publishing Trust, Wilmette, Illinois (out of print). A common greeting used among Bahá'ís, it translates into English as "God is All-Glorious." A form of The Greatest Name of God. Pronunciation: Allah-ho-Ab-ha.

7. Manifestation. A term used by Bahá'ís for unique Personages, Major Prophets or Messengers, and how They manifest perfectly the names and attributes of God. Each returns in spirit and a new human form. This occurred in the mid-19th century in both the Báb, a Shiraz merchant, and Bahá'u'lláh, a Persian nobleman. Bahá'u'lláh is a title meaning the Glory of God. Another title is the Ancient Beauty. Source: bahai-library.com

"Progressive revelation is a core teaching in the Bahá'í Faith that suggests that religious truth is revealed by God progressively and cyclically over time through a series of divine Messengers and that their teachings are tailored to suit the needs of the time and place of their appearance."
https://en.wikipedia.org/wiki/Progressive_revelation_(Bah%C3%A1%C A%BC%C3%AD)

8. "O Lord! Increase…" Bahá'u'lláh, *The Seven Valleys and the Four Valleys* (p. 34). Copyright 1945 and 1953, translated by Ali-Kuli Khan and Marzieh Gail, Bahá'í Publishing Trust, Wilmette, IL

9. "…asleep on My couch…" Bahá'u'lláh, *Epistle to the Son of the Wolf* (p. 11), translated by Shoghi Effendi, Copyright 1941, 1953 by the National Spiritual Assembly of the Bahá'ís of the United States, Bahá'í Publishing Trust, Wilmette IL.

10. "Should it be God's intention, there would appear out of the forests of celestial might the lion of indomitable strength whose roaring is like unto the peals of thunder reverberating in the mountains." Bahá'u'lláh, *Tablets of Bahá'u'lláh Revealed after the Kitab-i-Aqdas*, U.S Bahá'í Publishing Trust, pocket-sized edition Copyright 1988.

"The world is in travail, and its agitation waxeth day by day. Its face is turned towards waywardness and unbelief. Such shall be its plight, that to disclose it now would not be meet and seemly. Its perversity will long continue. And when the appointed hour is come, there shall suddenly appear that which shall cause the limbs of mankind to quake." Bahá'u'lláh, *Gleanings from the Writings of Bahá'u'lláh*, LXI, op cit.

11. "O God! Refresh and gladden my spirit. Purify my heart. Illumine my powers. I lay all my affairs in Thy Hand. Thou art my Guide and my Refuge. I will no longer be sorrowful and grieved; I will be a happy and joyful being. O God! I will no longer be full of anxiety, nor will I let trouble harass me. I will not dwell on the unpleasant things of life. O God! Thou art more a friend to me than I am to myself. I dedicate myself to Thee, O Lord."

'Abdu'l-Bahá, *Bahá'í Prayers*, Copyright 1954, 1982, 1985, 1991 by the National Spiritual Assembly of the Bahá'ís of the United States, Bahá'í Publishing Trust, Wilmette Illinois.

Note: The above is the correct version. In the narration I changed "my" to "his," which is not customary practice for Bahá'í prayers or writings.

Note: Although attributed to 'Abdu'l-Bahá, this prayer cannot be authenticated. It is still a favorite prayer used by innumerable Bahá'ís.

12. Regarding my cousin Muffie: In 1979 the terms "person with autism," "autistic," or "mentally challenged" weren't used. Thank goodness labels and stereotypes change.

13. "O my God! O Thou forgiver of sins, bestower of gifts, dispeller of afflictions! Verily, I beseech thee to forgive the sins of such as have abandoned the physical garment and have ascended to the spiritual world. O my Lord! Purify them from trespasses, dispel their sorrows, and change their darkness into light. Cause them to enter the garden of happiness, cleanse them with the most pure water, and grant them to behold Thy splendors on the loftiest mount." 'Abdu'l-Bahá, *Bahá'í Prayers,* op cit.

Our Bahá'í mentor, Bill Foster, encouraged us to memorize this. That way we could say it easily when visiting a graveyard or passing by one.

14. Invention idea. When I had left the house an hour earlier, I had no idea for an invention. The Versatile Sink (Mr. Private's words) came to me fully formed while riding down Route 295 to Inventions Submission Corp. An example of finding what I thought was divine inspiration.

15. Rational Soul. "The foremost degree of comprehension in the world of nature is that of the rational soul. This power and comprehension is shared in common by all men, whether they be heedless or aware, wayward or faithful. In the creation of God, the rational soul of man encompasses and is distinguished above all other created things: It is by virtue of its nobility and distinction that it encompasses them all. Through the power of the rational soul, man can discover the realities of things, comprehend their properties, and penetrate the mysteries of existence. All the sciences,

branches of learning, arts, inventions, institutions, undertakings, and discoveries have resulted from the comprehension of the rational soul." 'Abdu'l-Bahá, *Some Answered Questions*, chap. 58, para. 3.

16. "Thy Name is my healing, O my God, and remembrance of Thee is my remedy. Nearness to Thee is my hope, and love for Thee is my companion. Thy mercy to me is my healing and my succor in both this world and the world to come. Thou, verily, art the All-Bountiful, the All-Knowing, and the All-Wise." Bahá'u'lláh, *Bahá'í Prayers*, op cit.

17. OTIS. The State of New Jersey's centralized mainframe and statewide networking Information Technology organization. In 1998, OTIS became the Office of Information Technology (OIT), through Governor Christine Whitman's Executive Order (EO) No. 87, and later EO No. 42 (Corzine).

18. The technicolor vision I had in 1985 of climbing the steps to the Shrine of the Báb, in Haifa, became partial reality by 2001 when the nineteen terrace levels and steps were completed from the bottom to the top of the mountain. I had first seen the picture in my mind (soon forgotten), before the idea and later plans of the terraces was first shared with the Bahá'í World in August 1987. See a color photo at http://bahaiblog.net/site/2013/07/the-shrine-of-the-bab-and-its-significance/

The vision I had, although promised, is beyond my lifetime. The modernity and nobility of kings and queens are part of mankind's ordered life on this planet, and the purpose of government is to safeguard the interests of the whole human race. Manic when this vision occurred, it was a vision of what's been described in Bahá'í writings as humanity's coming of age, The Most Great Peace.

19. YMCA Indian Guides and Indian Princess Programs. In the 1980s "Native-American" was not common in my circles. In the 1950s with dozens of TV westerns it had been "Indians." The YMCA Indian Guides booklets described principles and aims that taught respect and understanding. However, people came to realize how culturally inappropriate such programs were despite positive intentions. By the year 2000 the programs were dropped and Adventure Guides without Native-American overtones was adopted instead.

20. "Truthfulness is the foundation of all human virtues. Without truthfulness progress and success, in all the worlds of God, are impossible for any soul." 'Abdu'l-Bahá, cited by Shoghi Effendi in *The Advent of Divine Justice,* Copyright National Spiritual Assembly of the Bahá'ís of the United States. Bahá'í Publishing Trust, Wilmette Illinois, U.S.A.

Re: courtesy: "I admonish you to observe courtesy, for above all else it is the prince of virtues. Well is it with him who is illumined with the light

271

of courtesy and is attired with the vesture of uprightness. Whoso is endued with courtesy hath indeed attained a sublime station." Bahá'u'lláh, *Tablets of Bahá'u'lláh Revealed after the Kitáb-i-Aqdas,* op cit.

21. "Is there any Remover of difficulties save God? Say: Praised be God! He is God! All are His servants, and all abide by His bidding!" The Báb, *Bahá'í Prayers,* op cit.

22. Kathy and Red Grammar song from *Teaching Peace* CD. Available from http://www.redgrammer.com/index.php/store/shop

23. "Blessed is the spot, and the house, and the place, and the city, and the heart, and the mountain, and the refuge, and the cave, and the valley, and the land, and the sea, and the island, and the meadow where mention of God hath been made, and His praise glorified." Bahá'u'lláh, *Bahá'í Prayers,* op cit.

24. Re: Spanish. In my childhood and youth, those who spoke it or had Spanish accents were called Spanish. Later, Hispanic, Latino, Latina, or Latinx would be common.

25. Kahlil Gibran, *The Prophet,* "On Love," Knopf, copyright 1923. This poem is in the public domain.

26. "He is God!

O peerless Lord! In Thine almighty wisdom Thou hast enjoined marriage upon the peoples, that the generations of men may succeed one another in this contingent world, and that ever, so long as the world shall last, they may busy themselves at the Threshold of Thy oneness with servitude and worship, with salutation, adoration and praise. "I have not created spirits and men, but that they should worship me." Wherefore, wed Thou in the heaven of Thy mercy these two birds of the nest of Thy love, and make them the means of attracting perpetual grace; that from the union of these two seas of love a wave of tenderness may surge and cast the pearls of pure and goodly issue on the shore of life. "He hath let loose the two seas, that they meet each other: Between them is a barrier which they overpass not. Which then of the bounties of your Lord will ye deny? From each He bringeth up greater and lesser pearls."

O Thou kind Lord! Make Thou this marriage to bring forth coral and pearls. Thou art verily the All-Powerful, the Most Great, the Ever-Forgiving."

'Abdu'l-Bahá, Marriage Prayer, also citing *Qur'án* 55:19-22, *Bahai Prayers,* op cit.

27. Baha'i Marriage Vows. The simple vow ordained by Bahá'u'lláh is said one partner to the other in the presence of at least two witnesses approved by a local Spiritual Assembly. Only one party must be a Bahá'í. The couple marries themselves since there is no Bahá'í clergy. The Religious Society of Friends (Quakers), have a similar practice.

28. "And then gave utterance to one mystic word, whispered privily by her honeyed tongue... And raised the call amidst the Celestial Concourse and the immortal maids of heaven...." Bahá'u'lláh, *Tablet of the Holy Mariner, Bahá'í Prayers*, op cit.

29. In order to guarantee that His Revelation would achieve its purpose of creating a united world—and to safeguard the unity of the Bahá'í community—Bahá'u'lláh appointed His eldest Son, 'Abdu'l-Bahá, as the Centre of His Covenant and ordained the establishment of the Universal House of Justice. In turn, 'Abdu'l-Bahá established principles for the operation of the Universal House of Justice and stated that after His passing [in 1921], the Bahá'ís must turn to His eldest grandson, Shoghi Effendi, whom He named Guardian of the Bahá'í Faith.

Both the Universal House of Justice [established in 1963], and the Guardian were tasked with applying the principles, promulgating the laws, protecting the institutions, and adapting the Bahá'í Faith to the requirements of an ever-advancing society.

https://www.bahai.org/shoghi-effendi/

Note: More than a dozen books exist about the Guardian. *The Celestial Burning* © 2012 by J.A. McLean is a masterful tome on Shoghi Effendi's writings and his use of hermeneutics and exegesis.

30. The Hail Mary. Well-memorized prayer by Roman Catholics. Along with the Lord's Prayer, prescribed for penance.

31. The Lord's Prayer. A venerated Christian prayer as revealed by Christ in both Matthew 6:9-13 and Luke 11:2-4.

32. From the Tablet of Visitation of Abdu'l-Bahá, *Bahá'í Prayers*, op cit.

33. Bahá'u'lláh, *The Hidden Words of Bahá'u'lláh*, Arabic #5. https://www.bahai.org/library/authoritative-texts/bahaullah/hidden-words/2#246296008

34. "It is incumbent upon the members of the House of Justice... to take counsel together regarding those things which have not outwardly been revealed in the Book, and to enforce that which is agreeable to them. God will verily inspire them with whatsoever He willeth, and He verily is the Provider, the Omniscient." Baha'u'llah, cited by Shoghi Effendi, *World Order of Bahá'u'lláh*, U.S. Bahá'í Publishing Trust, © 1938, 1955

35. Sadratu'l-Muntahá, *Qur'án* 53:14. "Tree beyond which there is no passing." Or "At the Lote Tree of the Utmost Boundary," symbolizing the supreme station of the Manifestation. It can mean the Persian custom of planting a tree at the end of a dead-end street.

36. 'Abdu'l-Bahá, quoted by Shoghi Effendi, *Bahíyyih Khánum, the Greatest Holy Leaf: A Compilation of Bahá'í Sacred Texts and Writings of the Guardian of the Faith and Bahíyyih Khánum's Own Letters,* Bahá'í World Centre, 1982 edition.

37. 'Abdu'l-Bahá, quoted from a letter from The Universal House of Justice, 26 November 2003, To the Followers of Bahá'u'lláh in the Cradle of the Faith (Persia/Iran)

38. Bahá'u'lláh, *Tabernacle of Unity,* 1. Tablet to Manikchi Sahib.

10.0 ACKNOWLEDGMENTS

I facilitate and/or take part in Writing Critique groups and they are invaluable. Chief among them is the Hamilton Creative Writers I sponsor every Monday; the Lawrence Creative Writers every Tuesday for a decade; and the Philadelphia Writers who meet monthly. The shared pieces and poems from a wide cross-section of talented writers and poets are priceless. Through them and their works I have learned a tremendous amount, and had my pieces critiqued and improved. In those sessions I have edited and reviewed over 3,000 pieces of prose or poetry.

Each writer in these groups is a mentor and friend, and all are welcome. We improve, support, educate, and encourage each other. You can find these groups and many others on **Meetup.com**.

Shout outs to the Princeton Writers Group at Princeton Library, the Writers sessions at Mercer County Library Lawrence Headquarters, and to Elliot Rubin's Zoom Poetry Group. Terrific folks—serious writers and poets, and no slouches—the best combination.

My Welsh friend Peter Murphy is a New Jersey treasure. A published poet and Bahá'í, he is the founder of Murphy Writing, now part of Stockton University. His own poetry, writing prompts, vision, expertise, organized writing courses, writers and poets retreats and annual conferences with a stable of knowledgeable instructors, have all added to my strengths and laid bare my weaknesses over many years, with much more to absorb.

Thank you, Peter, Amanda, and Taylor and so many I've met through them.

You can find their offerings at **murphywriting.com**

Made in the USA
Middletown, DE
03 July 2021

43504988R00166